CAMPUS RAPE CULTURE

This book looks at rape myths and rape culture within the university environment, examining the development of social identities in the creation and support of such culture. Building on a four-year research project, this book demonstrates how an understanding of rape culture and of the falsity of rape myths amongst students and staff at university is often at odds with an understanding of the degree to which sexual assaults take place, and of why they take place.

This book explores how traditionally held beliefs of sex roles between men and women, poor conceptions of consent processes, lack of available data, and an inability to see the full continuum of sexual assault limit the knowledge of sexual assaults inside the university community. Taken together the studies demonstrate how socialized social identities of masculinity and femininity hold power in how consent, sexual assaults, and sexual behaviors manifest through cultural values of rape myths and hook-ups. Universities are challenged to examine their sexual assault programming in connection to Title IX and beyond to create educational opportunities about rape culture and rape myths suitable for their students, faculty, and staff.

Written in a clear and direct style, this is essential reading for all those engaged in research about rape culture, sexual assault, and violence against women.

Jennifer L. Huck is an associate professor at Carroll University in Wisconsin. She obtained her doctorate from Indiana University of Pennsylvania in Criminology. She has worked in the criminal justice system as a legal assistant in prosecutorial and defense, and as a case manager for the Milwaukee Municipal Court. Her research interests include aspects of criminal justice policy and theory in connection with university students, women, and juveniles.

"Huck examines rape culture and rape myth acceptance in higher education through a series of studies. Currently, many in college and university settings are seeking to combat these issues in a meaningful way. If acted on appropriately, findings from this collection should help college and university communities become safer and protect their most vulnerable populations from sexual violence."
—Jason D. Spraitz, *Ph.D., Associate Professor of Criminal Justice, University of Wisconsin – Eau Claire*

"In a time when rape culture is more dominant than ever, this book dispels myths and exposes the reality of this issue. Huck poses many questions throughout, making even the most avid researcher question their own inherent biases. This book is a must for any college student, and honestly all of society."
—Katie Ely, *Ph.D., Associate Professor of Criminal Justice, Lock Haven University*

"Huck takes the reader on an educational journey, for all levels, through the varying sections of our culture, specifically highlighting important taboo topics of sexual assaults and rape culture. Through the use of pivotal research and thought-provoking questions, Huck positively challenges our cultural norms in hopes to solicit a critical cultural shift."
—Tiarra Irish, *LPC-IT, NCC, Catalpa Health and Wellness*

"With a thorough presentation of original, mixed-methodology research, Huck presents a deeper study of the circumstances that promote sexual assaults occurring on college and university campuses. Her examination of rape myths is grounded in theory that combines an understanding of feminism, culture, and identity and challenges existing systems of belief."
—Daniel Lee, *Ph.D, Full Professor of Criminology, Indiana University of Pennsylvania*

"With a laser focus on getting to the root causes, Jennifer Huck presents a critically important, much-needed, and participant-centered call to action for all universities to go beyond short educational programming on sexual assault to initiating an action-oriented dialogue and creating a lasting blueprint on how to 'chip away at rape culture's hold.' Jennifer Huck's work is not only a must-read for all those working at the university level, but all those who wish to 'move into identities of love, empathy, and compassion,' as she so eloquently puts it."
—Kate E. Masley, *Ph.D., Medical Anthropologist and Special Lecturer in Health Sciences, Oakland University*

CAMPUS RAPE CULTURE

Identity and Myths

Jennifer L. Huck

LONDON AND NEW YORK

First published 2022
by Routledge
2 Park Square, Milton Park, Abingdon, Oxon OX14 4RN

and by Routledge
605 Third Avenue, New York, NY 10158

Routledge is an imprint of the Taylor & Francis Group, an informa business

© 2022 Jennifer L. Huck

The right of Jennifer L. Huck to be identified as author of this work has been asserted by her in accordance with sections 77 and 78 of the Copyright, Designs and Patents Act 1988.

All rights reserved. No part of this book may be reprinted or reproduced or utilised in any form or by any electronic, mechanical, or other means, now known or hereafter invented, including photocopying and recording, or in any information storage or retrieval system, without permission in writing from the publishers.

Trademark notice: Product or corporate names may be trademarks or registered trademarks, and are used only for identification and explanation without intent to infringe.

British Library Cataloguing-in-Publication Data
A catalogue record for this book is available from the British Library

Library of Congress Cataloging-in-Publication Data
A catalog record has been requested for this book

ISBN: 978-0-367-48306-7 (hbk)
ISBN: 978-0-367-48307-4 (pbk)
ISBN: 978-1-003-03921-1 (ebk)

Typeset in Bembo
by codeMantra

CONTENTS

List of figures   *vii*
List of tables   *ix*

    Introduction   1

1   Interpreting the necessities: social identity, rape culture, and rape myths   12

2   Building rape myth perceptions – university community   35

3   Deconstructing student confusion and bewilderment   77

4   Creating identity in roles, statuses, and characteristics   104

5   Opening the university culture   127

    Conclusion   156

Research notes   *165*
Appendices   *171*
Index   *185*

FIGURES

2.1	Total rape myth scale items divided into sub-scales of rape myths	42
3.1	Definitions used in studies	84
5.1	Perceptions of sexual assault and programming	140
5.2	Perceptions of fear in participants' residences	141

TABLES

2.1	Study 3 Spring 2016 Survey Items Responses, Percentages and Means	43
2.2	Study 3 Spring 2016 Survey IRMA Scale	44
2.3	Independent T-tests of Scales Mean Differences in Study 3	46
2.4	Study 6 Fall 2017 Survey IRMA Items Responses, Percentages and Means	47
2.5	Study 6 Fall 2017 Survey IRMA Scale	48
2.6	Study 7 Spring 2018 IRMA Items Responses, Percentages and Means	50
2.7	Study 7 Spring 2018 IRMA Scale, Neutral Category Present	51
2.8	Study 9 Fall 2019 Rape Myth Percentages and Means	52
2.9	Study 9 Fall 2019 Survey IRMA Scale Means	53
2.10	Study 3 Spring 2016 IRMA Typical and Dichotomous Measures	54
2.11	Percentage of Combined Agreement in Studies	56
2.12	Percentage of Combined Disagreement in Studies	57
2.13	Study 4 Spring 2016 Faculty/Staff Survey Individual Items Percentages and Means	69
2.14	Study 4 Spring 2016 Faculty/Staff Survey IRMA Scale	70
4.1	Independent T-tests of Scale Mean Differences for Identity Variables, Study 3	110
4.2	Regression Analysis of Identity Variables in Study 9	115
4.3	Regression Analysis of Identity Variables in Study 3	116
4.4	Regression Analysis of Identity Variables in Study 6	116
5.1	Study 10 Fall 2019 IRMA Individual Items Percentages and Means	129
5.2	Study 10 Fall 2019 IRMA Scales	130
5.3	Study 10 Spring 2020 Survey Scales	130

5.4	Study 13 Spring 2020 Survey items responses, percentages and means	133
5.5	Study 13 Spring 2020 Survey IRMA Scale	134
5.6	Study 13 Spring 2020 Survey Scales	135
5.7	IRMA Individual Items Means for Comparison	137
5.8	Study Comparisons through Independent T-tests of Scale Mean Differences	138
5.9	Regression Analysis of Identity Variables in Study 13	140

INTRODUCTION

It was anticipated time could endure the trails of sexual assault that plagues many societies and cultures to create a way to limit these sexually aggressive acts toward women and men. However, time has taken a toll on sexual assault victims and survivors. The pain of sexual assault and the myths that perpetuate these actions make little discernment between the behaviors of the mid-1900s before the sexual and feminist revolutions and those which occur now in 2021. Sexual assaults still are not taken seriously enough by the public or the institutions meant to protect victims, a function of rape culture. Rape myths still exist as strength holds in stereotypes and justifications for why sexual assaults occur and why sexual assaults are defined as unproblematic.

Feminists and civil right protectors argued in the 1960s, 1970s, 1980s, and beyond that sexual assault was a way for patriarchal cultures to maintain power hierarchies between and within genders. Sexual assault became about more than the aggressive acquisition of sex and was attributed to the authority bestowed onto the attacker via the power lost by the victim. This developed and pushed the term *rape culture* into mainstream society, even though the nuances of the terms are not well understood. Rape culture also creates implicit biases through its connections to femininity, masculinity, sexual assaults, and rape myths. Arguments in the 1970s called for feminism and its ideals to create change and manifest equitable cultures where sexual assaults could be limited, yet this ideal has to be realized.

Instead, what has been created is a backlash against those who fight for freedom from victim blaming, rape myths, and rape culture. Women, mostly, and men want their victimization to be heard and avenged, but this is not happening now or seemingly in the near future. Strong perceptions and declarations of victim blame occur as a result of values and beliefs that hold victims accountable for the sexual assault instead of the aggressor. When people hear from friends, families, and strangers of their sexual assaults, empathy and compassion are not always the first response. Often people respond by asking or wondering what you did as a survivor to cause it. Victim blame is visualized and illustrated in simple comments made by others such as because she was drinking, because she kissed him first, because she wore a short skirt, or because she went to his house. Victim blame is also shown in the lack of fault attributed to the accused: he would not do that, he is a nice guy, he is a star athlete, or he is a good man. These grouping of statements posture anti-victim and pro-accused biases that trivialize both the sexual assault and the pain of the victim. This is the rape culture in action. As a society, we lack the ability to have faith in the victim because she is imperfect and to hold confidence that the accuser did not engage in a sexual assault because he is close to perfect.

Numerous recent books demonstrate these conflicting set of ideals against sexual assault. Krakauer (2015) details the Missoula University coverup led by law enforcement to protect student athletes who were accused of sexual assault and rape. Hundreds of victims were told not to talk as they would not be believed and would be accused of bringing negative actions against the university. The victims were told by the university and law enforcement that they would be responsible for the breakdown of the university system because they were raped. Miller and Armstrong (2018) show interconnected serial sexual assaults where women were not believed, and one recanted her story because the law enforcement thought she lied. The woman "Marie" was charged with making false claims once she recanted her rape story. Later, it was found Marie was telling the truth when the serial rapist was caught and charged with multiple rapes of various women. Gay (2018) provided many essays from women, men, and gender queer or transgendered individuals who detailed their accounts of being attacked and then revictimized by systems or people who did not believe them or argued they caused their own pain. In the book Violated (2017), the authors explain how many women were abused, assaulted, and attacked by Baylor's football players. Coaches and administrators heard of the cases and ensured that no one pressed charges, thus admitting to possible guilt but allowing the successful money-making football team to remain intact while the victims fell apart. Miller (2019) discussed her being raped by Brock Turner and how her world turned upside down in the aftermath. He became the victim who lost his education, scholarship, and swim team. The media and courts did not want to hear her victim story and accused her being unworthy for drinking at a college party instead of villainizing Turner because he sexually assaulted her when she was blacked out behind a dumpster.

These case studies do not stand alone. As suggested by Krakauer (2015) in her author's note, there are so many cases that go unknown, so many cases never reported, and so many cases not believed. Nass (1977), as an editor, brought together research and perspectives to show societal perceptions about rape. For instance, that to be raped is taboo (Donadio & White) and the result is victim blame

(Jones & Aronson). Additionally, in the Nass (1977) book, Hartwig claimed that rape victims are perceived as being at fault because our internalized, implicit, socialized sex roles accept male domination. This leads to the acceptance of rape myths and rape culture that create a false sense of justice for the accused – not the true victim. Subsequently, Sanday (1996) argued that implicit bias against women and the stereotypes of virginity impact the way society and institutions view women who claim rape.

Men, as the accused, often are given the benefit of the doubt as it is difficult to overcome a cultural history of not holding men, especially powerful men, high in social hierarchies, accountable. Women are dismissed and not believed as the case studies above demonstrate. Throughout the history of rape and sexual assault in the United States, it is shown repeatedly that the victim is to blame due to historical and situational context that has little to do with the actual victim. In fact, per Freedmand (2013), the history of sexual assault is filled with rationales and justifications that support the accusers especially when they are men; this history is not separate from criminal justice or university institutions.

This is not to state that all accused are guilty, and that due process of law should be ignored. Due process is the backbone of the justice system and always should be achieved but part of due process is honoring the victim as well as the accused. Both are part of the criminal justice system. Some of the legal cautionary tales can be found in book accounts of the Duke Lacrosse rape case (Cohen, 2014; Taylor & Johnson, 2007). You can also look into the stories of Justice Kavanaugh with sexual assault allegations from Dr. Christine Blasey Ford, Deborah Ramierez, and Julie Swetnick (Hemingway, 2020; Pogrebin & Kelly, 2019) – additionally, the claims against Harvey Weinstein or similar persons in Hollywood (Kantor, Twohey, & Lowman, 2019). These stories represent women coming against men who are perceived as more powerful than the accusers. Not only because they are males being accused by females but the power inherent in whiteness versus blackness, college student versus prostitute, lawyer against judge, and film producer against actresses. The mental assumption made when we hear about a woman accusing a man of sexual assault is that she is lying and of course he could not have done it. This is the rape culture.

Reading the book, *Justice on Trial*, you see the movement of a woman being scourged by many simply because she spoke up against a man. Granted, there are concerns with Dr. Blassey Ford's allegations that can make someone ponder to their truthfulness; namely, something that occurred in 1982 is hard to remember, unless of course it changed the path of your life as sexual assault does. Men and women talked down to her, questioned her worthiness, and of course blamed her for her own actions using mainly *it wasn't really rape* (because it was other forms of sexual assault) and *she lied* (because why did she wait so long to tell people). These core beliefs shame victims and teach women to not confess and keep all hidden.

As stated bluntly in *The Diversity Delusion*, if women do not come forward right away, the assault never happened as victims would always report this type of behavior. A lack of victim reporting does not showcase that rape culture does not exist, in face, against Mac Donald's claims that it resonates with the rape culture. In many of the interviews described later, I was one of the few who knew about their assaults and none of them reported it to law enforcement or campus authorities. This is due to the rape culture and not because of hidden agenda of fear mongering.

The way our systems, law enforcement and universities, handle allegations makes it problematic for victims to share their stories; rape myths and rape culture tell victims not to. The shame and stigma felt as a victim in the aftermath make it hard to provide voice to the incident. When people do tell of their assaults, many are met with poor reactions of victim blaming and more shame. The processes in place and the social handling of rapes make it improbable for victims to share their stories. How does one start to tell their more painful story to a stranger who is trained to be critical and impartial to your story as universities and law enforcement?

This is not supporting that we should ideally believe all accusations, but we should not assume accusers are liars. Due process in the courts must be held as part of the process; innocent until guilty must be upheld. Justice, due process, and our constitution must be upheld. But this is not an either/or game; you can believe a victim while waiting for the accused to go through appropriate steps to ensure that due process is secured.

Take a moment and play this mental game with me. If someone tells you they were mugged and their wallet was stolen, do you believe them? If someone texts you they were punched at a bar last night and have a black eye, do you believe they were assaulted? If someone tells you they were in a car accident and the other driver left the scene for a hit and run, do you think this happened? Most say "of course," so what is so different about sexual assault and rape. This benefit of doubt is given to most other accusers but why not in sexual assault? The quick answer is rape culture and rape myths – the long answers can be found in the many books, manuscripts, journals, presentations, and stories written about these topics, including this one.

Social narratives are built from the structures and guidelines provided by institutional powers in each society and culture. These guidelines or norms tell us how to operate in our daily lives by providing positive social cues of behaviors and beliefs. Many of these beliefs go unchallenged because socialization tells us to accept societal views as foundations to our cultural lives. When people share their assault stories, they are met with shame, anger, stigma, and blaming. This negatively reinforces anyone who desires to tell their story next; who wants to face that scrutiny.

The institutions of family, education, economy, and government provide these core behaviors and beliefs to create a common culture. Thus, institutions and individuals interact and communicate to develop the rules of life, including morality and ideas of right and wrong. It is through the processes of social narratives being built that create the ideas of victim blaming and patriarchal power at the base of rape culture and rape myths. Institutions and the individuals within them fight to perpetuate these myths and culture. It is the function of society and culture; change is not easy; it is tough to accept. Changing the values, attitudes, and beliefs appears to take unlimited time, but the time is now to continue the forward momentum.

The university environment has been examined dutifully as a social place where rapes and sexual assaults occur. Aligning with rape myths, university campuses are a place of parties, drinking, and learning adulthood. It is a place of chaos, learning about oneself, and testing boundaries of behaviors. It is about crossing lines and learning how to be an individual without parents watching. Universities are a place where a hookup culture rules sexual behaviors blurring lines of consent and sexual activity through sexual coercion and harassment. It is a place where adolescent norms are challenged while students become independent adults. Universities are not to blame for the sexual assaults and rapes that occur within their borders to their students; this is another artifact of the larger culture and the typical age of students. Universities are a place where many young adults are easily obtained for research efforts and as a learning institution a place that can aid in altering cultures. The rape culture seeps into all institutions; very few systems go unscathed.

Sexual assaults include sexually aggressive actions of kissing, grouping, or inserting without gaining consent. Sexual assault is a continuum with rape at the most serious end. Rape occurs in most jurisdictions when objects or body parts are inserted into holes of a body (e.g. anus, vagina). Sexual coercion is when someone uses their verbal prowess to talk another into engaging in sexual behaviors. A gray line is created between coercion and sexual assault especially when consent is not loud and clear. Sexual harassment is often verbal and occurs without sexual action. It is the unwanted verbal comments of sexual actions or continued requests of sexual behaviors. It might include quid pro quo requests of offering rewards for sexual behaviors. Sexual harassment can occur in the workplace as well as other situations.

Although roughly 10% of males are sexual perpetrators, research indicates that many more would engage in sexual assault behaviors if provided the chance and are certain of not being caught. Of the 10% of male sexual assaulters, around 50% are serial sexual assaulters, meaning that they have engaged in more than one sexual assault or rape. This does not include the numbers of transgender or non-cisgender individuals who are raped and assaulted. These males account for an estimate of sexual assault of 1 in 4 or 1 in 5 women on campuses. Rapes are higher and might be somewhere between 1 in 10 and 1 in 20. These estimates are difficult when people do not report the crimes or do not always know the definitions of assault. In the various surveys presented in this book, assaults range from 8.8% to 25% to 44.4% of the sample. Numbers are inconsistent but one rape or assault is too many as it alters the trajectory of life and the pain felt.

The university is a place for creating and upholding social identities. Universities environments guide students into adulthood through structured groups that create social beliefs, ideals, and wants. Groups for activities, studies, athletics, and

Greek life abound in most university campuses. Belonging to groups provides a path for students to define who they are and build identity structures that will last through life. These social groupings mold beliefs and norms created in the foundations of socialization. These groups are testing grounds for students to determine what beliefs are allowed, what gets hidden, and what becomes dismissed. Some of the attitudes include ideas about studying, cheating, drinking, drug use, sexual behavior, vacationing, partying, and sexual assaults. The selected groups help build adulthood socialization to forecast what ideals are upheld, including myths and culture.

These groups also have been accused of being the reason rapes and sexual assaults exist on campus while perpetuating the hookup culture. Hookup culture includes the ideals of not wanting or needed long-term serious relationships that lead toward marriage as people do not want to spend their energy on the commitment needed for this type of relationship. The hookup culture holds values of having fun in sexual connections regardless of relationship status as a goal. It focuses on sex and relationship connections built for the purpose of sex. The hookup culture and its focus on sex young people, especially men, in the culture feel as they must perform sexually or gain undesirable labels from others including being named weak or pussy. Women also have a sense of need to engage in sex as it is the norm, but often still are damned regardless of their actions being called prudes or whores depending on their path.

Hookups blur lines of sexual coercion and sexual assault; if nether person really wants to engage in sex but feels a need to because of hookup culture pressure, where does this lie. Many equate parties, drinking, and drugs as justification and necessities for hookups which are also active in sexual assaults scenarios. Thus, at a university when Greek life and athletics thrive in the party, culture sexual assaults are viewed as the groups' fault, not the university. This is inaccurate; it is rape culture and people succumbing to their socialization.

Although rape might not be caused by the rape culture, the response to sexual assaults is a direct connection to the rape culture. Universities have been deemed process agencies of sexually assault allegations while perpetuating the fear that if you attend college, you will be raped. This simplistic argument demotes the lives of young adults and shifts blame to an industry. We cannot forget that individuals are responsible for their actions even when their actions connect to their socialization. It is the system's responsibility to help limit the values and beliefs related to rape myths and rape culture while dismissing the myths and lies about causes of rape. Individuals and systems work together to build our lives.

The university provides a strong sample of young individuals who are more prone to be perpetrators and victims of sexual assault and rape because of their age and lifestyle. It is also an organized environment that allows for data to be collected more easily. In fact, this book argues that it is not the university lifestyle that manifests sexual assault and rape but the larger broader culture the university is within; it is the institutional social structure of the university that allows for sexual assaults to occur on its grounds to its students. Yet, this is not the fault of the university as rape and sexual assault occur everywhere and anywhere.

The purpose of this book is to demonstrate how social identities connect to the creation and support of rape culture and rape myth. It suggests that universities are a foundation to help motivate change in rape culture and must do more in educating college students to impact future generations. Social identities created through early socialization and short programs or education seminars at universities cannot expect to alter rape myth perceptions and culture long term. Thus, the role of the university is to provide education and support to illustrate the importance of shifting traditional and conservative beliefs about sex roles, sexual behaviors, consent processes, and definition of sexual assault to be less patriarchal and more feminist. This can be completed by addressing social identities that surround athletics, Greek life, and other organizations on campus by demonstrating the worth of honest and open masculine and feminine ideals. The ideals would encapsulate empathy and appropriate aggression or assertiveness.

To support this frame, the chapters described below showcase various research projects completed over the past four years. These projects use the features of rape myths and rape culture to measure the perceptions of university students. There were also interviews and focus groups to help understand the depth of the numbers and what students, faculty, and staff discuss surrounding the topics of rape myth and rape culture as well as consent and sexual assault definitions. Taken together, the studies support that socialized social identities of masculinity and femininity hold power in how consent, sexual assaults, and sexual behaviors manifest through cultural values of rape myths and hookups. Although most studies herein were from one university, one of the projects included a national sample of universities and another of a social media collected sample to illustrate that the voices in this book are common.

Gender construction of masculinity and femininity is developed through socialization and acceptance of roles that might be connected to sex. This is termed social constructionism and we must use our ability to see and define others through social experiences to see the patterns of how these identities are created. These patterns help us quickly view men versus women, female versus male, and boy versus girl. It also includes the various genders that are outside of the traditional dual-gender continuums. The basic foundational idea is that we watch those we grow up around to determine what it means to be a male or female and masculine or feminine. We take clues and develop ourselves from the positive and negative inputs we receive. Do people like it when I dress fancy or wear make-up or sit quietly? Do people like it when I play with trucks, wrestle with cousins, and wear dirt? These ideas become reinforced and we quickly attach it to gender alongside visual inputs. Visual identity includes hair length, clothing choices, make-up wearing, jewelry wearing, and others. This all connects to our society and culture, and as discussed later, creates the status and roles of our lives.

All of these ideas come together to answer broad questions I held: How does our society perpetuate the rape culture and rape myths? What is it about our socialization that develops identities that foster the continuation of rape myths and rape culture? How is it that we hold feministic ideals and promote ideologies of equity, but still address sexual assault in negative ways and poor form? What exists on the university campus, as a place that holds young adults, to help see future trends and the ideologies of students? Is the university a catalyst of change for rape culture and rape myths or does it stagnate these ideals?

Past research demonstrated how much still is not known about how to limit and prevent sexual assault on university campuses (Paludi, 2016). Many programs do not work beyond the short term in changing attitudes, and behaviors are even harder to alter (Foubert, 2000). Faculty, students, staff, and administrators do not know the prevalence and incidence of sexual assaults on their campuses because the numbers simply do not exist in convenient formats (Kruttschnitt, Kalsbeek, & House, 2014). The numbers do not exist for numerous reasons, including the inability to gather the numbers or university administrators not wanting to know the truth. Past research proposes that victim blaming has occurred throughout history and includes sexual assaults solutions for women – dress appropriately, act appropriately, do not put yourself in any perceived danger, and learn self-defense (Suarez & Gadalla, 2010). Programs and solutions often did not focus upon changing behaviors of perpetrators until programs such as except the Yes means Yes movement (Friedman & Valenti, 2019) and bystander intervention (Burn, 2009; Coker et al., 2011; McMahon, 2010) that requires peers to help peers out of potential sexual assault situations. These programs are often ill-equipped due to lack of funds and resources (Paludi, 2016). Title IX requires certain programs and trainings but once a university checks the box, little more is accomplished.

This work in this book started innocently enough with an outraged student who wanted to impact change in the programming on campus and ensure that students felt listened to and respected. We worked together through literature reviews, gathering data, mistakes in data collection, angst, anger, campus policies, long discussions, and eventual graduation of the student. I have brought more students in the mix to help keep their visions as part of the studies and knowledge collected; there is always a resounding concern that people do not care, students do not want to change, the university does not really listen, and that change must happen. This is what fuels this book and my data – a heartfelt belief that we must change and care enough to be the ones that make the numbers better, the reporting easier, the shame lower, and the compassion higher.

The book is about rape myths and rape culture within the university environment and corresponding culture, including the creation and development of social identities. It creates a narrative from one university through survey and interview data collected about rape myths, rape culture, sexual assault, consent, and identity creation. It provides a validity check about this university's experience through one national study, one social media study, and reliance on a literature review.

Rape culture is the creation of patriarchal systems that value male aggressions, dominance, and power over females which might result in violence, aggression, and sexual assault (Burt, 1980). Rape myths are misbeliefs and manifestations of justifications and excuses for why rape and sexual assault happen to women within the guise of male aggression and dominance. This includes victim blaming and beliefs that the man did not mean to harm the woman and that the victim is lying about the sexual assault. Social identity creation is the way individuals view themselves through certain lenses as connected to social roles, groups, and construction of self (Alexander & Wiley, 1981). This includes sports, Greek life, masculinity, femininity, political ideology, feminism beliefs, sex roles, consent, and conservativeness of sexual behavior. The book develops ideas of aggression and empathy as pathways to showcase one's identity in connection with rape myths, sexual assault, and rape culture.

The book brings together 14 quantitative and qualitative research projects undergone between 2015 and 2020, many of which focused on one university. The main university is a small private midwestern school with a religious connection. Its students are highly white, upper/middle class, and female. Men often come to campus to play sports in the division III conference. The national university sample includes private and public, small and large, and religiously affiliated schools. The social media sample is one created through the social media networks and includes a sample with higher levels of education than a true national sample. Taken together, these studies, displayed in the research note at the end of the book, demonstrate that change could be around the corner if we start pushing for it.

Findings suggest that the samples disagree with rape myths in their simplistic form and when directly asked. Interviews bring about the nuances of human nature in how we perceive our attitudes one way only to let our words show something else. The ideas of rape culture are acknowledged by the samples, and university environment is a place of safety. However, confusion exists in faculty, staff, and students as to the degree to which sexual assaults occur and why they happen. Traditionally held beliefs of sex roles between men and women, poor conceptions of consent processes, lack of available data, and an inability to see the full continuum of sexual assault limit the knowledge of sexual assaults inside the university community. The community cannot see the identity of the university being one that is unsafe or a place to be in fear.

Thus, sexual assaults cannot happen to the degree at this university that they occur at other schools; much less the statistic of 1 in 4 or 1 in 5 women will be sexually assaulted while a student. The false narrative of safety and a lack of it occurring here connects to a self-identity of pro-feminism and not wanting to be seen as a bad person as connected to peers. Students hold positive perceptions of their identity, including low aggression, mid-range empathy, confident self-esteem, and a disconnection to rape myths and rape culture. Yet, the data shows a naivety to sexual encounters, desires, consent, and sexual assault. This is problematic and allows for the university to be a socially bewildering place to rationalize sexual behaviors in light of hookup culture and rape culture.

This is not a book demonizing Greek life, athletes, masculinity, or males. It showcases concerns found in building identities and one way the confusion of identities manifests itself in the university environment. It sets to demonstrate that identity building through lifetime socialization impacts sexually aggressive behaviors but also allows for the university community to misinterpret sexual assault and consent because of the inherent desire to be safer or different than national statistics. This book's scope is to create one more chronicle in helping determine what could be done to progress culture away from negative masculine roles and out of dismissive patriarchal stories of sexual assault. This book can open a conversation inside universities for faculty, staff, administration, and students about how to change current ideals and programming.

The projects all use rape myths as measured by the shortened version of the Illinois Rape Myth Scale and rape culture as a means to measure perceptions of the university students, faculty, and staff. There were also interviews and focus groups to help understand the depth of the numbers and what students, faculty, and staff actually discuss surrounding the topics of rape myth and rape culture as well as consent and sexual assault definitions. Taken together, the studies support that socialized social identities of masculinity and femininity hold power in how consent, sexual assaults, and sexual behaviors manifest through cultural values of rape myths and hookups. Although most studies were from one university, one of the projects included a national sample of universities and another was a general social media sample to help illustrate that the case study is not a single story and this process is routine.

References

Alexander, C. N., & Wiley, M. G. (1981). Situated activity and identity formation. In Rosenburg, M. & Turner (Eds.) *Social Psychology: Sociological Perspectives*, pp. 269–289. Basic Books.

Burn, S. M. (2009). A situational model of sexual assault prevention through bystander intervention. *Sex Roles, 60*, 779–792.

Burt, M. (1980). Cultural myths and supports for rape. *Journal of Personality and Social Psychology, 2*, 217–230.

Cohen, W. D. (2014). *The price of silence: The Duke lacrosse scandal, the power of the elite, and the corruption of our great universities*. Scribner.

Coker, A. L., Cook-Craig, P. G., Williams, C. M., Fisher, B. S., Clear, E. R., Garcia, L. S., & Hegge, L. M. (2011). Evaluation of green dot: An active bystander intervention to reduce sexual violence on college campuses. *Violence against Women, 17*, 777–796.

Freedman, E. B. (2013). *Redefining rape*. Harvard University Press.

Foubert, J. D. (2000). The longitudinal effects of a rape-prevention program on fraternity men's attitudes, behavioral intent, and behavior. *Journal of American College Health, 48*, 158–163.

Friedman, J., & Valenti, J. (Eds.). (2019). *Yes means yes!: Visions of female sexual power and a world without rape*. Seal Press.

Gay, R. (Ed.). (2018). *Not that bad: Dispatches from rape culture*. Harper Perennial.

Hemingway, M., & Severino, C. (2019). *Justice on trial: Kavanaugh confirmation and the future of the supreme court*. Regnery Publishing.

Kantor, J., & Twohey, M. (2019). *She said: Breaking the sexual harassment story that helped ignite a movement*. Penguin Books.

Krakauer, J. (2016). *Missoula: Rape and the justice system in a college town*. Anchor.

Kruttschnitt, C., Kalsbeek, W. D., & House, C. C. (Eds.). (2014). *Estimating the incidence of rape and sexual assault*. National Research Council of the National Academies.

Lavigne, P., & Schlabach, M. (2017). *Violated: Exposing rape at Baylor University amid college football's sexual assault crisis*. Center Street.

McMahon, S. (2010). Rape myths beliefs and bystander attitudes among incoming college students. *Journal of American College Health, 59*, 3–11.

Miller, C. (2019). *Know my name: A memoir*. Penguin Books.

Miller, T. C., & Armstrong, K. (2018). *A False Report: A True Story of Rape in America*. Crown.

Nass, D. R. (1977). The rape victim. Dubuque, IA: Kendall/Hunt.

Paludi, M. A. (Ed.). (2016). *Campus action against sexual assault: Needs, policies, procedures, and training programs*. Abc-clio.

Pogrebin, R. & Kelly, K. (2019). *The education of Brett Kavanaugh: An investigation*. Portfolio.

Sanday, P. R. (1997). A woman scorned: Acquaintance rape on trial. Univ of California Press.

Suarez, E., & Gadalla, T. M. (2010). Stop blaming the victim: A meta-analysis of rape myths. *Journal of Interpersonal Violence, 25*, 2010–2035. doi:10.1177/0886260509354503

Taylor, S. & Johnson, K. C. (2007). *Until proven innocent: Political correctness and the shameful injustices of the Duke lacrosse rape case*. Thomas Dunne Books.

1
INTERPRETING THE NECESSITIES
Social identity, rape culture, and rape myths

This chapter explains the presumption that our social identities are built through socialization, including the knowledge within the rape culture and rape myths. Elements of us, especially that which is connected to masculinity and femininity, gender, and sex roles, are influenced by rape culture. It addresses ideas about who we are as a group, social system, infrastructure, and individual. The concepts of social identity, social constructionism, and socialization help work you through the building blocks of society and culture, and how the terms create values and beliefs connected to rape culture and rape myths. These values and beliefs might not be apparent to you at this moment as many of these values and beliefs are considered implicit or unconscious – we simply are not aware of them if we never try to become mindful of the ideas swimming around in our brain.

Social identities are the way we distinguish ourselves as individuals within particular groups while observing the society and culture surrounding us. This creation of self is completed within the groups and through the roles we identify with. Those identities which harbor a robust sense of belonging and purpose impact our perceptions of self and others the most. Social identity is created through the interactions and communications engaged during one's lifetime socialization experiences.

This book, thus, uses a symbolic interactionist framework. Symbolic interactionism comes from sociological and psychological thinkers such as Mills (1959/2000), Goffman (1978; 2009), Durkheim (1897/1961; 1933), Mead (1934), Blumer (1986), and Berger and Luckman (1966). Symbolic interactionism is the presumption that we become ourselves only through the connections we build with others. We are not true individualistic individuals, but persons who mesh ourselves into society and cultures. We become ourselves because of the groups we belong to, including those we are born into. Families, neighborhoods, housing, economic status, and educational opportunities build us at a young age through mechanisms known as the lottery of birth. Many parts of our foundational selves are not self-determined but socially determined by the social and cultural forces we are born into and then experience during our lifetimes. These opportunities for other life groups include higher education; sport and athletic groups; other extracurricular activities such as dance, theater, and music; and work opportunities. Take a moment to reflect on the groups that make you who you are – those that were important below the age of 8, those that created life as a teenager, those that made your young adulthood, and those you are in now. These groups make you – they provide you with roles and statuses that are part of the social hierarchy of life.

The paradigm of symbolic interactionism includes the theories used to develop ideas surrounding the curated power of rape culture and myths. First, situated identity theory presumes people want to be liked by the people who surround them; thus, social groups become environments of similar norms, values, and beliefs especially when group decision making is occurring (Alexander & Wiley, 1981). Second, expectation states theory argues that we hold stereotypes and conclusions about people in our groups that help us make decisions while using group members' strengths (Correll & Ridgeway, 2006). These conceptions we make of others impact how we make the decisions in our groups.

Situated identities are created through various groups and institutions. The main institutions are family, politics, governments, economic systems, and education. You can also include entities of military and criminal justice as these shape ideals of cultures and society. Situated identities are built from conceptions of gender through the continuums of masculinity and femininity. These ideas are shaped by movements of women and feminism as well as the backlashes formed in response.

Historical connections are explained to demonstrate how definitions of rape culture and rape myths shape the criminal acts of sexual assault and rape but then how these definitions make us through culture and symbolic interactionism. How a culture views rape and sexual assault matters. Our culture holds that assault, violence, rape, and subservience are a part of womanhood and being female. As such, rape cultures are the attitudes and beliefs that do not question sexual assault and in fact normalize it or argue that it is not important. Rape myths are ideals that presume women are to blame for sexual assaults; the myths blame the victim, suggest the victim is lying, or that the man did not mean to sexually assault the woman. Think about how this framing from socialization impacts sex roles of gender construction; what do these patterns develop identity and self-worth if rape is to be expected but then ignored?

The chapter is a generalized account of examining and connecting terminology that builds the foundation of the book. It explains how social identities perpetuate rape myths and rape culture but also deconstructs sexual assault definitions, consent, sex roles, and sexual behaviors. Relatedly, an argument is made that patriarchal socialization manifests some social identities supporting toxic masculinity or privileged manhood and the corresponding reduction in concern for sexual assaults and gender equity through consent, sex roles, and sexual behaviors. This creates poor consent practices and acceptance of one's sexuality; it blurs the line about what is and is not sexual assault. This then perpetuates rape myths and rape cultures especially considering what is known as the hookup culture of current college generations.

Identity creation terminology

We hold ourselves to be uniquely individualistic, a credence passed to us through culture and society. Communities, groups, families, and friends are important to our lives, but we portray ourselves as an individual within those groups. We see ourselves as a person before we see ourselves as the group. Rarely do we cross over into considering ourselves through a more complex sociological and psychological lens – or a social-psych framework. It demonstrates the use of a sociological imagination within a social constructionist framework using symbolic interactionism. In other words, this chapter discusses how to see ourselves within the structure of history and experiences lived as a society and culture through our individual selves (Durkheim, 1933; Mills, 2000). This format pushes you to see the creation of definition and worldviews through that social and cultural lens to thrust yourself to view the world through the eyes of others. The concepts establish that through our interactions and communication with the various people, groups, and institutions, our lives are created – our beliefs and behaviors are a product of the world around us (Goffman, 1978). One of the outcomes of this production, otherwise known as socialization, is the way we develop our thoughts while making behavioral decisions.

Socialization is the process within any culture that develops human children into appropriate members of their community. Socialization starts from the moment of birth usually through the association and assignment of gender or sex and the type of family born into. Ponder this for a moment – we become our gender before we are birthed. Gender reveal parties where you to eat blue cake or watch pink fireworks sets the yet to be born into a gender typology. Toys for future birthdays include dolls and sewing kits for girls and construction vehicles and cars for boys. (I would like to note I clearly remember owning dolls, action figures, and an orange garbage truck while wearing frilly dresses and dirt-filled shorts.) These assumption of roles showed you who you were to be before you even understood there was a you.

Socialization continues through life and its course of education, work, family, friends, economy, government, and other connections made. Socialization tells you the type of work you can do and the educational field you can pursue. How many male nurses exist? How many teachers are female, expect for gym? Why are there so many male CEOs? Our socialization is powerful and provides the scripts that rule our lives. These social scripts are developed in socialization process of learning through the people, groups, and institutions that develop a sense of self and your social identity. Thus, the fabric of your early life, the values and beliefs of your close family, friends and your educational system build the possible versions of you. These versions of you are your social identities; we hold more than one as we are different versions of ourselves when we are in various groups.

Your situated identity is developed during socialization from the groups and statuses you belong in that you perceive as being significant aspects of your life (Alexander & Wiley, 1981; Touhey, 1974). A situated identity helps you explain yourself when someone asks who you are and what do you do. The groups might change in significance throughout time, such as a soccer team being amazing when you are five years old to ten but then it becomes a group you no longer care about – it still makes you, you. Your identity is not static and can change depending upon the roles you are pursuing, the stage of life you are in, or the specific situation you are in. For instance, while growing up you held a role of athlete and that was how you mainly saw yourself. As you age into life, it becomes harder to connect with athlete as the options to join teams are limited. You then see yourself as an employee or parent or partner. Yet, Sunday morning pick-up games still allow you to focus and see yourself as an athlete. Another example, as a student, your teacher sees your studious side, whereas your friends get to view your goofy party side. These role changes help you portray yourself and choose identities that are specific to certain groups and the social environment.

Some identities become more salient than others and are regarded as a master status (Goffman, 1978; 2009). Statuses are all the character traits you hold due to your roles within groups. The master status is the identity you most align with or hold to be the most important. This is based partly on personal priorities of life and your social priorities based within your society and culture. You might be a mother, student, wife, daughter, and employee. Which status has the greatest priority might change from day to day or year to year based upon your interactions, goals, and outside forces of life. Each of those statuses includes roles (tasks) that must be accomplished for you to fit inside those groups and statuses. When in different situations, work versus home, different statuses mean more and take higher priorities. This shapes your identity – your role as an employee might be similar to your role as a mother but employers might not care about your identity as a mom. This is how your situated identities multiply and change; they are rooted into your current social context and environment.

Consequently, you construct who you are and how you are seen to some degree, but this might mean you need to only show part of yourself by hiding attributes of you. What you want to display is defined by society and culture as we want to be seen in a positive light. You cannot be labeled or viewed as a complete individual identity because the terms used connect to the society and culture you live within; what is seen as a positive label might change depending on the context, but some labels are hard to dismantle.

Some of my labels include: Professor. Mother. Wife. Daughter. Female. Criminologist. Scholar. Baker. Cooker. Gardener. Outdoor enthusiast. Reader. Dog, guinea pig, and chicken owner. Each of these labels means something to you after you read them. These labels provide a working conception of who you think I am. The order I wrote them also might indicate my priorities or how you see my priorities. But what if I provided a different set of labels: Feminist, Humanitarian, Social Drinker, Speeder, Shopper, and Arguer. How do you see my identity now? These labels provide truth in who I am but might give you caution if that was all that was known about me. Social identities are a mix of who we are and how we want people to see us. We do not let all people see all aspects of us at all times and we judge others based upon what we see or do not see in them.

We use labels as well as the status and roles publicly seen as shorthand guides to illuminate what we think we know about people. Certain labels hold more power than others when determining who a person is, if that person is trustworthy and if they should be allowed in my group. This is linked to one's master status. For instance, if you learn someone is a criminal, rapist, or victim – does that change the fact that they are a son, daughter, mother, father, or athlete? Not necessarily but we hold certain attributes as more important defining labels of one's situated identity (aka master status).

This perception of identity is also situationally dependent – are we in prison, school, work, home, playground, mechanic shop, grocery store? The situation connects with the identities of status and roles to build ourselves in light of the others in the situation. It is all encompassing. Social lives matter to our situated identity and the labels accepted as truths. We act how we want to be seen and how we think others will see us – it is a constant feedback loop when using symbolic interactionism and social construction as a reality builder. These labels impact the way we view the world and people while guiding various decisions.

Two theories within the structure of symbolic interactionism demonstrate how our situated identities build the decisions made during group interactions. Situated identity theory and expectation states theory are ways to see how labels, stigma, and attributes aid in decision-making processes of groups. Remember, symbolic interactionism assumes society and culture are created through interaction and construction. In our everyday events, large and small, we create the world and reality. We develop it through relationships within the society and cultural framework. Life is created and transfixed by the things we do with others and the perceptions developed from beliefs and behaviors of ourselves and others through imitation.

Situated identity theory examines the ways groups make decision together (Alexander & Knight, 1971; Alexander & Lauderdale, 1977; Alexander & Wiley, 1981; Touhey, 1974). The statuses and roles we see in our society connect to hierarchy levels depending upon the situation. Traditionally, the culture of the United States ranks the highest in the hierarchy those who are white, male, wealthy, heterosexual, and leaders. Subsequently, those who are people of color, female, poor or less wealthy, homosexual or non-heterosexual, and non-leaders are in the lower tiers of society. The intersectionality of your social status attributes combine create a personal identity; one that is viewed by your groups and demonstrates to them who you are. Hence, a white woman professional will be higher on the hierarchy than a black woman professional or a janitor who is white will be perceived lower in the status hierarchy than the bank teller who is white. The statuses combine to form quick snapshot judgments about the usefulness of a person.

To further complicate situated identity theory and its assumptions of the decision-making process, the identities we create in groups from the statuses held impact the decision-making process dependent on the group, its members, and the decision or task to be completed (Touhey, 1974). Situated identity theory further argues that we make decisions to make others happy in the group. People do not want to throw the group off balance and they will appeal to the top leaders of the groups or those that hold the most perceived power.

Hence, particular personas work better in certain environments, and socialization, as well as trial and error, helps us learn these techniques (Goffman, 1978). As discussed earlier, my role as a mother holds more meaning in my household decisions than being a female professor making decisions at work. At work, being a female professor can be viewed as a disadvantage to the male professors, unless the task at hand is perceived as a more female task, which is guided more by the second theory of expectation states. Regardless, when I am helping guide decisions, others use my situated identity to determine if my status and roles are useful to the task and I use my perceptions of the group to determine what task to engage in and what decisions to make. Situated identity theory suggests that we make momentary decisions about people based on roles and group conformity, we want to work with the status quo based upon perceived happiness of the group, and our group decisions defer to the hierarchy when determining what ought to be done to make a feel good decision. The group dynamics and members provide cues about what they prefer and how one is to act. This is why we act differently with various groups involved in discreet situations.

Expectation states theory clarifies the context for which situated identity theory functions. Expectation states theory presumes due to our culture and society, we know what statuses and attributes are viewed as positive and which are not due to assumed hierarchies (Berger & Wagner, 2007; Berger, Wagner, Webster, 2014; Correll & Ridgeway, 2006). We assess the situation we are in, the decision that needs to be made, look at the people around us, and determine who will help make the best decision. Thus, the type of people needed might change depending on the situational circumstance.

In this process, stereotypes from socialization are adhered to strongly because we create the decision helpers quickly within the context. We are only able to make such decisions in groups because of shortchange brain jumps that rely on schema and schemata. We look at the visual clues based on sex, gender, race, ethnicity, and any other attribute that are visual such as marital status or job title. Sometimes in longstanding groups, we can use past experiences to help build our decisions. If this is not available, we rely on stereotypes of identities and the hierarchies of society because our expectations from the verbal and non-verbal cues help determine the appropriate way to act (Berger & Wagner, 2007; Berger, et al., 2014).

To illustrate, whom we need to bake a cake (e.g. mother, female, wife) might be different from whom we select to build a bridge (e.g. male, engineer) and from who is perceived as knowing how to fix the dishwasher (e.g. father, male, husband) versus filling it (e.g. woman, girl). Expectation states theory suggests that decisions are stereotyped using bias secured throughout socialization. It also tends to keep decisions of in-groups and out-groups similar throughout time.

The two theories of situated identity and expectation states include an appreciation for implicit bias. Implicit or unconscious bias is the adhesive for actions, developments, and contexts within a society and culture. Implicit bias exists in all decisions and thought processes at the subconscious level. Biases are rooted into us so deeply that without examination, we rarely know its existence. These biases are formed at a personal level through socialization experiences but also are rooted in historical contexts of society and culture.

Implicit biases exist at various levels and connected to all statuses. Biases relate to perceptions of sex, gender, sexual orientation, race, ethnicity, weight, ability/disability, mental health, physical health, socio-economic status, and most other elements humans hold beliefs upon (cite). Biases are subconscious and created during socialization through feedback provided to us during experiences and interactions. We pick up on social cues of others or in books and movies to learn how we should interpret people and their attributes. We also learned connected values and beliefs about the attributes and the norms of hiding our thoughts or being able to express them. These beliefs impact daily routines, often without us knowing.

Implicit bias can start as prejudice, the thoughts, attitudes, and ideologies that share hierarchal beliefs and structures among status groups and roles. At times, these beliefs become discriminatory behaviors of an individual against the segments of social groups they are against or view negatively. Most of these biases are systemic and institutional, meaning that the large groups of a society or macro-level processes breed the biases in society and culture. The individual can then process it and let the cycle continue as the bias rests under the surface and rarely questioned or known to exist. These biases become ingrained in the foundation of social groups that we no longer see the bias as more than the society's status quo.

Taken together, these two symbolic interactionist theories assert that decisions are made by those who hold the most power in certain groups due to hierarchies of status symbols. The people who take the decision are chosen due to their perceived attributes. Those who will be listened to for advice, rules, and guidance might depend upon the decision being made but the structure of hierarchy remains strong. Much of this is unconscious and implicit; history, expectations, socialization, stigma, and status quo impact many decisions. This in many decisions, including that in criminal justice regarding rape – those who are white, male, rich, educated, and of European decent – will more likely be listened to and believed. This matters in the roles of court decisions and law enforcement actions with respect to who is a victim and who is a perpetrator. It is supported by these two theories and the purview of implicit bias that victims might not be believed or seen as accountable because of their statuses, typically being women and sometimes includes those women who are poor or racial minorities against accused males who might be male and rich and educated (think Brock Turner, Harvey Weinstein, and Justice Kavanaugh).

Rape culture and myth terminology

Historical trends dictated and developed the definitions of sexual assault and rape. One place to start is with the knowledge that sexual assault is a continuum of behaviors with rape being on the gravest end of the continuum. If rape is at the end of the continuum, the beginning could be sexual behaviors such as butt grabbing, forceful kissing, and groping that are unwanted. Rape is separated from other forms of sexual assault by the definitional characteristic of rape necessitating penetration of self or objects into bodily orifices, including mouths, anuses, and vaginas. Different legal jurisdictions (e.g. states, cities, and federal) hold various definitions for the levels of sexual assault, including how rape is defined. Sexual assault always includes sexual behavior that occurs without consent of both parties.

Consent is the providing approval for all steps in a sexual encounter. Consent can be murky and an implicit or assumed understanding between persons engaging in sexual behavior. Although we should want people who shout YES to participate in kissing and sex, this is not always the case (see *Yes means Yes*, Friedman and Valenti, 2019,). Consent to kissing is not the same as consent for oral sex and this is not the same as consent for sexual penetration. These are various steps in a sexual encounter that necessitate working through consent practices. Yet, as demonstrated later, the consent process becomes part of rape myths that can lead to sexual assaults without either party realizing it.

Sexual assault has a varied history of definition which leads in part to the confusion and lack of coordinated efforts by legal systems and society (Freedman, 2013). Governmental jurisdictions of federal and different states create their own definitions for what behaviors are sexual harassment, sexual assault, and rape. To note, it was not illegal nationwide for a man to rape his wife until 1993! Also, only women could be victims of rape until 2012 when the FBI finally defined men as possible rape victims because penetration could be of something other than a vagina. It was not until 2018 when the FBI declared that rape did not have to be considered forcible and that physical evidence of bruising or an altercation was not part of the definition. Certain states still define rape only as the penetration of a penis into a vagina so that fingers and objects do not constitute rape. This was the case in California when Brock Turner assaulted Chanel Miller, it was not rape because of the definition; this changed afterward. Thorough addresses of this definitional history are written in other books such as Brownmiller's *Against our Will* (1975).

The way a society defines behaviors determines who will be a criminal or in this case a rapist. Yet, to also be considered a rapist, you must be caught, prosecuted, and determined guilty. Without this action of the criminal law, the victim's voice is nothing more than accusations, words that often are perceived as untruths because of rape culture and myths.

Rape culture is present within the society of the United States and any other culture who perceives the dominion of patriarchy as a rationale for sexual assaults (Brownmiller, 1975; Burt, 1980). It creates assumptions that minimize the impact and effect of sexual assaults; men and others who victimize are not challenged and the behavior goes unrecognized. Rape culture also contains ideologies of sexism, genderism, homophobia, and misogyny.

Rape culture allows for the use of sexual coercion and harassment in everyday normal interactions. Actions that represent rape culture are considered norms and typical behaviors from certain segments of society, namely men. Rape culture acts as an implicit bias especially in the age of political correctness; we all know to be against rape but do little to act out against it or its tributaries. It is why locker room talk is championed and why boys will be boys. Rape culture allows boys to hit and kick a girl when they like each other while thinking this is appropriate. Rape culture triumphs in the nuances of conversations when men can list sexual conquests and be a hero, whereas women become slut-shamed and viewed as troublemakers for their sexual desires. Rape culture is the ability of bystanders to ignore actions that lead to sexual assault and rape because it is seen as not a big deal and nothing that needs an intervention (for instance, read Gay, 2019).

The rape culture also creates biases present in victim blaming that often occurs when people are accused. The victim is perceived as the problem because they tried to open the story on rape but also lying. Those who speak about rape are seen as troublemakers who are rocking the boat. Rape culture protects rape and sexual assault by building the walls that make it an unseen phenomenon by remaining in darkness. Rape culture does not triumph those who report sexual assault and rape to friends, families, universities, and law enforcement. Rape culture shuns and stigmatizes accusers and blames victims for ruining the life of the accused; this even continues once people are found guilty. Rape culture, thus, perpetuates and creates the correct social environment for rape myths to be created, marinated, and believed.

A place to start with rape myths is the contention of perceived victim blameworthiness. One accepted definition of rape myth that is connected well to the studies shown herein is "attitudes and beliefs that are generally false but are widely and persistently held, and that serve to deny and justify male sexual aggression against women" (Lonsway & Fitzgerald, 1994, p. 134). Thus, victim blame is a beginning to understand this complicated nuanced term. Rape myths hold fast in ideologies and assumptions of why sexual assaults occur, and thus often excuse the behavior.

Rape myths include the suggestion that sexual assaults occur when partying especially when someone (a woman) was drinking or using other drugs

(Johnston, 2013). Rape myths propose that people are raped only by strangers in dark alleys at night fulfilling what has been termed the blitz rape scenario. The blitz rape scenario or an accepted rape script foretells that proper rape is when the victims are seriously physically harmed by the attacker and the bruises, scratches, and blood let the world know the victim fought hard against the sexual encounter. This fighting proves that she did not want the sex and did all she could to let the rapist know. Without this physical proof, did the sexual assault really happen?

This depiction of the blitz rape script disallows for other rapes and sexual assaults to be noticed or affirmed (Bowie, Silverman, Kalick, & Edbril, 1990; Clay-Warner & McMahon-Howard, 2009). Rape myths build a world within rape cultures where acquaintance rape, date rape, party rape, and marital rape do not exist or at least are of little concern. Assault blurs among consent practices allowing for assumptions that if you are in a relationship, including friendships, then consent had to be provided or rightly was understood through tacit agreement during the sexual behaviors because it is assumed that only strangers rape people. Rape myths often ignore sexual coercion to gain approval of reluctant or non-participatory partners. Rape myths allow the true nature of sexual assault to go unnoticed, trivialized, and ignored.

Rape myths further confuse sexual assault by creating social expectations of what happens when someone, especially a woman, admits to sexual assault victimization (Lonsway & Fitzgerald, 1994; McMahon & Farmer, 2011; Payne, Lonsway, & Fitzgerald, 1999). Rape myths include beliefs of perceived victim blame, including the assertions of he didn't mean to rape, she is lying about the rape, she asked for the rape to happen, and the rape was not real rape. He did not mean to rape is a collection of ideas about thinking that consent was present, that he was drunk, or that he was so overcome by desire that he simply could not stop himself. She is lying includes the axioms that she is trying to get revenge at a man for breaking up with her, she wants notoriety, she wants to get a man in trouble, or she regrets having sex and claims rape. She asked for it to happen includes assumptions that she was acting out of her gender role by being too promiscuous or slutty. She kissed him or wore revealing clothing or did not say no loud enough or did not fight back hard enough.

It was not real rape includes ideas about consent in that the woman did not say no loud enough or that she was drunk or that she did not fight back from her attacker. All these principles advocate for the belief that it is the woman's prerogative to stop rape, not enjoy sexual activity, defend herself, and not dress in ways that turn men on (Burt, 1980; 1991; Edwards et al., 2011). Rape myths do not assume that men can stop rape by not raping; it is the woman's role to not become a victim by any means necessary. Hence, the blitz rape script scenario that deems a rape a true rape only when the woman victim yells and fights for her freedom.

Rape myths and rape culture put the onerousness on women without examining the true cause of rape – rapists. Rape myths discourage discussion and acceptance truth in sexual assaults in the use of power in sexual conquests. It denies the role society and culture have in developing environments ripe for excusing rapists for their actions. It fosters disbelief when victims tell their sexual assault stories and places the need for victims to defend themselves and prove their truthfulness. Rape myths do not provide opportunities for understanding about sexual assault because the myths suggest that it is the woman's fault for being raped and not the man's responsibility; she was raped because she stepped out of her sex role by acting against femininity and womanly social sexual guidelines.

Masculinity and feminism

Social roles and identities are the building blocks of how society and culture move along and allow us to make quick judgments while ascertaining knowledge about people through visible and assumed characteristics. Ultimately, this becomes an intersectionality of qualities such as age, race, ethnicity, sex, gender, marital status, professional status, socio-economic status, and even educational attainment. Intersectionality is the coming together of characteristics and assumed meanings of those attributes. We glean much of this from how people present themselves through preening of clothing, make-up, hairstyle, speech, and physical features especially of the face. Is the person wearing a ring and on which finger? Is the person wearing make-up? Does the person have long hair? Is the person wearing a dress or a power suit? Does the person have white skin? Does the person speak eloquently without slang? Does the person have gray hair or wrinkles? These attributes and more help society members discern what type of person they are and what categories they fit into.

These quick assumptions are based on personal and social socialization in which we learn stereotypes of roles and status. This includes our beliefs and our values toward these roles and statuses. As discussed above, these perceived statuses and roles allow people to make other oversimplifications about people with respect to their abilities, ideas, personality, intelligence, and overall worth. Certain statuses hold power in society and culture – such that in the United States those who are male, educated, wealthy, white, of European descent, and middle-aged but not yet senile, traditionally hold the top hierarchies of power distribution. As a patriarchal culture that holds strong values in sex roles and traditions, the social identities of men and women or males and females cannot be ignored when disentangling sexual assault, rape myth, and rape culture.

Much of this is seen as a polarized experience; you can be female and feminine or male and masculine, and the roles and rules cannot be crossed (Spruill, 2017). Gender roles of male and female are perceived as pervasive and static without gray areas. This neglects the reality of socially constructed experience where femininity and masculinity are two distinct continuums not one with pole ends of masculine and feminine (Murphy, 2004; Pagila, 2017). Instead, we might view one as a little feminine to a whole lot of feminine and a little masculine to a whole lot of masculine. These labels in themselves are then depicted through cultural association of what it means to be masculine and feminine and often ignore what else we can create and become.

Some traditional feminine questions would ask: Do you wear dresses? Do you use make-up? Are you sweet and silent? Are you coy and elusive? Some traditional masculine questions would ask: Are you strong? Do you wear suits? Do you like to get dirty? Do you fix cars? Are you powerful? Even writing these examples makes me cringe with stereotypical babble nonsense. Although these examples might help define masculinity and femininity, it does not provide answers about which of these people are male or female, although many would link responses to sex roles and gender association. As we know, boys can wear dresses with ruffles and play with trucks. Girls can play sports, fix cars, and bake a cake (like me!).

The role of femininity, as well as masculinity, is controlled and constrained by the social construction of gender roles. Although the role of femininity is changing, its traditional manifestations still reside in our viewpoints and ideologies of what it means to be female. Femininity at its core is about love, quietness, and empathy. Women are to be nurturing and caring. This is of and for others – nurturing to children and older family and caring for the needs of husbands and other men. Femininity is the ability to place others needs as part of her desires. This ability to care for others is the equation of love and viewed in terms of household chores. Raising babies, cleaning houses, making dinners, finding slippers, creating drinks, and being the perfect hostess is femininity. Doing all this while having coiffed hair, pressed dresses, and positive conversation is love as well as quietness. Femininity is deferring to men and letting them speak as well as rule the house. Femininity is docility and not questioning authority or the power and strength holds of men. Femininity is not holding jobs outside of the house as it makes the masculine breadwinner look weak. This traditional image of femininity has lost weight among younger generations as expressed in *Alpha Girls* and *Fight like a Girl*, but these conceptions still are ever-present.

Masculinity is expressed often as the opposite of femininity, but this is not reality through social constructionism (Lorber & Ferrall, 1991). It is not masculinity versus femininity but how much of each do you hold to create your gender through social construction and symbolic interactionism. Gender is socially created and as such we grab bits and pieces of both femininity and masculinity to create who we are and thus impact how society views us and how we perceive ourselves. Remember, this is the feedback loop of social identity. This identity is developed through socialization experiences of imitation, positive and negative reinforcement, and self-images. Thus, a person holds feminine traits and masculine traits simultaneously and perhaps even something outside of labels and these simplistic continuums.

Traditional masculinity and aggressiveness are viewed as a lack of empathy and dash of toxicity through power, aggression, and anger (Ford, 2018; Pagila, 2017). Masculinity has not shifted the same way femininity has through civil rights and feminism; it is static to the hindrance of males. Masculine identities are synonymous with strength and power. To be masculine means fixing cars, watching and playing sports, doing house maintenance, and keeping a woman (cite to manliness book and how to be a man and boys will be boys). Masculinity allows sexual actions regardless of marital status and men gain more status the more sexual conquests are gained. Males in this social construction express few emotions except for anger, happiness, and indifference. Masculine people do not care for children, do not cook, do not express empathy or sadness, and do not lose power. These characteristics are paramount to status and level of respect when being perceived as a man. Masculinity holds onto the role of breadwinner that he must work outside of the house to make money that affords everything the family needs. He controls the household through this money and power. Being masculine is rooted in ideas of "boys will be boys" and "don't cry." Masculinity conceptions are unforgiving and solid; there is little room for negotiation in a world where you need to be seen as tough.

Feminism has a colorful history that is not without conflicts and counterpoints. This is not a complete historical record of feminism but a brief highlight to appreciate the term feminism in how it is being accessed and connected within this book (for additional reads not noted elsewhere, see *Bad Feminist, feminism is for everybody, The Bridge Called my Back*, and *The Feminine Mystique*). The feminist movement or women's movement was a means to gain equitable treatment with acknowledging the social hierarchal gaps between men and women. Many thought that the gaps of housewife and breadwinner were biological creations making women inferior and unable to move outside of household chores. Girls were socialized to become mothers and wives and to not think beyond those roles. Girls education was downplayed, teaching them to read was pointless, and letting them attend school was a waste of money.

Boys were socialized to become employees and breadwinners with the luck of being husbands and fathers, but those roles were subservient to that of being economically successful. Economic success was key to keeping a wife and family (Ford, 2018; Murphy, 2004). While females were placed inside the household for chores, men were placed outside of the house so that inside the house became trophies of success as well. Having well-trained wife and children bolstered the man's success of running the household without acknowledging the work a female completed. Women and children were proprietary persons who had little say in their activities or household events.

Women sought more than their assigned birth roles; for instance, access to education, employment, and voting (Ford, 2016; Pagila, 2017). Women were determined to find a path that did not define them through men or children, and one that allowed for transactional power of self. The ideals of feminism allowed women and the world to see that females are more than mothers and wives and beyond nurses, teachers, and secretaries. The fight for equity through feminism provided prospects for female voices to be heard by gaining power restlessly denied.

The aspect this book chooses to focus upon is the power of claiming one's sexual desire and control over bodies. Men controlled many aspects of married life, including when, how, and where to have sexual relations. Society and culture made rules of when a girl or woman could marry, the price she earned in dowry, and the prospect of giving the man a boy in childbirth. Sexual coercion was often part of these relationships and was expected. Women were not to have control over their sexual beings. The men in their lives owned it, whether it was their father owning the virginity or the husband owning sexual power. If a woman did not have the ability to control her own sexual desires and doled it out on request through coercion or not, this often was implicit consent. Consent without bearing or truth, imagine the number of sexual assaults that occurred in relationships because it was the norm. This norm is a base of why sexual assaults in relationships is still trivialized and not taken seriously. How do you prove that your husband or boyfriend, or girlfriend or wife assaulted you especially at a time where domestic violence was also seen as a problem of the home and not society? This is partially why sexual assaults or "lesser rapes" or "unreal rapes" still mean so little to many in this culture.

National law did not recognize a husband's ability to rape his wife or a wife's victimhood until 1993 with Nebraska starting definitional changes in the last 1970s. Women seen as the property of their husbands and made to provide sexual services were not a matter of concern to law. This role of marriage included the ideal woman to play the docile female who held no sexual desire, while men were encouraged to conquest. This social role acceptance of hierarchy in sexual behavior resulted from historical struggles, including war, laws, dowries, and cultural attitudes.

As Brownmiller (1975) stated controversially in her book *Against our Wills*, sexual assault and rape had little to do with sex and were created by the desire of power over women. Rape was a catalyst for men holding onto power in their world and demonstrating control over much more than the women being raped. Rape was a tactic in war to illustrate the power of soldiers and countries over people. By domineering women, fear and supremacy were created. Men did not want their women (i.e. daughters, sisters, and wives) raped and made unmarriageable or outcasts of society. Sieged countries reluctantly ended battles and turned over areas of land to protect their women from tragic ends. It was not always the assault the women were being protected from but resulting loss of their female virginial sacredness. As such, it was still about men protecting their women and not creating a voice by or for women.

This eventually resulted in women fighting for equality in society through the need to exhibit ownership of their personal sexual worth. The feminist movement included rights to birth control and abortion as well as demonstrated control over their choices in acting on their sexual desires. The prolific stories of bra burning were incidental fights in women gaining control of what bound them; it became one means for women to showcase their freedom. This movement gave women authority over their bodies in deciding when to have sex for pleasure as well as when to have children, if they choose. This type of freedom opened more professional and educational paths as women saw themselves as something beyond mother, daughter, and wife. This is not to state that all is equal; women's roles still are fraught with complexities of role acquisition and competing demands as well as the proverbial glass ceiling.

Sex roles have changed during women's right movement and with the acceptance of feminism, but what it means to be feminism is not clear-cut or acceptable by all. Many within the fight for feminism and equity have not been able to agree with what the result should be in sexual liberation and sexual role movements (the bridge is my back book cite). The path of feminism and women's rights is not always agreed upon. Different situated identities need different fixes for equity to be created. There is not one way to achieve the goals of feminism in the fight for limiting the power of rape culture; in fact, some feminists denounce the terms rape culture and rape myths (Bevacqua, 2000; Charen, 2018; Keyser; 2019).

Thus, what still is prevalent in society is the vision of polarized sexes and genders. Polarity is seeing the world split in black and white or us versus them or conflictual groups. Polarity is divisive and creates the inability to see others as connected oneself. It disallows one to see the fight for feminism as being for all sexes and genders. It allows women to be against men and both to be against genders outside of cisgender labels. This polarity allows for the fights of feminism to lose intersectionality connections of poor women being against rich women and women who are white against those who are not. As such, the plight of Black women cannot be the same as that for white women much less that of what men see as the use of feminism. This leaves a segmented argument and power struggle limiting equity movements' abilities to shift paradigms and ideologies.

As Klein (2020) and Spruill (2017) argue, the 21st century could be better adapted at providing equity to humanity by limiting how polarity is viewed. Polarity thrusts equity movements wrongly into political actions. Once a political action, people can polarize the issues exponentially and it becomes a liberal versus conservative and democrat versus republican agendas. This polarization and oversimplification limits the power of movements in fights for equity because it places the changes desired against ingrown ideals of consensus morality decisions. Once issues become polarized and against the stronghold of morals, the equity concerns lose their punch in the movement. Once this happens, the movement loses power and forward momentum as it must fight against the backlash and moral convictions. To illustrate, one might have strong opinions against sexual assault and rape but if brought against a conservative ideology of anti-abortion – it is more difficult for feminist movements or their benchmarks to gain traction.

The result of this polarity is that women's issues are just that – something women need to contend with and find ways to overcome. It is not accepted by the larger society as needed paradigm shifts. Thus, the ability of feminism and women's movement to make changes in the past 100 years is nothing short of a miracle. The changes developed in sexual assault laws and regulations have been won but these have not altered the consensus of society and culture. Rape culture still exists. Rape myths still believed. Sexual coercion still occurs. Victims still are blamed. Men still are studs, while women are sluts. Abortions still are questioned as are birth control methods and Plan B. Men still conquest women.

Sexual harassment still is as part of the workplace. Rape still occurs without reports and convictions. The power of sex still is held by men and acquisitioned by women.

University environment and sexual assault

Title IX since 1972 regulates the duties and roles of university faculty, staff, and administration in reporting sexual assaults, including rape. The rules dictate mandatory reporters (i.e. almost everyone who is a university employee) and appropriate channels for reporting alleged or suspicious sexual assaults of students. Most universities have Title IX coordinators who aid in the regulatory behaviors, including running conduct hearings or investigations when allegations among students occur. The Clery Act was developed in 1990 to ensure universities reported all numbers of sexual assaults, rapes, and sexual harassments that happened on campus grounds to its community. The intent of these regulations was to encourage reporting of sexual assaults on campuses to make campuses safer, but it has largely missed this target.

Regulations were changed in 2020 almost reversing the course of Title IX by reducing its structure for university investigatory hearings and limiting mandatory reporters. For instance, athletic coaches no longer are mandatory reporters, whereas this role remains for faculty. The burden of proof has shifted away from the accused to the accuser in the conduct hearings increasing the weight of the victim to explain themselves and have undisputable proof that the sexual assault occurred. Universities can select how they will proceed and can create stricter rules than Title IX, but it is too early to know what universities will choose or the ramifications of the changes.

Title IX was a welcomed approach to protecting and educating students about sexual assaults on campuses. It also created the need for universities to demonstrate self-protection qualities while educating certain groups (i.e. fraternities and athletics) in how to make the university safer. Universities developed education for its freshman often in the form of a large presentation often through mind-numbing slides. This allows universities to claim that they met the requirements of Title IX and educated all students about the concerns of sexual assault, how to protect themselves, and how to report sexual assaults on campus, including who is a mandatory reporter. Universities also needed to run campaigns for its athletes and fraternity members falling prey to the assumption that this is who engages in sexual assaults.

Title IX is deemed problematic by some scholars and universities. It creates a university conduct structure where they are to investigate sexual assault allegations internally and do not have to provide information to law enforcement (cite). This internal investigation places emphasis on truth-seeking and not counseling or fixing the situation for either party. One concern is that it demonizes universities and places too much emphasis on allegations, sexual misconduct, and rapes. It makes universities appear to be more unsafe than other parts of society and institutions. As Mac Donald (2018) and Johnson and Taylor (2017) proposed, this is negative for the university and wastes precious resources on conduct hearings and victim response teams. It makes students fearful of attending the school and adds to discontent of universities not doing enough to stop the rape crisis. It perhaps even leads to concerns of hiding sexual assaults as made apparent in books like *The Hunting Game* (Dick & Ziering, 2016), *Violated* (Lavigne & Schlabach, 2017), and *Missoula* (Krakauer, 2016).

However, even prior to Title IX, universities connected with groups and programming to help educate about sexual assaults. In the 1980s and 1990s, these education efforts included lots of self-defense training for women and discussion about how to self-protect on campus, the ideals of victim blaming and rape myths. Ideas of not wearing skimpy clothing, not drinking heavily, not walking by yourself late at night, and not encouraging men relied on rape myths to protect women students. In the 2000s and 2010s, additional efforts were developed following the yes means yes movement and bystander intervention. Knowledge about rape myths was growing to encourage universities to develop novel ways to prevent sexual assaults.

The *Yes means Yes* (Friendman & Valienti, 2019) movement encouraged smart and demonstrable consent – you want people to say yes to sexual behaviors and not just implicitly agree. Consent is a powerful tool that many currently in college can define and recite what should be done during sexual encounters. You want your partner to say yes to the questions you ask about what behaviors are allowed. You should have conversations before and after sexual behaviors to know what was acceptable. You should not force your partner into anything sexual as saying nothing is the same as saying no; implicit consent might exist, but you need to know what you are doing is fine with your partner. However, college students still are confused how to actually do engage in appropriate consent (Freitas, 2018) without feeling weird. In a hookup culture, where your partner might not be well-known, and the intent is sex, consent becomes even murkier and hard to grasp. It is a learned process.

Many universities succumb to the belief that the masculine world of sports and fraternities creates appropriate spaces for sexual assault to occur. Many studies and educational efforts focus on these two groups with the assumption that if you can stop the behaviors of these men, sexual assaults will decrease on college campuses. Consequently, many resources and campaigns are delivered to these groups on campuses disregarding female organizations and athletics as well as other student organizations to promote positive masculinity. Although fraternity members and athletes are to blame for some sexual assaults, it is not as simple as assuming these groups solely are responsible. Remember groups have norms, values, and beliefs that might be congruent to rape myths and rape culture, but rapes are individual actions and behaviors.

For instance, Hechinger (2017) provides details about a fraternity that teaches men how to be true gentlemen but also informally compliments sexual conquests and power over females. As a group, this fraternity condones sexual conquests and to a degree sexual assault. Yet, not all brothers in the fraternity are rapists and assaulters. It might be encouraged and trivialized as women who attend the parties know what they are getting themselves into, but it is still an individual action. The group holds norms and beliefs that the individual must decide if that is part of their personality, identity, and actions. Remember, our groups are part of our decision-making processes; we want the other members of our groups to like us and be content with the decisions made. Working in these groups makes sense but not blame in totality. Blaming these masculine groups fosters the ideals of rape myths about who society should fear – large groups of men – and discounts acquaintance rapes and date rapes of which many have nothing to do with these two groups.

One reason athletes and fraternities are singled out is because of their connection to parties, beer, and freedom (Sperber, 2000). Rape culture perpetuates that rapes and sexual assaults occur when people are drunk and acting scandalously testing out their independence by living social life of being a university student. When individuals are perceived as not protecting their safety, especially when women are drinking in skimpy clothing surrounded by young men, she is asking to be raped. It developed into the rape myths of he didn't mean to and she was asking for it. These victim blaming perceptions develop false stories of when and how rape can occur. Rape does occur during parties by fraternity members and athletes, but it also occurs while in a dormitory with a close friend while watching a movie or off-campus to non-university students in the same age group.

Unsafe in the Ivory Tower (Fisher, Daigle, & Cullen, 2010) demonstrated the reasons students and university employees must understand the problems of sexual assault and remove themselves from the ideologies of implicit biases surrounding when, where, and why rapes or sexual assaults occur. The dark side of university life marks clearly the concerns but not moving beyond the false definitions of real rape. Although official numbers are most likely incorrect due to unrecording, university environments can make themselves more supportive by showing faculty, staff, and especially students how to define sexual assaults and how to react when they undoubtably occur. As many of the case studies show, if students feel comfortable in telling their rape and sexual assault stories, the shame can lessen and moves others to let their stories out.

Another concern of university life that connects with rape myths, rape culture, and sexual assaults is the hookup culture. This phrase demonstrates the desire of people to engage in sexual behaviors outside of serious or monogamous relationships. The hookup culture moves away from the traditional norms of building a long-term relationship that could lead to marriage and favors short-term connections that allow human sexual needs to be met. It places the creation of relationships on the back-burner slogans such as one-night stands and friends with benefits. It allows for the mutual understanding that sex is a given when hookups and connections are created.

Wade (2017) describes her research about this new culture of sex in *American Hookup: The New Culture of Sex on Campus*. She explains that this might be the new way to create enjoyable sexual relationships without the need for relationship building. The purpose is to not want a long-term relationship by building meaninglessness in the hookup. The steps of this meaningless hookup include drinking, partying, finding an object, and starting the hookup through kissing, grinding, dancing, or other initiations. For many, the purpose of partying on college campuses is to find hookups. However, this is not always the goal and it places much pressure on males and females to hookup and score so that they are not seen as wimps. Sexual conquests still are important, but the idea is that there is less of a need to hide desire.

The dark side of the hookup culture is that it connects with the rape culture and the lack of building consent practices. The hookup culture alongside partying or dating apps or Netflix and chill develop situation where sex is assumed and questions about consent do not need to be asked. It places extra pressure or sexual coercion into the gathering because people feel like they must have sex for the hookup to be successful or be labeled a prude or a tease. Women might also still be viewed as a slut in the hookup culture, while men gain positive views of being studs. The concern is that without clear-cut consent practices and assumptions that sex will occur; blur the lines of sexual assault.

Phillips (2017) in *Beyond Blurred Lines: Rape Culture in Popular Media* described college campus as breeding grounds for rape culture as well as its discrediting. The mixture of young adulthood, media portraying sex as inevitable on campus, and the need for freedom or independence builds the expectation of hookups. People do not presume that the rape culture impacts their daily lives by their university being unsafe. Especially when myths tell us that sexual assaults are physical altercations of demented strangers in dark alleys. When the story we tell ourselves about rapes does not include quiet dorm rooms and friends, we are disallowing ourselves to see the negative power of a hookup culture. That hookups go sour and this allows for men to say that sex occurred while women scream assault or that victims might not even know that they were assaults due to blurred lines and ideas of what a sexual assault is. The power of media in shaping the discourse around sexual assaults is strong in providing the imagery of so-called real rapes.

In some interviews, women discussed their thoughts about the hookup culture. For instance,

> I think there is in my feelings from what I've seen from one of my friends said some of my friends is that there's less focus on what really is scenario where you should be able to give him physically and emotionally OK with these things are happening like being high or being drunk have many friends will engage in sex while drunk and they're like I mean I felt a little dirty afterwards but I'm OK I felt like this there like I it's kind of like this well I have this experience now and that's important because now I'm more experience and experience is important.

She demonstrated that hooking up on this campus happens a lot and is fueled by alcohol. That by being under the influence you have an excuse for your actions in satisfying sexual desires with semi-anonymous people. It is a way to gain sexual experience without feeling too overwhelmed by the prospect of being in an unknown situation. Alpha girls want to have control and mastery in all aspects of their life.

Another woman interviewee reinforces that the alcohol fueled hookups on campus and its potential downside.

> You get into situations where you don't know what happened, maybe you are spiraling into things and place yourself in a weird position. I know of a situation of a friend. She was extremely intoxicated and she was dancing all over the party all night long in front of me. She left with someone and I didn't know where they went. She was a virgin before that night. They had sex but in her mind he raped her. He said he took her to her dorm and left without touching her. But she is unclear and knows something happened. I don't know who to believe. In this world of hook up culture and alcohol, how do you know.

Hookups have a negative side especially when fueled by alcohol, hormones, and adrenalin (Johnston, 2013; Wade, 2017). Although the purpose is to have fun in a non-committal manner, sexual assaults occur during them. When people are intoxicated and unsure about proper consent mechanisms or cannot slur together words, rape happens.

According to the book, *Drink* (Johnston, 2013), part of college life and rape myths is the commitment to drinking by men and women. Females used to drink less and not try to outdrink male counterparts. Binge drinking is part of the college environment and culture and females, wanting equity, engage in it more than ever, binge drinking among females is on the rise in college populations. Mix this with other risk-taking behaviors and hookup cultures provide an opportune moment for assaults to occur. Some scholars will use this to blame women for being stupid in making poor decisions and blame them for their assaults. Others will say that women need to be smarter not in a victim blame manner but in the way we wear seatbelts in cars and helmets on bikes. Despite advances and desires for equity, society is not there yet. Protection still is merited even if it is not fair.

Summary

My argument in this book is that our culture creates definitions of right and wrong through socialization. We learn how to act, speak, and think largely due to early socialization from family and then school and peers; this evolves into workplace learning and all other connections made, including social groups and organizations. These connections define who we are and thus how we respond to situations such as sexual assault.

The rape culture and ideas of rape myths are now part of mainstream conversations and discussion, even though many do not recognize full definitions. The same with sexual assault and consent; the words are meaningful, but few appreciate the nuances of the terms and what they truly mean. Ideals of feminism, femininity, and masculinity provide contexts for socialization of what women and men (or girls and boys) are to do situations. This makes the world of dating and hookups even more confusing in the shadows of gray, especially when we deem ourselves safe and invincible as many young college students do.

By accepting the world of aggressive men and docile females, by presuming even consensual sex has moments of coercion and male domination, by groups starting this is appropriate actions and behaviors – individuals are at a loss for when sexual assaults occur. When assaults do occur, people barely admit it to themselves much less accepting the stigma and shame by sharing the experience with others. In a patriarchal and misogynistic environment; female victims still are battle against themselves when reporting rapes or sexual assault. Socialization tells women to accept the power of men, in all forms including silence of sexual assault especially when those sexual assaults do not align to the blitz rape scenario.

The studies explored in the remaining portion of this book help support this argument as well as demonstrate the need for more research. This research needs to move beyond heteronormativity explanations of myths and culture. It also needs more movement in university walls to gather strength in appreciating the subtilties of intersectional populations as many studies rely on samples that are majorly white and upper middle class. More work, especially qualitative, needs to be accomplished with males and ideals of masculinity to draw connections. Also, additional variables work to develop a social psychological foundation of appreciating sexual assault, its movements, and cultural forces.

This book is not suggesting that rape culture is the only entity that generates rapes and sexual assault. Crime causation is difficult to measure and develop appropriate theories that align with individual rationales. Criminology acknowledges that crimes and deviance occur due to biological, sociological, and psychological reasons. These three paradigms of thoughts built the foundations of criminology and its theoretical constructs through the modern appreciation that sociological, psychological, and biological traits create tendencies to engage in crime. When people hold particular traits, they are more or less likely to engage in deviance and crime, but it is never certain that crime will happen. There is no magic equation or recipe that states when and if an individual will act in criminal behaviors. These theories are built through research that examines mostly men and boys to see why people are more likely to engage in crime. This is based on statistics and narratives of patterns. Thus, we have theories about crime. We have theories and beliefs about the causation of sexual assault and rape; the rape culture is part of it.

The rape culture is one means our society develops cultural norms, behaviors, values, and artifacts. It helps dictate appropriate gender and sex roles, including rules for how people are to act in family, education, careers, and relationships. Rape culture builds traditions within institutions of family, education, government, employment, and others to state what is appropriate to occur in these groups. I am concerned with sexual assaults and rapes, but the rape culture is devastating beyond this outcome – it shapes the worlds of females and males into binary simplicity and creates negative outcomes for both. Women have a higher rate to be assaulted but both men and women are impacted through their psychological well-being which manifests into their physical and biological health. This book showcases one element of rape culture while integrating it with the nuanced identities we create.

References

Alexander Jr, C. N., & Knight, G. W. (1971). Situated identities and social psychological experimentation. *Sociometry, 34,* 65–82.
Alexander Jr, C. N., & Lauderdale, P. (1977). Situated identities and social influence. *Sociometry, 40,* 225–233.
Alexander, C. N., & Wiley, M. G. (1981). Situated activity and identity formation. In Rosenberg, M., & Turner, R. H. (Eds.). *Social psychology: Sociological perspectives* (pp. 269–289). Transaction Publishers.
Berger, P., & Luckman, T. (1966). *The Social Construction of Reality.* Anchor Books.
Berger, J., & Wagner, D. G. (2007). Expectation states theory. *The Blackwell Encyclopedia of Sociology,* 1–5.
Berger, J., Wagner, D.G. and Webster, M. (2014), Expectation states theory: Growth, opportunities and challenges. In Thye, S. R. & Lawler, E. J. (Eds). *Advances in Group Processes* (Vol. 31, pp. 19–55), Emerald Group Publishing Limited. https://doi.org/10.1108/S0882-614520140000031000
Bevacqua, M. (2000). *Rape on the public agenda.* Northeastern University Press.
Blumer, H. (1986). *Symbolic interactionism: Perspective and method.* University of California Press.
Bowie, S. I., Silverman, D. C., Kalick, S. M., & Edbril, S. D. (1990). Blitz rape and confidence rape: Implications for clinical intervention. *American Journal of Psychotherapy, 44,* 180–188.
Brownmiller, S. (1975). *Against our will: Men, women, and rape.* Ballantine Books.
Burt, M. R. (1980). Cultural myths and supports for rape. *Journal of Personality and Social Psychology, 38,* 217–230.
Burt, M. R. (1991). Rape myths and acquaintance rape. In Parrot, A. & Bechhofer, L. (Eds.), *Acquaintance rape: The hidden crime* (pp. 26–40). John Wiley & Sons.
Charen, M. (2018). *Sex matters.* Crown Forum.
Clay-Warner, J., & McMahon-Howard, J. (2009). Rape reporting: "Classic rape" and the behavior of law. *Violence and Victims, 24*(6), 723–743.
Correll, S. J., & Ridgeway, C. L. (2006). Expectation states theory. In DeLamater, J (Ed.) *Handbook of social psychology* (pp. 29–51). Springer.
Dick, K., & Ziering, A. (2016). *The hunting ground.* Skyhorse Publishing.
Durkheim, E. (1933). *The division of labor.* Trans. G. Simpson. Macmillan.
Durkheim, E. (1897/1961). *Suicide.* Glencoe.
Edwards, K. M., Turchik, J. A., Dardis, C. M., Reynolds, N., & Gidycz, C. A. (2011). Rape myths: History, individual and institutional-level presence, and implications for change. *Sex roles, 65,* 761–773.

Fisher, B. S., Daigle, L. E., & Cullen, F. T. (2010). *Unsafe in the Ivory Tower*. Sage.
Ford, C. (2018). *Boys will be boys: Power, patriarchy and toxic masculinity*. Oneworld.
Ford, C. (2016). *Fight like a girl*. Oneworld.
Freedman, E. B. (2013). *Redefining rape*. Harvard University Press.
Freitas, D. (2018). *Consent on campus*. Oxford University Press.
Friedman, J., & Valenti, J. (Eds.). (2019). *Yes means yes!: Visions of female sexual power and a world without rape*. Seal Press.
Gay, R. (2019). *Bad feminist*. Verlag.
Goffman, E. (2009). *Stigma: Notes on the management of spoiled identity*. Simon and Schuster.
Goffman, E. (1978). *The presentation of self in everyday life*. Harmondsworth.
Hechinger, J. (2017). *True gentlemen*. Public Affairs.
Johnson, K. C., & Taylor Jr., S. (2017). *The campus rape frenzy: The attack on due process at America's universities*. Encounter Books.
Johnston, A. D. (2013). *Drink*. Harper Wave.
Keyser, A. J. (2019). *No more excuses*. Twenty-First Century Books.
Klein, E. (2020). *Why we're polarized*. Avid Reader Press.
Krakauer, J. (2016). *Missoula: Rape and the justice system in a college town*. Anchor.
Lavigne, P., & Schlabach, M. (2017). *Violated: Exposing rape at Baylor University amid college football's sexual assault crisis*. Center Street.
Lonsway, K. A., & Fitzgerald, L. F. (1994). Rape myths. In review. *Psychology of Women Quarterly, 18*, 133–164.
Lorber, J. E., & Farrell, S. A. (1991). *The social construction of gender*. Sage.
Mac Donald, H. (2018). *The diversity delusion: How race and gender pandering corrupt the university and undermine our culture*. St. Martin's Griffin.
McMahon, S., & Farmer, G. L. (2011). An updated measure for assessing subtle rape myths. *Social Work Research, 35*, 71–81.
Mead, G. H. (1934). *Mind, self and society* (Vol. 111). University of Chicago Press
Mills, C. W. (2000). *The sociological imagination*. Oxford University Press.
Murphy, P. F. (Ed.). (2004). *Feminism & masculinities*. Oxford University Press.
Pagila, C. (2017). *Free women free men*. Pantheon Books.
Payne, D. L., Lonsway, K. A., & Fitzgerald, L. F. (1999). Rape myth acceptance: Exploration of its structure and its measurement using the *Illinois Rape Myth Acceptance Scale. Journal of Research in Personality, 33*, 27–68. doi:0092-6566/99
Phillips, N. D. (2017). *Beyond blurred lines*. Rowman & Littlefield.
Sperber, M. (2000). *Beer and circus*. Henry Holt and Company.
Spruill, M. J. (2017). *Divided we stand: The battle over women's rights and family values that polarized American politics*. Bloomsbury.
Touhey, J. C. (1974). Situated identities, attitude similarity and interpersonal attraction. *Sociometry, 37*, 363–374.
Wade, L. (2017). *American hookup: The new culture of sex on campus*. WW Norton & Company.

2
BUILDING RAPE MYTH PERCEPTIONS – UNIVERSITY COMMUNITY

Rape myths are attitudes, perceptions, beliefs, values, and actions that perpetuate the trivialization of sexual assaults and victim blaming (Lonsway & Fitzgerald, 1994). Rape myths form narratives to limit the seriousness of rapes and those who fall victim to them. These myths are a cornerstone to rape culture and both feed from each other. The myths exist because of rape culture and rape culture continues because the myths hold power. There is an intuitive sense to be against rape myths but even when people utter claim to being against them, the myths resonate and are given voice. It is this reverberation that concerns this book. People know that we should not blame the victim, but we are quick to do so, especially when the victim encapsulates particular identities. Rape myths lie in the bottom of a drawer ready to be used when necessary but not always in the most glamorous manner.

Rape myths are those ideals that proclaim the victim's responsibility in being raped by suggesting a woman being at fault for when a man overpowers her sexually (Burt, 1980; Lonsway & Fitzgerald, 1994). Traditionally, rape myth studies ignore homosexual rapes or rapes of a man due to the nature of rape myths being stereotypical proclamations of rape. Some suggestions for reading about this topic are *Male on Male Rape* by Scarce (2008); *Male Rape is a Feminist Issue* by Cohen (2014); and *Queering Sexual Violence* by Patterson (2016). Rape myths argue that the man did not mean to do it or that she lied about it happening or that it was her fault or that it was not really rape. These myths have foundations in misogynistic and patriarchal ideological systems; they exist in societies where men are viewed as more powerful and where men culturally are against women gaining power toward equity. This means as an individual, people agree that women are good and deserve power in the workforce and men can change diapers and clean the house, but collectively our culture still fights against women. Rape myths are anti-feminist to their core (Brownmiller, 1975; Conaghan & Russell, 2014; Suarez & Gadalla, 2010); they attack equity and love between people to keep us polarized (Spruill, 2017).

We all hold attitudes, values, beliefs, and perceptions about the actions that we engage in numerous times a day. Behaviors root themselves in socialization and are developed in direct and indirect ways throughout life. Beliefs about who can cook or sing or run or wrestle or not wear a shirt in public. Attitudes about females being unstable and males being strong. Perceptions about sexual behaviors and sex roles – who should start sexual behaviors and who should stop sexual encounters. Behaviors should correspond to those beliefs, attitudes, and perceptions but that is not always the case. We often engage in acts that are against perceptions or attitudes because we know that the behaviors that correspond with the belief might not be judged positively. Think of what was proposed about expectation states theory and situated identity theory – we want people in our groups to like us by our actions, so we behave how we think our confidents want us to act. Thus, actions might go against beliefs, which makes measuring social attitudes and perceptions difficult.

Actions are not alone in acting out against beliefs; stated perceptions can also go against our held beliefs in accordance to who we are with and whom we are trying to impress. Rape myths are perceptual shortcuts that help us view the action of rape and sexual assault as well as its causes. The way to measure rape myths is through scales of measurement; the studies herein use the Illinois Rape Myth Acceptance (IRMA) scale (McMahon & Farmer, 2011). These IRMA scales (i.e. rape myths, she asked for it, it wasn't really rape, she lied, and he didn't mean to) are measured by asking people to rate their views on individual statements that characterize the rape myths. This is the creation of terms and variable in research. The rater is doing their best to look at the statements to tell researchers answers to the statements. In light of rape myths and their implicit nature, we are often asking about perceptions that have never been thought about before.

When was the last time you had an in-depth conversation about the rape myths you believe in and why? You are reading this book, perhaps you have some knowledge about rape myths and how they are surveyed and perhaps you discuss these topics over dinner like I do. Yet, the nuances of the terminology are not well known unless they have been examined, questioned, and critiqued. As Phillips (2016) argued, we know the words rape myth, rape culture, and victim blame, but do not always attribute much meaning to the terms. These are words that have lost meaning and are not much more than recognizable axioms of society.

As a culture, rape is viewed as bad and that it's not the victim's fault. However, we also believe that it is the victims' fault and actions by so many, including the legal system, university administration, and family, trivialize the harmfulness of rape and sexual assault. Books are written about how rape and sexual assault is worried about too much, and time and money should be spent on other more important things like learning Shakespeare (Mac Donald, 2018). This is the rape culture speaking. Socialization generates implicit biases inherent for misogyny, patriarchy, and anti-feminism to allow for the continuation of stated beliefs and assumptions of behavioral causes. It is why women are slut-shamed and men are hailed as sexual heroes. It is why men in many cultures can be promiscuous pre-marriage, but their matrimonial women must be virgins. It might be why we do not believe in rape myths, but our actions and ideas show otherwise.

Feminism has been fought for, argued against, and turmoiled over. The idea that women must move their own agenda forward is connected inherently to rape myths and rape culture. Rape myths and rape culture presumptions hold reason and rationale for ideological constructs of feminism; we need feminism to rid cultures of rape myth and rape culture. As Brownmiller (1975) roared in her groundbreaking book, rape and its surrounding perceptions of it being an acceptable act against women to show power and finesse always have been about overthrowing women and showing them their weaknesses while men demonstrate their strengths.

When women and others who hold perceived weaker identities of social hierarchy such as Blacks and homosexuals are raped, it is of even less concern (Brewer & Smith, 1995; Brownmiller, 1975; Echabe, 2010). Women are not perceived powerful entities, but women are and should be recognized as such. Rape myths and rape culture propagated from this assumption of civilizations that the powerful can do what they crave to while the underlings of society are to be controlled and subservient (Higgins & Silver, 1991). It is of little concern to the society, even though it should be of grave concern, when those lower in the hierarchy are traumatized and hurt; it does not disturb power.

The women's movement and feminism loudly said NO to the continued ignorance and insignificance of sexual assault. The war was declared when woman shouted that this is not acceptable, sexual assaults must stop, and we are equals. Once women and others of lower power gain equity and justice, harm should be lessened. It is harder to hurt someone you perceive as an equal and worthy of respect.

However, here in the 21st century, we still are arguing and debating about the worth and perceptions of rape myths and the false narratives that support those myths (for instance, see Casey, 2020; Kipnis, 2017; Mac Donald, 2018). These ideologies exist to perpetuate rape myths and rape culture as it continues to develop for the next generation through unchecked socialization. If women become true equals, the question goes, what becomes of men? Men also gain worth even though they might lose some esteemed privilege of manhood.

Before the research, you should think about a recent scenario. A military officer, Vanessa Guillen, was sexually harassed and assaulted by men in her unit. She stayed silent for some time but then began using the chain of command to tell her story. After threats from various men in her unit and others, she disappeared. Her body was later found mutilated and dismembered. Then in July 2020, female professor and formal military personnel, Betsy Schoeller, posted this statement to social media: "sexual harassment is the price of admission for women … if you're gonna cry like a snowflake about it, you're gonna pay the price." Take a moment to think this story through. A woman serving the United States was harassed and raped in 2019 and 2020. She bravely spoke out to the military, received threats, and refused to stay quiet. She was then brutally murdered, her body hidden. Only so that a woman could say it was her fault for joining the ranks, of trying to be one of the boys, of not allowing the boys to be boys, and of snitching against your own. Schoeller claimed that Guillen was assaulted, raped, and murdered because of her personal decisions to join the military and speak truths. This is what rape culture, rape myths, and victim blaming look like in the 21st century.

This is the cost of feminism women and men feel (Ford, 2016; 2019; Kindlon, 2006; Murphy, 2004). You can try to join social groups traditionally held for the other sex such as women joining the military and men becoming stay at home dads. Even though we preach a tough game of opportunity and individualism, the battle to cross sex roles is fraught with harm. Books by Ford, *Fight like a Girl* (2018) and *Boys will be Boys* (2019), demonstrated the turmoil men and women face living in a post-civil rights movement era. Girls are still humiliated over their bodies, sexual desires, and womanhood. Boys still fight to be tough, aggressive, and macho without being able to show their true underlying feelings. All genders ascribe to the rape culture and rape myths that are found prevalent in the United States as well as the United Kingdom and Australia. The solid truth is that rape myths, rape culture, and idealisms of patriarchy have done a doozy to us all. We must work through the pain and ugliness of culture to move to the other side where women and men can be freer.

I must explain a bit about myself and potential biases in conducting this research. I am a female, cis gender, married professor who teaches criminology through a foundation of sociology. I have been a student for a long time and stayed in the university environment to work; this means I have been in the university setting almost my entire adult life. I have also worked in law firms where I have perceived the pain and hurt of boys and men when they are accused of sexual assaults and rapes. I worked in a court system where I helped prostitutes (who also usually are mothers, sisters, daughters) regain aspects of their lives. I worked with men who have sexual assault criminal histories and listened to their stories. I have held the hands of friends, family, students, peers, and colleagues while wiping tears while they recount stories of sexual assault.

Additionally, as many females, I have been sexually harassed plenty of times in my life, including as an employee especially in lower status jobs when I was in college – all the colleges. I have been sexually assaulted on lower ends of the continuum of ass or breast grabs or forcible kisses. I have stories from bars of inappropriate touches and people protecting me. I hold stories of women close to me and their stories of harassment, assault, and rape. I hold stories of what occurs on university campuses before I started this research as a student and as a professor who hears stories from students. All of this is why I do this research, including a student who wanted to do some research with me under ideals of changing the system. I hold some natural bias about how I want the university to look. It would be great to paint my research as showing a lack of rape myths, but the research did not present itself that way and so that is not the story I can tell.

My heart and love are in this research and that might not make me always objective in the points I make or what I view as conclusions, but as any researcher, I try my best. I read lots of books and articles; I checked my ideas with those interviewed and students who aided me in the research process. In the end, this is vital to share by adding more thoughts and reality to appreciating rape myths and rape culture in our world.

Rape myth measurement

We can identify rape myths in the manners of speech and actions of everyday life. Researchers built ways to measure rape myths since the 1980s and formulated trusted reliable means to see the perceptions of rape myths. More than one scale still is used in research endeavors outside of this book. In these studies, the IRMA scale (McMahon & Farmer, 2011) was employed. It was selected due to its value in measuring attitudes of college students and of its length being only 22 items. It was converted into a 24-item scale by adding two key items missing from the IRMA measurement after a few rounds of using the scale. Language in the statements was altered to make the survey about adult women and not girls as the university population is of adults. This scale is appropriate for university samples as it is easy to read and use for participants and can fit on a single page. This allows for a quicker response to the items, hoping for more truthful perceptions (Dillman, Smyth, & Christian, 2014). Also, other scales can be used in the survey when the survey of interest is not too complicated or lengthy. See Appendix C for the altered scale used in these studies. The ideas presented in this chapter are from surveys and interviews about campus life through perceptions of students, faculty, and staff.

The evolution of rape myth scales was started by Burt in 1980 with the call to action of researchers to start engaging with these ideas. At the start, it was a general call that wafted into universities and student lives. The first scales were lofty and long. They also held low content, criterion, and construct validity (McMahon & Farmer, 2011). Essentially, this means that the scales did not measure rape myths in a manner that was both predicable and true. A lot of this stemmed from problematic wording and poor item connection to sample. In other words, researchers were being researchers using jargon and clinical terminology. This is not how the culture at large understands sexual roles, behaviors, and assaults. The statements used to measure needed to align with the populations being studied (Dillman, Smyth, & Christian, 2014). If I walked up to a 20-year-old and asked them if they have necked recently, would they know what I was referring to – do you?

The items of the scale were created through various tests by various researchers (Farmer & McMahon, 2005; Hinck & Thomas, 1999; Lonsway & Fitzgerald, 1994; 1995; McMahon & Farmer, 2011; Payne, Lonsway, & Fitzgerald, 1999).

Rape myth scales were developed mostly in the 1980s and 1990s to find ways to measure the terms scholars were writing about theoretically. It is known in social science; if you cannot measure something, it does not exist. Although the concepts of rape myth and rape culture are social constructions the terms and attributions of them are real just as we create meanings for in our society for concepts such as money, depression, and happiness. The rape myth scale has been through various versions and edited throughout time to ensure the language connects to the intended user or survey participant.

Original versions were closer to 80 items and meant to survey the general population such as that written by Payne, Lonsway, and Fitzgerald (1999) who created the first long version of the IRMA scale. It held around 70 statements for survey participants to rank as strongly agree, agree, neutral, disagree, and strongly disagree. The goal was to determine the proportion of populations that accepted rape myths. Researchers soon realized that university students provided appropriate samples per their age and experiences with sexual assault and rape. As different versions were tested, the items decreased to 50 and 45 to fit length requirements, reliability goals, and student attention spans.

Then in the 2000s, it was altered by Farmer and McMahon (2005) and McMahon and Farmer (2011) to make it shorter and more suitable for college students and researchers. Researchers rephrased statements and worked alongside college students to get terminology correct. There was a need for definitions, conceptions, and items to align with the sample. By using words and statements the sample understood, the rape myth scales became more reliable and valid or more consistent and closer to the reality of life. This is necessary to produce good research, and why the first few surveys were trial runs of the measure to ensure wording and terminology made sense in the population used. Study 3 was the first long survey using the IRMA scale, but it was not until study 9 that finalized the scaled and survey; even now, there are things to be changed for the next reiteration of the study.

Research is an evolving process. The studies herein continue to demonstrate reliability for IRMA and validity even with the additional terminology changes. Although reliability coefficients of Cronbach were measured as highly reliable, there was a need to check validity. Reliability is about consistent responses through various distributions of measures, whereas validity checks the correctness of the variables. Is IRMA measuring perceptions of rape myths?

One check was the neutral category for responses. There is disagreement in the survey community if participants should be forced to answer ideas they might have never pondered before (Albaum, 1997; Armstrong, 1987; Croasmun & Ostrom; 2011; Dillman, Smyth, & Christian, 2014; Edwards & Smith, 2014). From the discussion that follows in this chapter, it seems best if IRMA is studied with the lack of a neutral category. With most studies, a neutral category is present between agree and disagree to allow respondents who do not have strong connections either way to still answer quickly and easily. Yet, by forcing people to make a response of agreement or disagreement, reality appeared favored.

Studies 6 and 7 demonstrated the shift of using the neutral responses versus not placing neutral category as an option. The first survey did not have the neutral category the second one in spring did. Although there was not an exact match of samples, freshman seminars were used as a sample tool for both the fall and spring semesters. More people moved to agreement; thus, neutral responses were hiding people who agreed, and, of course, who disagreed. This slight level of agreement or disagreement moved many people off the fence. It also created more missing items on the survey; people, students, and faculty/staff, increased not responding to questions they were uncomfortable answering. Yet, the number of missing was not high enough to be of concern to outweigh the benefit of gaining real responses.

Another shift made was in the wording of some of the individual scale items. These were made in the 2018 and 2019 surveys. Some of this was in consultation to other researchers but also from looking at what people wrote on the margins of the surveys with respect to gender. Students wrote on the versions of the survey about male victims or transgender victims to demonstrate that the world of rape myths is gendered. It is acknowledged that IRMA is made with the intent of measuring rape myths in the consideration of the current rape culture. This means male perpetrators and female victims. Item 23 was added stating, "only females can be victims of sexual assault and rape." It assesses the belief of who can and cannot be raped gathering information about rape culture ideology. Working in all items was altered to make girls into women and boys/guys into men. This shifts the focus to adults but also the IRMA was more likely to use the term girls than boys as men were men or guys; this is biased and perpetuates genderism and misogyny.

The last change was adding item number 24 to the scale, "if consent is given once, consent for sex is always there." It was an early measure of control before the last survey in 2019 that placed a consent scale. When determining the alpha levels of the 22-item versus 24-item scale, there is no appreciable significant difference. Yet, when I report the measures in this book, I use the traditional 22-item scale with items 23 and 24 being single measured variables.

The total rape myth scale as measured in my last version is found in Appendix C. The 24 items are shown and displayed as they were in the survey. The first 22 items taken together form the *total rape myth scale* that measures how the sample perceives rape myths as a complete idea. The sub-scales shown in Figure 2.1 with their individual items are *she asked for it, he didn't mean to, it wasn't rape,* and *she lied*. The sub-scales are used to determine connections to specific rape myths and beliefs. People might not perceive agreement or disagreement with the whole scale or sub-scales. By dividing the sub-scales and using each as its own variable, usually a dependent variable, you can ascertain more precise perceptions about rape myths. By looking at Figure 2.1, you can see the nuanced differences between each sub-scale creating different versions of rape myth views.

SUB-SCALE	ITEMS FROM IRMA
SHE ASKED FOR IT	1. If a woman is raped while she is drunk, she is at least somewhat responsibility for letting things get out of hand 2. When women go to parties wearing slutty clothes, they are asking for trouble. 3. If a woman goes to a room alone with a guy at a party, it is her faulty if she is raped. 4. If a woman acts like a slut, eventually she is going to get into trouble. 5. When women get raped, its often because the way they said "no" was unclear. 6. If a woman initiates kissing or hooking up, she should not be surprised if a guy assumes she wants to have sex.
HE DIDN'T MEAN TO	7. When guys rape, it is usually because of their strong desire for sex. 8. Guys don't usually intend to force sex on a woman, but sometimes they get too sexually carried away. 9. Rape happens when a guy's sex drive goes out of control. 10. If a man is drunk, he might rape someone unintentionally. 11. It shouldn't be considered rape if a guy is drunk and didn't realize what he was doing. 12. If both people are drunk, it can't be rape.
IT WASN'T RAPE	13. If a woman doesn't physically resist sex – even if protesting verbally – it can't be considered rape. 14. If a woman doesn't physically fight back, you can't really say it was rape. 15. A rape probably doesn't happen if a woman doesn't have any bruises or marks. 16. If the accused "rapist" doesn't have a weapon, you really can't call it rape. 17. If a woman doesn't say "no" she can't claim rape.
SHE LIED	18. A lot of times, women who say there were raped agreed to have sex and then regret it. 19. Rape accusations are often used as a way of getting back at guys. 20. A lot of times, women who say there were raped often led the guy on and then had regrets. 21. A lot of times, women who claim they were raped have emotional problems. 22. Women who are caught cheating on their boyfriends sometimes claim it was rape.

FIGURE 2.1 Total rape myth scale items divided into sub-scales of rape myths.

Student perceptions of rape myths

The research note section at the end of the book includes more specific data about the studies including research questions, statistical tools and tests, demographic data, and other information deemed pertinent to your understanding the methodological tools of data collection and analysis. All studies were approved by IRB and completed in compliance with research protocols.

The initial purpose of the studies was to gather information about the university in connection to students, faculty, and staff perceptions of rape myths and connected characteristics. Study 1 demonstrated a need for research alongside the literature review. Study 2 illustrated the appropriate use of IRMA in the sample and questions that could be asked to gain warranted data. The process unfolded a disbelief in rape myths when measured directly but an aptitude to use them in conversations surrounding the topic.

Study 3 – The third study was deployed in 2016 after glitches were fixed with the first two pre-tests. The survey was distributed to students in freshman-level seminar courses and senior-level seminar courses. This allowed a sample that included even distributions of freshmen and juniors/seniors. The sample was 316 students, mostly female, approximately 1/4 involved in athletic teams on campus, and less than 10% involved in Greek life. Most did not remember ever attending a campus program about sexual assault, even though all freshmen are required to do so during freshman welcome week. Of the 1/3 who remembered attending campus programming about sexual assault, most (73%) remember only attending one event. The event most remembered was one containing a personal story of human trafficking.

This version of the IRMA scale included neutral-level responses: strongly agree, agree, neutral, disagree, and strongly disagree to the 22 items of the rape myth scale. This study had the intent to determine the level of rape myth acceptance and if programming attendance or upperclassman status impacted the level of rape myth acceptance. Most individual items on the scale were disagreed or strongly disagreed with as shown in Table 2.1. The scales also show a sample that does not accept rape myths; see Table 2.2. However, these averages and percentages also illustrate a minority who agree or strongly agree with the items.

TABLE 2.1 Study 3 Spring 2016 Survey Items Responses, Percentages and Means

Scale	Items – Rape Myth Statements	SA	A	N	D	SD	Mean
She asked for it	1 If a woman is raped while drunk, she is at least somewhat responsible for letting things get out of hand.	2.2	5.7	15.8	23.7	52.2	4.2
	2 When women go to parties wearing slutty clothes, they are asking for trouble.	1.9	9.2	15.5	25.3	48.1	4.1
	3 If a woman goes to a room alone with a guy at a party, it is her own fault if she is raped.	0.6	3.8	10.4	23.1	61.7	4.4
	4 If a woman acts like a slut, eventually she is going to get into trouble.	3.5	18.7	24.1	25.3	28.2	3.6
	5 When women get raped, it's often because the way they said "no" was unclear.	1.3	4.7	11.4	26.3	56.0	4.3
	6 If a woman initiates kissing or hooking up, she should not be surprised if a guy assumes she wants to have sex.	5.4	18.0	25.6	20.3	30.1	3.5
He didn't mean to	7 When guys rape, it is usually because of their strong desire for sex.	4.7	22.5	33.2	17.7	21.2	3.3
	8 Guys don't usually intend to force sex on a woman, but sometimes they get too sexually carried away.	2.8	20.6	28.5	25.6	22.2	3.4
	9 Rape happens when a guy's sex drive goes out of control.	4.1	11.4	22.2	26.9	35.1	3.8
	10 If a guy is drunk, he might rape someone unintentionally.	4.4	13.6	26.9	22.8	32.0	3.6
	11 It shouldn't be considered rape if a guy is drunk and didn't realize what he was doing.	1.6	5.7	9.2	20.6	63.0	4.4
	12 If both people are drunk, it can't be rape.	4.7	3.8	16.8	21.8	52.2	4.1

(Continues)

Scale	Items – Rape Myth Statements	SA	A	N	D	SD	Mean
It wasn't really rape	13 If a woman doesn't physically resist sex – even if protesting verbally – it can't be considered rape.	0.9	3.8	4.1	17.4	73.7	4.6
	14 If a woman doesn't physically fight back, you can't really say it was rape.	1.3	2.2	2.5	13.6	80.1	4.7
	15 A rape probably doesn't happen if a woman doesn't have any bruises or marks.	0.6	0.3	0.6	8.9	89.6	4.9
	16 If the accused "rapist" doesn't have a weapon, you really can't call it rape.	0.9	0.3	0.6	6.3	91.8	4.9
	17 If a woman doesn't say "no" she can't claim rape.	2.2	10.8	22.5	27.5	36.1	3.9
She lied	18 A lot of times, women who say they were raped agreed to have sex and then regret it.	5.7	11.7	34.5	27.2	20.3	3.4
	19 Rape accusations are often used as a way of getting back at guys.	4.4	14.2	27.8	25.9	27.5	3.6
	20 A lot of times, women who say they were raped often led the guy on and then had regrets.	3.8	10.8	29.7	27.5	27.2	3.6
	21 A lot of times, women who claim they were raped have emotional problems.	4.4	13.9	23.7	25.3	32.6	3.7
	22 Women who are caught cheating on their boyfriends sometimes claim it was rape.	3.8	19.6	33.5	20.6	22.5	3.4

TABLE 2.2 Study 3 Spring 2016 Survey IRMA Scale

Scale	Alpha	Possible Range	Midpoint	Actual Range	Mean (Std. Dev.)
Total rape myth scale Items 1–22	0.922	22–110	66	53–110	87.29 (14.13)
She asked for it Items 1–6	0.820	6–30	18	8–30	24.09 (4.65)
He didn't mean to Items 7–12	0.750	6–30	18	9–30	22.72 (4.49)
It wasn't rape Items 13–17	0.788	5–25	15	7–25	22.89 (2.81)
She lied Items 18–22	0.896	5–25	15	5–25	17.75 (4.81)

* Any score below midpoint marks agreement with scale.

For the individual items in the IRMA scale, in study 3, all items have means above 3 and most are above 3.5. This indicates disagreement with the rape myth statements. A few statements are under 3.5 suggesting neutral affinity such as item 22 (women who are caught cheating on their boyfriends sometimes claim it was rape), item 8 (guys don't usually intend to force sex on a woman, but sometimes they get too sexually carried away), and item 7 (when guys rape, it is usually because of their strong desire for sex). These statements thus are scored as lower-level neutral statements moving toward agreement. Looking at these statements, they remove the blame from the rapist or assaulter and place it either on a lying female, physical desire, or strong manliness. These statements being more neutral show that students are conflicted.

With study 3, there are three items that have strong levels of disagreement holding means at or above 4.7. Items 14 (if a woman doesn't physically fight back, you can't really say it was rape), 15 (a rape probably doesn't happen if a woman doesn't have any bruises or marks), and 16 (if the accused "rapist" doesn't have a weapon, you really can't call it rape). These three items are part of the *it wasn't really rape* scale. These items illustrate that students do not see rape as only the most horrific stories involving weapons, beatings, and heavy physical bruising or bleeding, the blitz rape script. Many sexual assaults and rapes do not contain these measures and instead rely more on physical force and sexual coercion.

In connection with the individual items of IRMA, the 2016 survey has two scales that scored near neutral or that the mean is closer to the midpoint. The two scales of *she lied* and *he didn't mean to* are created by the same items explained above. Somewhere in the rape culture, students hold biases that men simply do not intend to rape and it "just happens," while the women accusers are liars. This is socialization at work; it creates biases and presumptions about actions. Women let rape happen and profess too much when they come forward to report it.

For the scales, independent t-tests were conducted with the variables of class standing and remembering program attendance. Results of these statistical measures are depicted in Table 2.3. Class standing was connected statistically to the scales of *total rape myth, she asked for it, he didn't mean to, and she lied*. For the variable of remembering attendance at a sexual assault program, *he didn't mean to* scale was the only scale where means varied significantly. Independent t-tests suggest that remembering program attendance or being of a certain class standing impacts the mean-level scores of the rape myths. It compares means between the various levels of each variable to see if meaningful differences exist. If meaningful differences exist, you can assume that the variable of comparison (i.e. class standing) is impacting the other variable (i.e. rape myth).

The class standing variable is upper-level students versus lower-level students. All relationships are negative. This suggests that for the sample in study 3, underclassmen are more likely to disagree with rape myth scales and upper-level students have a mean value that is lower indicating a more neutral response or perhaps more agreement.

The variable of program attendance is not if a person attended a specific program but if the individual remembered attending any program about sexual assault or rape while a student at the university. This connection is negative as well. Thus, those who remember attending a program were more natural on the scale or perhaps more agreeable to the scale.

TABLE 2.3 Independent T-tests of Scales Mean Differences in Study 3

	Lower-Level Students		Upper-Level Students		Independent T-test	
	M	SD	M	SD	t	df
Total rape myth	85.407	1.073	90.052	13.509	−2.819★	296
She asked for it	23.473	0.359	25.008	4.101	−2.878★	308
He didn't mean to	22.279	0.324	23.382	4.549	−2.122★	307
It wasn't really rape	22.851	0.196	22.919	3.011	−0.210	310
She lied	17.179	0.352	18.634	4.622	−2.631★	310
	Does not remember program attendance		Remembers program attendance		Independent T-test	
	M	SD	M	SD	t	df
Total rape myth	86.500	13.755	89.214	14.703	−1.551	295
She asked for it	23.881	4.486	24.647	4.847	−1.364	307
He didn't mean to	22.351	4.487	23.510	4.453	−2.158★	306
It wasn't really rape	22.795	2.923	23.059	2.588	−0.774	309
She lied	17.519	4.619	18.290	5.147	−1.327	309

★$p \leq 0.05$; ★★ $p \leq 0.001$.

Taken together, these variables are not stating that the more programs you attend about sexual assault or holding a higher age or having more education results in higher levels of disagreement to the rape myth scales. After doing many studies and finding similar results, it appears that upper-level students and those who remember attending programs are more able to perceive their biases and rationales for sexual assault. They are more open to state this is what I think about rape myths. It shows that as people gain education and lose ignorance, they are able to share cultural myths we are not supposed to believe in. Students have an understanding about socialization and culture, and they are willing to share their connection to the biases learned through socialization. Rape myths can be changed but only once we are educated enough and have enough experiences to visualize their existence.

Study 6 – This study was completed in the fall semester of 2017. The study connects to study 7 as it was completed in two phases over two semesters. The main goal of study 6 was to determine the level of rape myth acceptance of students when the neutral category was removed from the IRMA scale. The sample held 187 students of whom were mostly female and divided among freshmen and seniors.

Table 2.4 shows the individual items from IRMA in the Fall 2017 survey. For the individual items measured as strongly agree (1), agree (2), disagree (3), and strongly disagree (4), a mean at or above 3 shows disagreement with the statement. Any mean below 3 shows agreement as there is no neutral category in this survey measurement. Only two items (7 and 8) that have means less than three

TABLE 2.4 Study 6 Fall 2017 Survey IRMA Items Responses, Percentages and Means

Scale	Items – Rape Myth Statements	SA	A	D	SD	Mean
She asked for it	1 If a woman is raped while drunk, she is at least somewhat responsible for letting things get out of hand.	1.1	4.3	25.7	6.9	3.63
	2 When women go to parties wearing slutty clothes, they are asking for trouble.	2.1	8.6	16.6	72.7	3.60
	3 If a woman goes to a room alone with a guy at a party, it is her own fault if she is raped.	0.5	2.7	17.6	79.1	3.75
	4 If a woman acts like a slut, eventually she is going to get into trouble.	2.7	18.2	32.1	46.5	3.23
	5 When women get raped, it's often because the way they said "no" was unclear.	2.7	8.6	20.9	67.9	3.54
	6 If a woman initiates kissing or hooking up, she should not be surprised if a guy assumes she wants to have sex.	4.8	21.9	36.9	35.3	3.04
He didn't mean to	7 When guys rape, it is usually because of their strong desire for sex.	4.3	37.4	34.2	23.5	2.77
	8 Guys don't usually intend to force sex on a woman, but sometimes they get too sexually carried away.	2.1	29.4	39.6	28.9	2.95
	9 Rape happens when a guy's sex drive goes out of control.	2.7	15.5	36.9	44.4	3.24
	10 If a guy is drunk, he might rape someone unintentionally.	3.2	25.7	28.9	42.2	3.10
	11 It shouldn't be considered rape if a guy is drunk and didn't realize what he was doing.	0	3.7	17.6	78.1	3.75
	12 If both people are drunk, it can't be rape.	1.6	4.8	19.8	73.3	3.66
It wasn't really rape	13 If a woman doesn't physically resist sex – even if protesting verbally – it can't be considered rape.	0.5	1.6	13.4	84.0	3.82
	14 If a woman doesn't physically fight back, you can't really say it was rape.	0.5	0	9.1	89.8	3.89
	15 A rape probably doesn't happen if a woman doesn't have any bruises or marks.	0.5	0	7.0	92.5	3.91
	16 If the accused "rapist" doesn't have a weapon, you really can't call it rape.	0.5	0	3.2	96.3	3.95
	17 If a woman doesn't say "no" she can't claim rape.	1.6	9.6	28.3	60.4	3.48
She lied	18 A lot of times, women who say they were raped agreed to have sex and then regret it.	2.7	17.1	48.3	31.0	3.09
	19 Rape accusations are often used as a way of getting back at guys.	2.	15.5	12.8	39.0	3.18
	20 A lot of times, women who say they were raped often led the guy on and then had regrets.	2.1	12.3	40.1	45.5	3.29
	21 A lot of times, women who claim they were raped have emotional problems.	3.2	13.9	34.8	48.1	3.28
	22 Women who are caught cheating on their boyfriends sometimes claim it was rape.	1.6	21.4	46.5	30.5	3.06

and four items (7, 8, 10, and 22) are at or below 3.10. Eleven of the items have agreement from 15% or more of the sample. Item 7 has the highest level of agreement at 41.7%. Items 7 (when guys rape, it is usually because of their strong desire for sex), 8 (guys don't usually intend to force sex on a woman, but sometimes they get too sexually carried away), 10 (if a guy is drunk, he might rape someone unintentionally), and 22 (women who are caught cheating on their boyfriends sometimes claim it was rape) have the highest levels of agreement. Most of these items form the *he didn't mean to* scale of IRMA, which coincides with study 3. Additionally, item 22 is from the *she lied* scale that also held higher levels of agreement and neutral responses. This builds the reliability or trustworthiness of these measures for this population.

Items with the highest levels of disagreement and means form the *it wasn't really rape* scale. Items 13 (if a woman doesn't physically resist sex – even if protesting verbally – it can't be considered rape), 14 (if a woman doesn't physically fight back, you can't really say it was rape), and 15 (a rape probably doesn't happen if a woman doesn't have any bruises or marks) held the highest levels of disagreement and strong disagreement. This is important and does illustrate that this sample does appreciate the varying types of sexual assault and rape and it is not all a blitz rape scenario. Blitz rape scenarios tend to be the stranger rape in a dark alley where the victim was beaten and heavily physically assaulted and harmed by the rapist. This rape script is often viewed as the normal "real" rape, but it is the least prevalent. This sample is aware that rape comes in more than one form, which is a positive improvement in our culture and society.

The scales of IRMA for study 6 demonstrate, as assumed, disagreeableness to the actual rape myths created in the scales. These are displayed in Table 2.5. The total rape myth scale has a high mean of 82.84, which is about 30 points higher than the midpoint illustrating a higher disregard for the rape myths. This sample does not agree with the total rape myth scale as well as the smaller scales

TABLE 2.5 Study 6 Fall 2017 Survey IRMA Scale

Scale	Alpha	Possible Range	Midpoint	Actual Range	Mean (Std. Dev.)
Total rape myth scale Items 1–22	0.911	22–88	55	39–95	82.84 (9.53)
She asked for it Items 1–6	0.832	6–24	15	6–24	20.79 (2.27)
He didn't mean to Items 7–12	0.658	6–24	15	11–24	19.48 (2.79)
It wasn't rape Items 13–17	0.782	5–20	12.5	5–20	19.04 (1.69)
She lied Items 18–22	0.871	5–20	12.5	5–20	15.89 (3.18)

* Any score below midpoint marks agreement with scale.

represented in IRMA. All means are above the midpoints sharing student disagreement. The scale closest to the midpoint is the she lied scale and then the he didn't mean to scale. This makes sense as the individual items in these scales hold the most variety of responses and the higher percentages of agreeableness to the individual items.

Study 7 – This survey was completed in the Spring of 2018 and is connected to study 6. Study 7 examined the level of rape myth acceptance of students when the neutral category was used in the IRMA scale items. The sample includes 147 students of whom were mostly females and freshmen. This allowed for comparison of means with and without neutral responses between this study and study 6. The samples were not a matched set, meaning the freshmen in each survey might not be the same students expected by chance.

Examining the survey items for study 7, shown in Table 2.6, is different than study 6 and more like study 3 as the neutral category exits. Participants could choose from strongly agree (1), agree (2), neutral (3), disagree (4), and strongly disagree (5). Means reflect the individual scores so that 3 marks neutral, 4 and above is disagree, and 2 and below is agree. Twelve of the items have means between 3.20 and 3.94. The other means are at or above 4.3. This reflects the nature of neutral categories; many more items sit in the neutral zone of not having a solid direction of rape myth perception. Only three items have means below 3.5, suggesting a low level of neutrality that is moving toward agreement. Items 6 (if a woman initiates kissing or hooking up, she should not be surprised if a guy assumes she wants to have sex), 7 (when guys rape, it is usually because of their strong desire for sex), and 8 (guys don't usually intend to force sex on a woman, but sometimes they get too sexually carried away) are all part of the *he didn't mean to* scale. This again builds the reliability of studies 3 and 6 using the IRMA scale for this sample.

The four items with the highest means are at or above 4.70. These items are numbers 2 (when women go to parties wearing slutty clothes, they are asking for trouble), 11 (it shouldn't be considered rape if a guy is drunk and didn't realize what he was doing), 15 (a rape probably doesn't happen if a woman doesn't have any bruises or marks), and 16 (if the accused "rapist" doesn't have a weapon, you really can't call it rape). This is similar to the rape myths concepts from study 6; most speak the truth about the gravity of the rape and physical harm before it can be called a rape. Item 2 discussed the need to allow women to wear what they want and not be harassed for it. It lives directly in the world of misogyny and patriarchy creating the rape culture that women are to blame especially when slutty, drunks who kiss men. This artifact of the rape culture needs to be dismantled, and this sample shows a pattern to strong disagreement.

Table 2.7 shows the scale descriptive statistics for study 7. Per usual, the scale means demonstrate disagreement with the rape myths scales as measured by IRMA. The scale is reliable but the *he didn't mean to* scale has a low alpha rating suggesting that this sample has divergent responses in this scale. This is explained by looking at the individual items and seeing the various swings in the responses

TABLE 2.6 Study 7 Spring 2018 IRMA Items Responses, Percentages and Means

Scale	Items – Rape Myth Statements	SA	A	N	D	SD	Mean
She asked for it	1 If a woman is raped while drunk, she is at least somewhat responsible for letting things get out of hand.	1.4	6.1	7.5	24.5	60.5	4.37
	2 When women go to parties wearing slutty clothes, they are asking for trouble.	1.4	4.1	12.9	19.0	62.6	4.7
	3 If a woman goes to a room alone with a guy at a party, it is her own fault if she is raped.	2.7	2.0	8.8	15.0	70.7	4.5
	4 If a woman acts like a slut, eventually she is going to get into trouble.	5.4	11.6	15.0	30.6	36.7	3.82
	5 When women get raped, it's often because the way they said "no" was unclear.	1.4	3.4	13.6	24.5	56.5	4.32
	6 If a woman initiates kissing or hooking up, she should not be surprised if a guy assumes she wants to have sex.	5.4	18.4	27.2	21.1	27.2	3.47
He didn't mean to	7 When guys rape, it is usually because of their strong desire for sex.	8.8	16.3	35.4	20.4	16.3	3.20
	8 Guys don't usually intend to force sex on a woman, but sometimes they get too sexually carried away.	4.1	15.0	32	28.6	19.0	3.44
	9 Rape happens when a guy's sex drive goes out of control.	5.4	8.8	23.8	24.5	34.0	3.75
	10 If a guy is drunk, he might rape someone unintentionally.	2.0	13.6	26.5	21.1	35.4	3.75
	11 It shouldn't be considered rape if a guy is drunk and didn't realize what he was doing.	0.7	1.4	10.2	20.4	66	4.85
	12 If both people are drunk, it can't be rape.	0.7	2.7	17.7	23.8	55.1	4.30
It wasn't really rape	13 If a woman doesn't physically resist sex – even if protesting verbally – it can't be considered rape.	1.4	2.7	2.7	17	74.1	4.63
	14 If a woman doesn't physically fight back, you can't really say it was rape.	0.7	0.7	2.7	14.3	81.0	4.75
	15 A rape probably doesn't happen if a woman doesn't have any bruises or marks.	0.7	0	0	12.9	86.4	4.84
	16 If the accused "rapist" doesn't have a weapon, you really can't call it rape.	0.7	0	0	6.1	93.2	4.91
	17 If a woman doesn't say "no" she can't claim rape.	3.4	7.5	21.1	27.2	40.1	3.94
She lied	18 A lot of times, women who say they were raped agreed to have sex and then regret it.	2.0	11.6	29.9	34.0	20.4	3.60
	19 Rape accusations are often used as a way of getting back at guys.	4.1	8.2	21.1	33.3	31.3	3.81
	20 A lot of times, women who say they were raped often led the guy on and then had regrets.	0.7	8.2	31.3	23.8	34.0	3.84
	21 A lot of times, women who claim they were raped have emotional problems.	8.2	8.2	21.1	21.8	38.1	3.76
	22 Women who are caught cheating on their boyfriends sometimes claim it was rape.	2.7	15.0	26.5	25.2	27.9	3.62

TABLE 2.7 Study 7 Spring 2018 IRMA Scale, Neutral Category Present

Scale	Alpha	Possible Range	Midpoint	Actual Range	Mean (Std. Dev.)
Total rape myth scale Items 1–22	0.788	22–110	66	56–101	99.00 (12.82)
She asked for it Items 1–6	0.821	6–30	18	9–30	24.86 (4.55)
He didn't mean to Items 7–12	0.311	6–30	18	12–72	23.32 (5.81)
It wasn't rape Items 13–17	0.691	5–25	15	9–25	23.06 (2.43)
She lied Items 18–22	0.832	5–25	15	7–25	18.64 (4.30)

* Any score below midpoint marks agreement with scale.

of those who agree and disagree as displayed and discussed prior. All means are well above the mean point suggesting a solid level of disagreement in this sample.

Study 9 – This study occurred in Spring 2019 to assess the student body about rape myths and the connection of identities constructs. This study is discussed with greater detail more in Chapter 3 but is used here to show the rape myth data with the largest sample of 597. The neutral category was not used in this survey and responses were strongly agree (1), agree (2), disagree (3), and strongly disagree (4). As with the earlier studies, students, as a group, do not agree with the rape myths. The item results are displayed in Table 2.8.

As with the other studies, the blanket statement of disagreement with the myths does not adequately explain the data. We need to examine those who do not disagree. There are 11 items of concern that resulted in higher percentages (greater than 15% of the sample) of agreement. Items 4 (if a woman acts like a slut, eventually she is going to get into trouble), 6 (if a woman initiates kissing or hooking up, she should not be surprised if a guy assumes she wants to have sex), 8 (guys don't usually intend to force sex on a woman, but sometimes they get too sexually carried away), 9 (rape happens when a guy's sex drive goes out of control), 10 (if a guy is drunk, he might rape someone unintentionally), 17 (if a woman doesn't say "no," she can't claim rape), 18 (a lot of times, women who say they were raped agreed to have sex and then regret it), 19 (rape accusations are often used as a way of getting back at guys, 20 (a lot of times, women who say they were raped often led the guy on and then had regrets), 21 (a lot of times, women who claim they were raped have emotional problems), and 22 (women who are caught cheating on their boyfriends sometimes claim it was rape). Of these items (6, 10, and 19), three are above 20% and two items (8 and 22) are above 30%. Like the other studies, these items create the *he didn't mean to* and the *she lied* scales. It appears that these two scales are the ones with the most support.

TABLE 2.8 Study 9 Fall 2019 Rape Myth Percentages and Means

Scale	Items – Rape Myth Statements	SA	A	D	SD	Mean
She asked for it	1 If a woman is raped while drunk, she is at least somewhat responsible for letting things get out of hand.	0.8	9.3	26.1	63.8	3.53
	2 When women go to parties wearing slutty clothes, they are asking for trouble.	0.3	5.9	28.7	65.0	3.58
	3 If a woman goes to a room alone with a guy at a party, it is her own fault if she is raped.	0.2	2.0	26.6	71.2	3.69
	4 If a woman acts like a slut, eventually she is going to get into trouble.	1.5	18.9	38.2	40.2	3.18
	5 When women get raped, it's often because the way they said "no" was unclear.	0.0	3.5	33.7	59.4	3.56
	6 If a woman initiates kissing or hooking up, she should not be surprised if a guy assumes she wants to have sex.	2.2	25.8	38.7	33.3	3.03
He didn't mean to	7 When guys rape, it is usually because of their strong desire for sex.	5.1	7.1	36.1	21.7	2.74
	8 Guys don't usually intend to force sex on a woman, but sometimes they get too sexually carried away.	1.0	29.9	42.9	26.2	2.94
	9 Rape happens when a guy's sex drive goes out of control.	2.4	19.1	42.1	36.5	3.13
	10 If a guy is drunk, he might rape someone unintentionally.	1.9	25.2	37.1	35.9	3.07
	11 It shouldn't be considered rape if a guy is drunk and didn't realize what he was doing.	0.7	3.5	30.1	65.7	3.61
	12 If both people are drunk, it can't be rape.	1.4	6.8	37.5	54.4	3.45
It wasn't really rape	13 If a woman doesn't physically resist sex – even if protesting verbally – it can't be considered rape.	0.5	2.5	21.92	71.4	3.68
	14 If a woman doesn't physically fight back, you can't really say it was rape.	0.0	0.8	20.4	78.8	3.78
	15 A rape probably doesn't happen if a woman doesn't have any bruises or marks.	0.0	0.7	16.9	82.4	3.82
	16 If the accused "rapist" doesn't have a weapon, you really can't call it rape.	0.0	0.0	15.1	84.9	3.85
	17 If a woman doesn't say "no" she can't claim rape.	1.2	14.3	39.6	44.9	3.28
She lied	18 A lot of times, women who say they were raped agreed to have sex and then regret it.	2.0	17.4	53.7	26.9	3.05
	19 Rape accusations are often used as a way of getting back at guys.	1.9	21.6	47.0	29.5	3.04
	20 A lot of times, women who say they were raped often led the guy on and then had regrets.	0.7	14.9	50.4	34.0	3.18
	21 A lot of times, women who claim they were raped have emotional problems.	2.7	16.2	43.2	37.9	3.16
	22 Women who are caught cheating on their boyfriends sometimes claim it was rape.	2.1	32.6	42.9	22.5	2.86

TABLE 2.9 Study 9 Fall 2019 Survey IRMA Scale Means

Scale	Alpha	Possible Range	Midpoint	Actual Range	Mean (Std. Dev.)
Total rape myth scale Items 1–22	0.915	22–88	55	48–88	73.44 (9.03)
She asked for it Items 1–6	0.813	6–24	15	8–24	20.58 (2.93)
He didn't mean to Items 7–12	0.718	6–24	15	11–24	18.95 (2.92)
It wasn't rape Items 13–17	0.794	5–20	12.5	12–20	18.42 (1.91)
She lied Items 18–22	0.855	5–20	12.5	5–20	15.32 (2.99)

* Any score below midpoint marks agreement with scale.

Some items 70% of the sample selected strongly disagree. These items are 3 (if a woman goes to a room alone with a guy at a party, it is her own fault if she is raped), 13 (if a woman doesn't physically resist sex – even if protesting verbally – it can't be considered rape), and 14 (if a woman doesn't physically fight back, you can't really say it was rape). Two different items had more than 80% of the sample strongly disagree: items 15 (a rape probably doesn't happen if a woman doesn't have any bruises or marks and 16 (if the accused "rapist" doesn't have a weapon, you really can't call it rape). The items of 13, 14, 15, and 16 partially create the *it wasn't really rape* scale along with item 17. Item 17 holds higher percentages in the agreement categories to make the scale show lower disagreement.

The scales for study 9, see Table 2.9, build reliability in the IRMA measure as the findings are similar to the prior studies with smaller samples. All the means are above the midpoints and at high enough scores to suggest disagreement with the scales. The *she lied* scale is the closest mean to the midpoint but still three points higher demonstrating disagreement. The total rape myth scale has a high mean, almost 20 points above the midpoint, like all of the others. This is a positive and warranted outcome of any of these rape myth studies. It is just more thought-provoking to dissect those who do agree with the rape myths as a deviant portion or perhaps the more truthful portion.

Removing neutral responses

The purpose of neutral as a survey response category allows participants safety in their responses and to not think hard about their perceptions (Armstrong, 1987; Edwards & Smith, 2014; Guy & Norvell, 1977). In rape myth research, it allows survey takers to not agree or disagree with tough statements and can make the equivalent of it does not matter to me or I do not know what I think. At times,

TABLE 2.10 Study 3 Spring 2016 IRMA Typical and Dichotomous Measures

IRMA Scale	Typical Measurement Percent at or Below Midpoint	Dichotomous Measurement Percent at or Below Midpoint
Total rape myth	10	30
She asked for it	16	31
He didn't mean to	17	47
It wasn't rape	3	9
She lied	36	59

it can lessen the number of non-responses, as it did in the surveys of this study. When neutral was removed from the scale, some items had more participants who decided not to provide a response. This happened the most for the items in the *it wasn't really rape* scale.

The following shows one way to think about neutral categories in rape myth surveys. The conclusion presented is to not use them as it seems to distort the data from what participants think if they take an extra second to decide on agreements or disagreement perceptions.

Study 3 – When conducting the first full-scale study, percentages of people responding to the individual items in the neutral category were noted and pondered about. By using the typical measures of strongly agree, agree, neutral, disagree, and strongly disagree, there were more truthful perceptions lurking in the neutral category. Researchers (Dillman, Smyth, & Christian, 2014; Edwards & Smith, 2014; Hawkins & Coney, 1981) have noted in different types of studies that using a neutral category allows respondents to hide their true perceptions and not think about the level of their agreement to statements and ideas participants might not have ever thought about before. When people engage in surveys, participants want to be as quick and lazy as possible; the neutral category allows them to do so.

As shown in Table 2.10, when the single items were collapsed into disagree or not disagree (includes strongly agree, agree, and neutral), a higher percentage of respondents were not in disagreement with the scales. This suggests that students do not disagree with the scales as much as the means suggest in typical measurement of IRMA. Three times as many students do not disagree with the *total rape myth scale, he didn't mean to scale, and it wasn't rape scale* in the dichotomous measures than in the typical measures. The scales of *she asked for it* and *she lied* are close to twice as many students who do not disagree with the rape myths when measured with dichotomous items. Neutral perhaps is hiding people who slightly agree with the myths, and this is a problem with the measurement tool. In obtaining knowledge about difficult social constructs as rape myths, researchers want to get as close to reality as possible in the measurement device and the responses provided. This builds reliability and validity while reducing measurement error. In short, do you want to know that most people disagree or despise rape myths or that they just do not agree with it as the neutral category exists. This middle ground is not helpful in creating programing responses from data.

Studies 6 and 7 – These studies were created to test the usefulness and effect of the neutral category in rape myth measures. This is a small analysis to engage in a way to think about how people perceive rape myths and what happens when answers are forced by removing the easily selected neutral category. Yet, this is an area of unconscious thought and implicit bias. People might have never thought about these ideas before, and when forced to on a survey, people will select answers based on what is comfortable which is the neutral fence sitting category.

One way to digest the differences of the studies is to examine the percentages of agreeableness and disagreeableness to the statements. Tables 2.11 and 2.12 display percentages of agreement and disagreement to the IRMA items from studies 3, 6, 7, and 8 so that you do not need to flip through the book to find the numbers again. Studies 3 and 7 had the neutral category available for students in their response; studies 6 and 9 did not. In both of the tables, the percentages of agreeing or disagreeing are combined, strongly agree with agree and disagree with strongly disagree. This effectively moves the neutral category out of the tables as well as those who answered neutral and allows for a quick visual comparison.

Studies 6 and 7 were created for comparison but 3 and 9 provide additional data and a reliability test to see outliers in the comparison studies. For one type of comparison, you can look at the total percentages of agreement and disagreement in each table to find those items that had a difference of 10% or more between neutral surveys and non-neutral response surveys. The hypothesis for this exploration in removing neutral was that respondents would move more toward agreeing with the rape myth statements, but these two tables illustrate the opposite. Without the neutral category, students shifted toward disagreement.

From this simplistic analysis, items to pay attention to are 7, 8, 10, and 19. These items, when looking at study 6 (no neutral category), have at least a 10% higher level of agreement than study 7 (neutral category) and often study 3 (neutral category). Item 19 has 36% higher agreement in study 6 than study 7. Item 7 has 16% higher agreement in study 6 than study 7. Item 10 is 13% higher in study 6 than study 7. Item 8 has a 12% higher agreement in study 6 than study 7. Most of these items are in the *he didn't mean to* scale except item 19 which is part of the *she lied* scale. Both of these had more movement in levels of agreement and disagreement in the items in all of the studies, with higher levels of agreement overall than other items and scales.

The disagreement percentage comparison is displayed in Table 2.11. This comparison table displays many items than the agreement table that have differences between the neutral and non-neutral response categories in the studies. Sixteen out of the 22 items have percentage difference of 10% or more between studies 6 and 7. Items 1, 3, 4, 6, 7, 8, 9, 10, 11, 12, 17, 18, 19, 20, 21, and 22. A few of the differences to note, such as item 6 that has a 24% difference between study 6 and study 7; there is more disagreement in study 6 that does not have a neutral category. Item 8 has a 23% higher level of disagreement in study 6 than

TABLE 2.11 Percentage of Combined Agreement in Studies

Scale	Items – Rape Myth Statements	Study 3*	Study 6	Study 7*	Study 9
She asked for it	1 If a woman is raped while drunk, she is at least somewhat responsible for letting things get out of hand.	7.9	5.4	7.5	11.1
	2 When women go to parties wearing slutty clothes, they are asking for trouble.	11.1	10.7	5.5	6.2
	3 If a woman goes to a room alone with a guy at a party, it is her own fault if she is raped.	4.4	3.2	4.7	2.2
	4 If a woman acts like a slut, eventually she is going to get into trouble.	22.2	20.9	17.0	20.4
	5 When women get raped, it's often because the way they said "no" was unclear.	6.0	11.3	4.8	3.5
	6 If a woman initiates kissing or hooking up, she should not be surprised if a guy assumes she wants to have sex.	23.4	26.7	23.8	28.0
He didn't mean to	7 When guys rape, it is usually because of their strong desire for sex.	27.2	41.7	25.1	12.2
	8 Guys don't usually intend to force sex on a woman, but sometimes they get too sexually carried away.	23.4	31.5	19.1	30.9
	9 Rape happens when a guy's sex drive goes out of control.	15.8	18.2	14.2	21.5
	10 If a guy is drunk, he might rape someone unintentionally.	18.0	28.9	15.6	27.1
	11 It shouldn't be considered rape if a guy is drunk and didn't realize what he was doing.	7.3	3.7	2.1	4.2
	12 If both people are drunk, it can't be rape.	8.5	6.4	3.4	8.2
It wasn't really rape	13 If a woman doesn't physically resist sex – even if protesting verbally – it can't be considered rape.	4.7	2.1	4.1	3.0
	14 If a woman doesn't physically fight back, you can't really say it was rape.	3.5	0.5	1.4	0.8
	15 A rape probably doesn't happen if a woman doesn't have any bruises or marks.	0.9	0.5	0.7	0.7
	16 If the accused "rapist" doesn't have a weapon, you really can't call it rape.	1.2	0.5	0.7	0.0
	17 If a woman doesn't say "no" she can't claim rape.	13.0	11.2	10.9	15.5
She lied	18 A lot of times, women who say they were raped agreed to have sex and then regret it.	17.4	19.8	13.6	19.4
	19 Rape accusations are often used as a way of getting back at guys.	18.6	48.2	12.3	23.5
	20 A lot of times, women who say they were raped often led the guy on and then had regrets.	14.6	14.4	8.9	15.6
	21 A lot of times, women who claim they were raped have emotional problems.	18.3	17.1	16.4	18.9
	22 Women who are caught cheating on their boyfriends sometimes claim it was rape.	23.4	23.0	17.7	34.7

*Studies 3 and 7 have neutral categories.

TABLE 2.12 Percentage of Combined Disagreement in Studies

Scale		Items – Rape Myth Statements	Study 3*	Study 6	Study 7*	Study 9
She asked for it	1	If a woman is raped while drunk, she is at least somewhat responsible for letting things get out of hand.	75.9	94.6	85.0	89.9
	2	When women go to parties wearing slutty clothes, they are asking for trouble.	73.4	89.3	81.6	93.7
	3	If a woman goes to a room alone with a guy at a party, it is her own fault if she is raped.	84.8	96.7	85.7	97.8
	4	If a woman acts like a slut, eventually she is going to get into trouble.	52.3	78.6	67.3	78.4
	5	When women get raped, it's often because the way they said "no" was unclear.	82.3	88.8	81.0	96.4
	6	If a woman initiates kissing or hooking up, she should not be surprised if a guy assumes she wants to have sex.	50.4	72.2	48.3	72.0
He didn't mean to	7	When guys rape, it is usually because of their strong desire for sex.	38.9	57.7	36.7	57.8
	8	Guys don't usually intend to force sex on a woman, but sometimes they get too sexually carried away.	47.8	68.5	47.6	69.1
	9	Rape happens when a guy's sex drive goes out of control.	62.0	81.3	58.5	78.6
	10	If a guy is drunk, he might rape someone unintentionally.	54.8	71.1	56.5	73.0
	11	It shouldn't be considered rape if a guy is drunk and didn't realize what he was doing.	83.6	95.7	86.4	95.8
	12	If both people are drunk, it can't be rape.	74.0	93.1	78.9	91.9
It wasn't really rape	13	If a woman doesn't physically resist sex – even if protesting verbally – it can't be considered rape.	91.1	97.4	91.1	97.0
	14	If a woman doesn't physically fight back, you can't really say it was rape.	93.7	98.9	95.3	99.2
	15	A rape probably doesn't happen if a woman doesn't have any bruises or marks.	98.5	99.5	99.3	99.3
	16	If the accused "rapist" doesn't have a weapon, you really can't call it rape.	98.1	99.5	99.3	100.0
	17	If a woman doesn't say "no" she can't claim rape.	63.6	88.7	67.3	84.5
She lied	18	A lot of times, women who say they were raped agreed to have sex and then regret it.	47.5	79.3	54.4	80.6
	19	Rape accusations are often used as a way of getting back at guys.	53.4	51.8	64.6	76.5
	20	A lot of times, women who say they were raped often led the guy on and then had regrets.	54.7	85.6	73.8	84.4
	21	A lot of times, women who claim they were raped have emotional problems.	57.9	82.9	59.9	81.1
	22	Women who are caught cheating on their boyfriends sometimes claim it was rape.	43.1	77.0	53.1	65.4

*Studies 3 and 7 have neutral categories.

in study 7. Items 21 and 22 are 23% and 24% higher in disagreement to the items in study 6 than in study 7. Item 19 has lower levels of disagreement in study 6 than in study with a 13% difference but remember item 19 has higher levels of agreement in study 6.

These tables showcase differences in the surveys which used neutral and those that did not. To determine if the differences were statistically significant, independent t-tests were run after the five IRMA scales were scaled against its values via POMPS (see explanation in Research notes) in studies 6 and 7. The results of the t-tests indicate significant differences in some of the scale means. The *total rape myth scale* and *wasn't rape* scale are significant at the stronger threshold of p value 0.05 and the *asked for it* and *she lied* scales were significant at the threshold p value of 0.1. The *didn't mean to* scale was not significant.

For *total rape myth scale*, there was a significant difference in the scores for study 6 (M = 80.47 SD = 13.89) and study 7 (M = 77.27, SD = 14.57) conditions; $t(313) = 1.983$, $p = 0.048$. For the *it wasn't rape* scale, there was a significant difference in the scores for study 6 (M = 93.62, SD = 11.33) and study 7 (M = 90.31, SD = 12.34) conditions; $t(326) = 2.541$, $p = 0.012$. For the *she asked for it* scale, there was a significant difference in the scores for study 6 (M = 82.16, SD = 18.15) and study 7 (M = 78.58, SD = 18.94) conditions; $t(326) = 1.737 p = 0.083$. For the *she lied* scale, there was a significant difference in the scores for study 6 (M = 72.62, SD = 21.17) and study 7 (M = 68.19, SD = 21.52) conditions; $t(325) = 1.859$, $p = 0.064$. There was no significant statistical difference in the *didn't mean to* scale; the scores for study 6 (M = 74.86, SD = 15.54) and study 7 (M = 72.17, SD = 24.23) conditions; $t(321) = 1.212$, $p = 0.226$.

All of the scales held higher means in the Fall 2017 study (study 6), which did not allow students a neutral response to the IRMA items. In the study when a neutral response was not possible, students proclaimed higher disagreement, which is what was shown in the individual item percentage differences. This suggests that when students were forced to choose where their perceptions lied on the IRMA, they moved toward disagreement.

The *he didn't mean to* scale did not hold a significant difference between the means in the studies. Looking at the results of the individual items and scales from the studies, this does make sense. This scale consistently held higher levels of neutral and agreement than other scales. This scale seemed to be the most congruent within and between the various versions of surveys and studies.

The shift to disagreement in the surveys might suggest an issue with social desirability bias. Social desirability bias is the likelihood someone will select responses on a survey because they think they are the "right" choice. A quick five-second conversation with oneself demonstrates how social desirability bias works: I know I should not agree with sexual assault and rape nor should I blame the victim. The researcher is standing in the room and will collect my survey so I will disagree as I know I should. Other students are in the room and what if they see me making agreement to these things? They might not like me. Essentially, it is suggesting that social identity theory is working, and symbolic interactionism is doing its job in helping socially construct our lives, thoughts, attitudes, and actions.

Taken together, the exploration of the neutral category in IRMA shows that using a neutral response option might not be the best. It appears to lower the validity of the measure as it creates a response error. Students were likely not neutral but did not want to respond or be forced to provide their opinion. The results of non-neutral IRMA items and scales shifted more toward disagreement. Whether this is an honest response or a socially constructed response is hard to ascertain.

The quantitative analysis of IRMA does show that people are most likely to disagree with the statements and thus supporting the reliability of the IRMA. This means that people disagree with rape myths and are apt to show their lack of support especially for the *it wasn't really rape* scale. This shows that students accept multiple definitions of sexual assault, as discussed in Chapter 3. The issue might still be whether IRMA is valid or is it an accurate measurement of how researchers define rape myths and the connected rape culture. Is IRMA measuring what we want it to measure or is it measuring something else?

These statements and scales provide an appropriate measure of rape myths and the underlying rape culture. It is difficult to measure attitudes and perceptions that people might hold when it includes implicit bias and strong socialization to hold specific beliefs and values. A dip into the interviews of students does show that the measurement might not capture all the subtle nuances of rape myths in how people discuss them and wrestle with the terms themselves. It is the difference between being asked straight-forward a belief about rape and then slowly discussing how the conceptions and constructs come together and are displayed in real life.

This is the purpose of engaging in qualitative and quantitative methods about the same subject. A mixed-method study (Creswell, 1999; Creswell & Creswell, 2017) has the ability to lessen the weakness of each method through the strengths of the other. The questions that remain in the numerical assessments of the IRMA and surveys can be answered through interviews and focus groups when students are willing to engage on the topic. By holding conversational interviews, students provided information indirectly about their views on rape myths and rape culture that could not be found via surveys. They helped plug in the holes through in-depth stories given to researchers from guided questions.

Therefore, to make sense of the numerical data, I conducted two different sets of interviews which were conducted for data collection with students about rape myths and rape culture in Spring 2018 and another in Spring 2020. Taken together, 14 female students were conversed with about key ideas relating to this research. In Spring 2018, students conducted the audio-recorded interviews while I was in the room to take notes and answer follow-up questions. These interviews were in direct connection to the IRMA data collected to determine a more in-depth analysis of what the numbers might mean. The Spring 2020 audio-recorded interviews were conducted of victims/survivors to detail their stories in connection to key terms, including rape myths and rape culture; I conducted these interviews in confidence.

Rape myths were known and appreciated in the way that women heard the term. Women students remarked that they have heard the term used but unsure of their exact meaning. When asked to describe the myths, remarks were about alcohol, shaming, and that a woman is a slut when raped. They also strongly conclude that rape myths were bogus and should not be believed but spoke about how society cannot make the beliefs go away.

One story is of a woman who was raped when using a dating app such as Tinder. She enjoyed sexual relationships and was fine giving the idea that she wanted sex through the app. She was active in the hookup culture and would not have called herself a novice when the assault happened at 17 years old. This is a good time to assess your own implicit bias – what do you think about this woman or technically woman? What sort of morals does she hold? Does she connect with the puritan culture of the United States? Would you blame her for being raped? It is hard to be honest with yourself about this. As a society, we need to dig deep to assess ourselves before we move forward. Many might think her a slut or a whore or promiscuous. What if she was a boy or a man? These subtle perceptions hidden in those ideologies are rooted rape myths in a rape culture. This is what is being fought against – this is what needs to change.

Hidden underneath the idea of rape myths is the knowledge that we should perhaps ignore them because they are not real, and we should not believe in them. There was a battle expressed among students during interviews the appreciation of not knowing clear definitions or examples of rape myths, but demonstrating a disregard for a lack of knowledge because the rape myths should not exist. Students thought if we are not supposed to believe in them why should I know them clearly. If we do not know them, then people will not abide by the rape myths. This is a concern of implicit biases be it sexism, genderism, racism, classism – the sweeping of ideas under the rug. An idea similar to this is colorblindness – if we do not see color, then racism must not exist, and the rules will change magically. This did not work for racial equality and it will not work for sexual assault. The more we ignore rape myths, the more power they are given.

This can be shown with a story told during my first interviews with students on campus. A student told us about how her family viewed sexual assault, feminism, and femininity verses masculinity. She grew up in a family that had little open dialog about sex, consent, and sexual assault. It was not easily discussed. Femininity and masculinity were taught in the stereotypical manner, but she questioned the appropriateness of this normed behavior. Women were to be docile and kind. Men were to be rough and aggressive. Girls loved pretty pink things. Boys love trucks and guns. What struck me was how she connected these normed sexual identities to rape myths. The student interviewee noticed that boys were taught that aggression was acceptable, and that boys and men need to seek out powerful leadership positions. These male attributes moved into to sexual practices and abridged rights and power of women. Girls were taught quietness and peacemaking. What this means for rape myths is that they are true. Women are to be submissive and give into sexual coercion. Men take sex as a prize and women are to be accepting and accommodating.

Let us travel into another story – a student who was raped repeatedly by her father and brother while growing up. A mother who ignored what was going on. The assaults started when the girl was 5. This pattern showed her what was to be learned about sexual behavior. This girl learned the meekness of females and the strength of males. She learned that sex was to be taken by men and given freely by women or consequences and physical pain would result. Hence, she gave it freely away in high school and it took life in college with a stable boyfriend and lots of therapy to see the destructive pattern developed as a result of being assaulted in a rape culture.

Rape myths as measured in the studies are the perceptions that men do not mean to rape, women lie about rape, that the action was not rape, and she deserved. The story identified above as well as the interviews of college students demonstrates that rape myths impact various layers of our lives. The survivors of rape hide themselves in the shadows of stereotypes and norms of femininity/female and masculinity/male. The victims become the implicit results of socialization. Although the story highlights a dark example of how rape myths are learned, the first scenario demonstrates how society and culture share the validations of awful actions without much thought of consequences.

These types of justifications provide people with the ability to accept sexual assaults, harassment, and coercion. People accede to the erosion of consent as trivial and normal. This is a line you must work to understand and see. In the introduction, you tested your social judgments by seeing me through my different labels. Earlier in this chapter, you examined your perceptions and conclusions as you read about a woman using a dating app for the sole purpose of sex. Now, move yourself into a place of accepting that we hold rape myths as truths even if it is implicit or subconscious; it is still part of us as a culture and an individual. The rape culture ensures the rape myths are part of our social world and experiences. For instance, while writing this book, I came across a story in the media about a woman who was sexually assaulted by her employer or boyfriend or friend or someone she knew; I missed that part. My first gut-check reaction was why did she do that, and then utter disgust followed with a smirk chuckle of – there is the rape culture doing its thing. Even in the midst of my knowledge and research, my brain goes there because I am part of this culture. The sooner we accept that and not fight it, the better we can limit it impacting others.

These rape myths become a means to analyze our world and the actions that can occur within. Rape myths are ways we categorize life and make sense of its atrocities. By victims accepting these myths, it provides guidance during an uncontrollable time. It makes sense out of the broken norm (e.g. sexual assault or rape) but showing women how to respond – distrust, shame, stigma, and silence. Rape myths and culture also show that it is the victims' fault for falling prey; it is their fault for it happening. The logic is thus, as long as I do not engage in actions that make me more prone to sexual assault victimhood, then I will be safe. If I believe in the rape myths, I know how to protect myself. However, it is not that simple.

Rape myths are an evolution of gendered sexuality and vision of power usage in patriarchal heritages (Brownmiller, 1975; Burt, 1980). If women are to be quiet and weak, the very act of talking about sexual assault is wrong – *she must be lying*. If men are supposed to be powerful and aggressive, they can take what they want – *it wasn't really rape*. If men do not see sexual coercion that leads to sexual assault as a problem due to a lack of consent – *he didn't mean to rape*. If a woman steps outside her bounds by wearing proactive clothing or kissing a man or not being a virgin – *she asked for it and deserved it*. This is the rape culture at its core allowing for the rape script to survive through the acceptance of rape culture.

How this connects to the idea of a rape-free society (similar to a color-blind society) is that we do not actually see rape or rape myths for what they are. Most of the woman interviewed supported this as do the quantitative studies – rape myths are not perceived; they are disagreed with, but ever so present under layers of misogyny. The interviews showed that rape myths and rape culture are confusing. The women students were not sure what to believe or how to explain rape myths beyond their existence. Women were able to talk about the larger myths that it is the woman's fault or alcohol and parties are to blame but could not articulate the subtle distinctions found in most rape myth scales.

This was present in the last of the first set of interviews. She was a student leader on campus. Came from a conservative family who believed in virginity until marriage and was unsure how to cope with what happened and what her family would do to learn she was not the girl she pretended to be. During her freshman year on campus, she was raped. She was at a party hanging out with friends and ended up spending more time with a guy in the group. They were drinking, dancing, kissing, and having a fun time. They moved things to a quieter room to talk and maybe watch a movie. Like so many stories of assault, this is not what happened. He kept pressuring her to go further (e.g. sexual coercion): to take off her clothes, to let him see her body while he undressed. She told him no. She told him to stop. She asked to leave. Through physical force, he would not let her go until he was done. She does not remember many of the details of the rape but knows it happened and knows her virginity was taken from her. She cried during telling the story as I was one of the first people she told. She had explained that night to a few friends who slut-shamed her, told her she wanted it, told her she was asking for it, told her she should not have gone into his room if she did not want sex, told her she should have not kissed him and led him on, told her she should accept what she did and not lie about it. This made her stay quiet about the experience because her friends used rape myths and the rape culture to blame, shame, stigmatize, and silence her.

It is remarkable how younger generations support the idea that it is the older generations that purport sexism, classism, racism, and all the other isms. I hear it in my classes, I read it in papers, I discuss it during office hours. Our generation is not the one to blame as we think differently (better) than those *old people*. In many of the interviews and data from the surveys, a strong credence existed in feminism as defined by equality of genders and sexes (see also, Ford, 2016; 2019; Kindlon, 2006; Klein, 2020; Spruill, 2017). It is a justification tool used to protect our self and social identities. It is not us; we are good people. It is their fault for letting it happen; what a powerful tool of socialization.

This learned skill creates a gap between acknowledging what happened not being your fault but believing the rape myths to actualize that it was your fault. Victims talked of themselves as an expressed other now that they held the shame and stigma of being raped. Something they wanted to hide but also revealing and working through the pain would help secure a stronger life. Most feared that by telling their story, the pain would be too much for others. The trust destroyed by the sexual assault prompted their silence and lack of divulging their victim status to friends, family, university officials, law enforcement, therapists, and professors. Socialization provides a storyline about who we are as a woman, and if we are the strong emboldened females of this generation, we should not be raped or feel pain from it.

Another version of the rape myths that came across in the interviews was the implicit ability for women to protect themselves against rape at all times, especially in exposed moments. The surveys showed that the university was perceived as safe. The interviews suggested that the university was not susceptible to sexual assault and sexual violence as other campuses. It was small, friendly, midwestern, religious, private, and not a party school. This kept the women convinced that this school was safer than others. Upper-level students saw the university as less safe than underclassmen in the survey, which I think is due to experiences undergone and witnessed. All women in the interviews, even the couple who were raped by students on campus, still perceived the campus as safe and protected against many of societies' social ills.

Yet, these women made so many remarks about alcohol, stranger danger, safety plans, key carrying, victim blaming, slut shaming, and self-defense. It was clear that the women interviewed felt a need to protect themselves and their friends. Women said that the campus was safe but still needed to engage in protective acts to ensure they did not get raped. Some women postulated that it was an ingrain mechanism taught in our society. Some women blamed other women for not protecting themselves enough and that was why rapes occurred. Some women felt that women needed to be smarter to outwit potential assaulters whether on campus or off, but more actions were taken when off campus or at parties especially if drinking, doing drugs, or by themselves.

Most women interviewed discussed their need for protection while being in public. Many had pepper spray and emergency alarm or whistles. A few carried sharp objects like knives and scissors with them in backpacks or pockets or cars. Students talked about the need for knowing self-defense tactics and how to play safe. This was all done to not be raped. Yet, all the survivor and victim stories were told in ways where no weapons or tactical gear was used against the assailants. Why – I can tell you are asking yourself this question. Because – most stories of assault and rape hold assailants who are trusted – friends, lovers, boyfriends, girlfriends, family, hookups, and others. Pepper spray, keys between the fingers, and whistles are ready in public spaces not bedrooms and dorm rooms.

As a whole, we still believe in rape myths and perpetuate them; we might not realize it beyond subconscious thoughts in how it impacts attitudes, beliefs, perceptions, and actions. This was a road to follow in the interviews; the origination of rape myths and the power the myths hold in society despite feminism and women's struggle for rights. So why in 2020, when so many younger people believe that sexism is dead and working worlds both in the home and out of the home are equally one, do we still have place for myths? The interviews answered: because so many things in our society show that they still should exist. We have slut shaming, dress codes for girls but not boys in schools, dress codes to limit breast viewing, narratives that allow locker room talk and boys to be boys. The society we live in still provides much power to showing women their place in society in and out of the bedroom.

One story depicted this thought pattern from a survivor of more than one sexual assault, at least one in high school and more than two by a boyfriend during her freshman year at college. Her stories were simple. In high school, there was a friend of a friend who liked her, and she might like him. She went to his house in the summer and ended up in his bedroom. They flirted, talked, kissed while watching a movie. She was wearing typical short shorts of high school and a tee-shirt. He was trying to rub her legs and move up the shorts as well as enter her shirt. She kept telling him no. She kept moving farther away from him. She was 15 and did not know what to do. She did not want to look like a prude or a slut, and she did not want to let her friends down who helped set up this date. She also did not want to do anything more than kiss. He eventually used his body weight to tackle her on the floor, forcibly kissed her, and undressed both of them. She screamed and yelled – he told her it would do no good. No one would stop him – even though people were in the house and outside in the yard. She eventually gave in, closed her eyes, wished for the pain to stop, got dressed, and ran home – no one in the house or yard looked at her when she left. At home, she hid evidence of the sexual assault such as bloody underwear in a garbage can. She told no one about this until years later, and still has not told many; I am one of the few.

These are her words:

> I don't wanna have sex Right now and he's like well what am I gonna see you next I follow along my god so is like so there's but even then there's like an inherent pressure yeah otherwise they'll like leave you if you don't like the filter needs how do you think that may be relates to like sexual salt and the ideas surrounding all of this that I wouldn't like say it is sexual but I think it can lead to it definitely and make people feel like obligated to fulfill their partners needs if they don't want to do that

which I guess in a way is sexual salt because it's kind of against your will but you're not like verbalizing it and I feel like you keep it to yourself it's kind of like not claiming yeah so it's almost like a coercion experience talking you into it.

Her other encounter with sexual assault was during her freshman year at college with a boyfriend who attended a different school and was known in her neighborhood as a *great guy*. They dated for about two years and were sexually active. They had shared in consensual sex. She described herself as not a very sexual being, especially due to the sexual assault in high school. She believed that long relationships required sex but that partners should respect desires of when one does and does not want to engage in sex. However, her partner often used sexual coercion to talk her into sex. Phrases such as "this is how I know you love me" or "everyone does it" or "I have manly needs" were some of his favorites in quilting her into sex. When this happened, she would talk to her groups of girlfriends who stated that this is how sex worked in relationships – they all had sex when they did not want to in order to make the relationship happy or to avoid fights or discontentment from their male partners. Consequently, she assumed this behavior was normal, not a version of assault, and continued to give in. Eventually, she stopped giving in. She wished it was due to empowerment, but she said it was depression and she really did not want to. She was tired of it and hoped he would understand. So, he raped her. He held her down, forced her clothes off, unnoticed her screaming, disregarded her saying no numerous times, held her down harder when she hit and kicked. She left his house, retreated into a new world of shame and stigma impacting her grades and relationships. She eventually broke up with him – but it was weeks after the rape. At that time, he tried to have sex again, tried ever coercion he could think of, and she finally left in a hurry to escape his domineering power.

Her words explaining the relationship and how it moved along:

> Yeah I think where it all starts kind of like kind of defines the fight the rest of the relationship or like even if it's just like continuously hooking up you know friends with benefits thing there's like still a standard there I feel like we're like whoever is the dominant person in the relationship male or female like whatever they want there yet and do you what do you think that does to try and understand just sleep very much like to marry more difficult than it should be you know because well I think there's a room it's really hard to define sexual salt and consent because it's different for everyone.

People want others to love them and take care of them. The dominant person uses this affection to gain sex in relationships. The coercion of love, support, relationships, and the human need to not want to be alone is how powerful people use love for sex.

Women survivors and victims believed that the sexual assaults, including rapes, were their fault. That something in the situation could have been avoided if they were smarter about protecting themselves, by not showing up to party or date, by yelling louder and fighting harder. That the people who raped them were kind and loving and just did not know how to control themselves and of course they did not mean to assault the victim. That the victim should have known better than to show up to someone's house to watch a movie. That the victim should have used the dating app and then met the person at their house. These women fell victim to rape myths. Myths of him not meaning to or her not understanding the situation (akin to her lying about it) or her leading him on. Myths about consent not being enforced and she should have made sure he listened. They spoke with the fluency of myths without knowing that it was myths they were speaking.

Part of the reason is that all of the women's stories were not part of the accepted rape scenarios of our society or the blitz rape (Bowie, Silverman, Kalick, & Edbril, 1990; Clay-Warner & McMahon-Howard, 2009). A blitz rape occurs when the woman was assaulted by a stranger, in a dark alley, physically beaten and bloodied; she fought toughly against it, screamed at the top of her lungs, and almost died. In rape and sexual assaults, we categorize what a true rape is and what is not. We fail to acknowledge acquittance rape or date rape, marital or relationship rape, and non-physically harmful rape as rape. These situations become viewed as misunderstandings of consent (Freitas, 2018). As a society, we have transformed enough to know that these true rapes are not the fault of the victim, but we fail to acknowledge that this itself is a myth. Women fail to acknowledge the role of myths on their own sexual assault history, a topic discussed more in Chapter 3.

The concern thus is that students do not even see what they presume. Their beliefs are hidden even to themselves. Strong subconscious waves are denied truth in measuring with the scales. This could be positive in that students are less likely to act upon the ideals they hold deep about causes of sexual assault. But it also means that the implicit bias has a foundation that emerges when students discuss rape myths and rape culture that are not addressed in the scale. The scale cannot find these subtle details that lie under the surface.

If rape myths are implicit biases, it is a concern with programming and change. If we do not know or cannot admit to our core foundation assumptions about beliefs, attitudes and behaviors do not change. Implicit biases are strong elements in our core socialization that exist from the culture and society in which we live. Hence, from these student studies, students agree with rape myths, perhaps not in the exact manner described in the IRMA. This means before programming can occur to change rape myth conceptions, students need to see that they hold the beliefs. This is an obstacle that will be fought with pushback. Who wants to admit to believing in rape myths? Who wants to stand up and proclaim that they believe in victim blaming and sexual coercion? From the scales used in my studies – not many.

Faculty and staff perceptions of rape myths

Faculty and staff perceptions are part of the puzzle in figuring out rape culture on a campus. As an educated body, faculty and staff should be aware of sexual misconduct and assault on their campus. By knowing numbers and safety concerns, they are better equipped at promoting awareness and proactive movements against sexual assault. Most studies about rape myths rely on convenient student samples and do not gather data from faculty and staff. This is a concern as faculty and staff are mandatory reporters and are part of the process in making a university safer.

As noted in Chapter 1, Title IX and the Clery Act coordinate the type of response universities and colleges in the United States must undergo about the sexual misconduct on their campus. Title IX is for the equitable treatment of sexes and genders in any educational environment and rooted in athletics when first created in 1975. Changes were enforced in 2020 to loosen the regulations of sexual misconduct in universities, including less conduct hearings, and victims need to share more proof of their allegations. Universities are able to create stricter standards, but it is uncertain how many and which ones will do so.

Title IX makes faculty and staff mandatory reporters at most universities and provides for only a few personnel on campuses to be confidential reporters, usually mental health treatment professionals, clergy, and public safety or security. One concern of faculty and staff is that if they are encouraging reporting of sexual misconduct by students, numbers in the Clery Reports are accurate, reliable, and depict reality. However, many campuses do not want the numbers portrayed to be accurate or depict reality because the truth of numbers behind sexual assault and misconduct makes universities appear unsafe (Dick & Ziering, 2016). Many students do not report their victimhood out of stigma and shame, so most numbers reported by law enforcement or universities are low.

There is a dark figure of crime in all crime numbers (Kruttschnitt, Kalsbeek & House, 2014). There is no way to know the raw numbers of arsons, car jackings, murders, robberies, assaults, and rape. Numbers are limited by who reports the crimes and what happens to the report once the alleged victim is finished detailing their story. From various types of crime data collection, we acknowledge knowing about 50% of the total crime that occurs on average. Some crimes such as murder are reported more often, so police and researchers know that number clearer. Sexual assault and rape are crimes that go unreported to the highest degree with estimates that 80–90% are unreported. Let that sink in – out of 100 sexual assaults, maybe 10 to 20 are reported to law enforcement. When people share their victimization, they are likely to speak with close friends and family who will not shame the victim or think the victim is lying. Hence, the rape myths shape the undisclosed cases of rape, which people then inaccurately use to state that rape culture does not exist.

Universities have hidden their numbers of sexual misconduct, sexual assault, and rape for decades. The documentary film and book *The Hunting Ground* (Dick &

Ziering, 2016) made people wince at the actions undergone by ivy league schools such as Harvard to maintain low numbers of sexual misconduct and rape. Similarly, Missoula, Baylor, Stanford, and others (Dick & Ziering, 2016; Fisher, Daigle, & Cullen, 2010; Krakauer, 2016; Lavigne & Schlabach, 2017; Miller, 2019) disallow law enforcement to engage in investigatory duties about rapes involving students. What university wants to be the one that tells its true statistics first? What university wants to declare how unsafe it is for females (and all others) to attend their university? It is in the prime economic interest of universities and the perceived security of students for these numbers to stay inaudible.

Faculty and staff, also known as campus security authorities in research, provided data in surveys. Quantitative surveys were distributed to faculty and staff meetings (study number 4) and focus groups were a follow-up to the surveys with volunteers of a faculty and staff in study 5. The survey showed that employees of the university did not believe in the rape myths and in fact were in higher disagreement to the myths than students. Focus groups though showed that the story behind the numbers was not simple to grasp.

Study 4 – The faculty and staff ($n = 75$) of the university were objectively in disagreement with the rape myths as measured in the survey through IRMA. This study used the neutral category in responses to IRMA statements along with strongly agree, agree, disagree, and strongly disagree. As you can see in Table 2.13, few of the items have strongly agree as a chosen response by participants and there are five items that have null percentage of respondents in the strongly agree and agree categories. All items hold means high into the strongly disagreement levels with only item 8 (guys don't usually intend to force sex on a woman, but sometimes they get too sexually carried away) being below 4.0 at 3.90 due to a high level of neutral responses. Also, item 4 (a woman acts like a slut, eventually she is going to get into trouble) holds the highest level of agreement at 14% of faculty and staff. Faculty and staff were more likely to be neutral or disagree with the items than students as observed in percentages.

Comparable to the student surveys, the items in the *it wasn't really rape* category held the highest amount of disagreement and were most of the items where no agreement was marked. From this scale, items 13 (if a woman doesn't physically resist sex – even if protesting verbally – it can't be considered rape), 14 (if a woman doesn't physically fight back, you can't really say it was rape), 15 (a rape probably doesn't happen if a woman doesn't have any bruises or marks), and 16 (if the accused "rapist" doesn't have a weapon, you really can't call it rape) held the highest means all above 4.85. Items 3 (if a woman goes to a room alone with a guy at a party, it is her own fault if she is raped) and 11 (it shouldn't be considered rape if a guy is drunk and didn't realize what he was doing) share high means at 4.85 and 4.87, respectively.

The scales of IRMA for the faculty and staff study demonstrated high levels of disagreement and hold the highest means among those surveys with the neutral category. This is not surprising as the individual items illustrated high disagreement and extremely low levels of agreement. Table 2.14 displays the ranges and

TABLE 2.13 Study 4 Spring 2016 Faculty/Staff Survey Individual Items Percentages and Means

Scale	Items – Rape Myth Statements	SA	A	N	D	SD	Mean
She asked for it	1 If a woman is raped while drunk, she is at least somewhat responsible for letting things get out of hand.	0.0	2.7	5.6	14.7	77.3	4.67
	2 When women go to parties wearing slutty clothes, they are asking for trouble.	0.0	5.3	2.7	14.7	77.3	4.64
	3 If a woman goes to a room alone with a guy at a party, it is her own fault if she is raped.	0.0	0.0	2.7	9.3	88.0	4.85
	4 If a woman acts like a slut, eventually she is going to get into trouble.	2.7	12.0	10.7	14.7	60.0	4.17
	5 When women get raped, it's often because the way they said "no" was unclear.	0.0	1.3	4.0	14.7	80.0	4.73
	6 If a woman initiates kissing or hooking up, she should not be surprised if a guy assumes she wants to have sex.	0.0	12.0	13.3	26.7	48.0	4.11
He didn't mean to	7 When guys rape, it is usually because of their strong desire for sex.	1.4	5.5	21.9	19.2	52.1	4.15
	8 Guys don't usually intend to force sex on a woman, but sometimes they get too sexually carried away.	1.4	8.2	28.8	21.9	39.7	3.90
	9 Rape happens when a guy's sex drive goes out of control.	0.0	5.4	13.5	16.2	64.9	4.41
	10 If a guy is drunk, he might rape someone unintentionally.	0.0	5.5	24.7	19.2	50.7	4.15
	11 It shouldn't be considered rape if a guy is drunk and didn't realize what he was doing.	0.0	0.0	2.7	8.0	89.3	4.87
	12 If both people are drunk, it can't be rape.	0.0	1.3	2.7	12.0	84.0	4.79
It wasn't really rape	13 If a woman doesn't physically resist sex – even if protesting verbally – it can't be considered rape.	0.0	1.3	1.3	8.0	89.3	4.85
	14 If a woman doesn't physically fight back, you can't really say it was rape.	0.0	0.0	2.7	0.0	97.3	4.95
	15 A rape probably doesn't happen if a woman doesn't have any bruises or marks.	0.0	0.0	1.3	0.0	98.7	4.97
	16 If the accused "rapist" doesn't have a weapon, you really can't call it rape.	0.0	0.0	1.3	0.0	98.7	4.97
	17 If a woman doesn't say "no" she can't claim rape.	1.3	4.0	6.7	16.0	72.0	4.53
She lied	18 A lot of times, women who say they were raped agreed to have sex and then regret it.	0.0	4.1	24.3	16.2	55.4	4.23
	19 Rape accusations are often used as a way of getting back at guys.	0.0	5.5	16.4	24.7	53.4	4.26
	20 A lot of times, women who say they were raped often led the guy on and then had regrets.	0.0	2.7	16.2	18.9	62.2	4.41
	21 A lot of times, women who claim they were raped have emotional problems.	0.0	1.4	16.2	14.9	67.6	4.49
	22 Women who are caught cheating on their boyfriends sometimes claim it was rape.	0.0	1.4	20.5	17.8	60.3	4.37

TABLE 2.14 Study 4 Spring 2016 Faculty/Staff Survey IRMA Scale

Scale	Alpha	Possible Range	Midpoint	Actual Range	Mean (Std. Dev.)
Total rape myth scale Items 1–22	0.923	22–110	66	60–110	99.65 (10.77)
She asked for it Items 1–6	0.801	6–30	18	13–29	27.17 (3.64)
He didn't mean to Items 7–12	0.767	6–30	18	16–29	26.31 (3.53)
It wasn't rape Items 13–17	0.624	5–25	15	15–25	24.28 (1.57)
She lied Items 18–22	0.923	5–25	15	12–25	21.78 (3.81)

*Any score below midpoint marks agreement with scale.

means of IRMA scale for faculty and staff. The ranges were similar to all other surveys, but the percentages are well above neutral.

Total rape myth scale is the only scale that had a participant score less than the midpoint of 66; literally one person held a total score of 60 out of 110. For the study, 18.3% held the highest score for the scale and another 42.2% scored at 100 or more with 98.6% scoring at or above the midpoint. *Asked for it* scale held 32.0% of respondents at the highest level of disagreement and another 45.3 at or above 25. All respondents are above the midpoint scale, scoring 13 or above. *He didn't mean to* scale has 26.4% at the highest score in the scale, another 44.5% at or above 25. All respondents are at or above the midpoint of 16. *It wasn't rape* has 68.0% of respondents in strong disagreement and all respondents have scale score at higher than the midpoint at 15 or more. *She lied* scale has 42.5% of respondents in strong disagreement and all respondents have scale score at the midpoint or higher. Thus, all disagree with the scales.

These employees professed that the school was safe and there was little reason for fear on the campus. They also boldly disagreed with the IRMA scales. Faculty and staff on average strongly disagreed with the rape myth total rape myth scale as well as the four subsidiary scales of *she asked for it, he didn't mean to, it wasn't rape*, and *she lied*. Also, similarly to students, there were some items that tended to have more neutral answers almost as if people wanted to agree but knew they should not agree. Remember we know not to believe in rape myths, and it might take more subtly to realize how people perpetuate the myths and how they are part of our subconscious identities. Therefore, the focus groups were conducted. We needed to hear how people spoke about the myths through stories not solely numbers.

Study 5 – Focus groups were conducted with three volunteer groups, one staff and two faculty groups. The groups convened to build a small quick community that were willing to discourse about the topic of rape culture, rape myths, sexual assaults, and the perceived university life. After four general questions were discussed and the conversations died out, a video was shown. This video was created by a student as a PSA for other students. The creation of the video is interesting in itself – the student made with my knowledge and blessing, but I was not part of the production. She was pulled into conduct hearings once student affairs were made known of her advertisement flyers because she was not distributing them through the proper channels. The result of the conduct hearings was nothing much to the student, but it froze the project allowing only two students to be in the video. The student wanted to make sure something was done with the video so it was used here to disengage what employees think about the role of sexual assaults, myths, and culture on the campus once seeing the aftermaths portrayed.

These campus security administrators came together in their conversations with some overarching themes. The campus is safe or at least safer than those big universities that are known for sports, fraternities, and parties. The campus is quiet, and our students are kind Midwesterners who would not hurt others especially at this private, religious school. If there was a big concern of sexual assault on campus, I would know. I do not hear much about rape on this campus, so it must be safe. Faculty and staff even through marked as Title IX mandatory reporters were not knowledgeable about sexual assaults on campus or the hookup culture or social life beyond classrooms and offices. Some faculty were able to bring generalities into the discussion about what they knew about sexual assault. A few staff could do the same generally and speak specifically about this university because it was their job to know the information. Yet, sexual assault fell to the same stereotypes involved with the myths.

Once the video was shown where two people shared the aftermath of their rapes on campus, faculty and staff were alarmed and outraged. The video illustrated the pain, stigma, hatred, red tape, and questioning experienced by the victims with the tag line "it happens here." The video stories did not fit with the focus groups conceptualizations of students on this campus. How could our students be so mean toward the victims? How could our students tell these victims it was their fault? How could our students be called liars? How could they be told that they enjoyed the sex and he did not mean to do it? How could they be called temptresses, whores, and sluts? How could the rape myths be so alive? They saw in the brief video, the truths beyond rape cultures and social stereotypes that people on their campus were not only victims of sexual assault but of rape myths.

As much as faculty did not think that the university was connected to rape culture and myths and sexual assaults, the video opened their eyes. The video displayed the reality of it happening on this nice midwestern campus and how myths made students react to their friends and peers. Faculty and staff watched with jaws open and hands covering mouths and hearts. Tears were in their eyes, and mine. Heads shook in wonderment. Pain shot from their eyes.

The video also contained some national university statistics about sexual assault and rape. This was where the faculty and staff started their discussion. Those numbers cannot be right nationally. Those numbers are not right for our university. What are the numbers for our university? But I have never known a student who was assaulted? But maybe I have and just did not know. This is similar across other universities. People want to see their place as safe and strong and without turmoil. Work and home should be safe places not to be feared. Part of the issues of sexual assault on campuses is the reckoning that this crime happens everywhere even if you do not hear about it. It is not about fear mongering but safety ensuring, which is a role of administration on campuses.

It was fascinating being in the room where some of the faculty and staff became woke to this idea. It was moments of aspiration, anger, fortitude, and disbelief. Disbelief in how students responded and that the focus group members were ignorant of this life. Once contemplated the video, faculty and staff took their roles as mentors and guardians of education to task. They rationalized why they did not know was because faculty and staff are out of students' lives; this part of life is not shown in the academic classroom. Its effects are seen through missing classes, poor grades, lack of connection to subject material, inability to participate in class, and a sense of vague depression or withdrawal. Without students being able to open up to the reason behind the mood and grades shifts, many are left to assumptions of the student not caring enough for this class or not trying hard enough. Instead of realizing, it is the student who cannot engage in school because of the trauma they are witnessing and processing.

The survey shed some light on this procurement of woke eye-widening. Most of the faculty and staff disagreed with rape myths and viewed the campus as safe for students and themselves. This dissonant cognition was captured more by the neutral responses in the survey. Two scales held more neutrality than others with single items perceived as neutral by 16% to 28% of respondents. Neutral response is indicative of one who is not disagreeing with the statement but also not comfortable agreeing with the statement. The items in the scales of *he didn't mean to* and *she is lying* were most neutral suggesting that close to 1 in 5 or 1 in 4 campus security authorities had a hard time pronouncing disagreement. These respondents did not want to provide complicit agreement to the statements but were fine saying that they did not disagree.

The focus groups by no means came to a point where faculty and staff engaged in victim blaming or stated that victims lied about sexual assault or that men did not mean to rape their victims. They hedged around the ideas that sometimes when alcohol and drugs are involved, things become complicated and assaults might happen. Is this similar enough to saying that it was the beers' fault? And if it is the beers' fault, it would not be the man's fault? And if she was so drunk perhaps, she consented when she didn't mean to? So, it's not that she is lying, she doesn't remember the details. This could be the professional ways of saying "she lied" and "he didn't mean to" or least expressing neutrality of these ideas.

I must point out that the focus groups were concerned about sexual assaults and wanted to do something, anything, to help make progress on campus especially after the video was shown. These employees wanted to cease the disease of rape myths and rape culture to build acceptance of victims and their stories.

Believing in rape myths and purporting them do not make a person wrong, immoral, or judged; it makes them part of this society and culture.

Campus programming shifting rape myth perceptions

Students, faculty, and staff all discussed campus programming and its need to build. Currently, this campus completes the requirements of Title IX in educating its freshmen, athletes, sororities, and fraternities. It also engages with students through Take Back the Night, sexual assault awareness month, denim day, and other events hosted by faculty such as guest speakers. There is signage around campus to alert students about how to confidentially speak about personal sexual assaults and who are mandatory reporters. The university counseling center works alongside the local women's clinic and shelter to support rape victims and survivors. The residential staff in dormitories aid in explaining processes and procedures to students as well as lead discussions about consent, safe sexual practices, and sexual assault.

Faculty and staff go through mandatory training about sexual assault on campus and the proper channel for mandatory reporters when students discuss events of sexual assault or rape. The office for victims is open to discuss resources and concerns with faculty and staff for education but this often centers on appropriate reporting and numbers on campus. There is a committee on campus comprising faculty, staff, public safety, and the Title IX coordinator which meets once a semester to discuss needs on campus and programs offered.

Part of the student survey was measuring the way programs impacted rape myth viewpoint. Specifically, did the number of programs a student remember attending limit agreement or enhance disagreement with the rape myths? The answer was no. First, most students (%) did not remember ever attending a presentation about sexual assault or rape including athletes who go through additional programming. This is despite the fact that all students attend Title IX training as freshmen. Of those who remember events, it was a human trafficking speaker or rape survivor that was remembered along with Take Back the Night. None of this showed promise of lower rape myth perceptions and rape culture adherence even though the programs were rated by students as good programing.

Faculty focus groups shared little knowledge about programming on campus geared toward students and spoke little more than the Title IX compliance trainings completed yearly. Many were unable to dictate how to proceed as a mandatory reporter when a student came to them. Many were nervous about the thought of a student coming to them about this topic. Staff who worked with students were more knowledgeable but the other staff in the groups recognized since they do not work directly with students; they know little about sexual assaults on campus.

What all said about the campus was that more educational opportunities were necessary. Peer programs were spoke about highly by faculty, staff, and students. People wanted the information and wanted to be able to secure a safer campus.

74 Rape myth perceptions

Many wanted to learn bystander training, once it was explained to them, to help people in distress before, during, or after a sexual assault occurred. People also wanted numbers. They wanted to know how big of a program sexual assault was on the campus to see benchmarks of improvement. They wanted to know that the campus cared about students and found real ways to support them. Many stated if you supported and educated students, faculty, and staff, the university would know the truth and be more inclined to do something about it. By keeping sexual assault in the shadows, people can rely only on beliefs, hearsay, and experiences.

By not actively seeking out the truth, the truth binds us all. It is outlandish to me, now that I study campus sexual assault, how much we do not know and do not study. Universities are filled with researchers, who do not examine one of the more horrific behaviors of campus life. In some way, we accept the rape culture in that rapes and sexual assaults are bound to happen. This is part of life. What we neglect to acknowledge is what this does to generation after generation of college students and employees. Universities need to build in resources to help ease shame and stigma that allow victims to overcome the obstacle of not reporting their sexual assaults to anyone. None of the women survivors told law enforcement except for the child case. Few told family or friends or boyfriends or girlfriends, but they told me. Many want their story heard and recognized to do good. People want the members of the university to help and provide compassion. As *Campus Action* book supports, we need victims to work with university employees who can work with students who can provide administration knowledge who, in turn, prioritizes evidence-based programming and wholistic education. What most universities do now is a bandage; we instead need to stop allowing the wounds to happen.

Summary

As a culture and society, we know how to response negatively to rape myths. When asked directly, people will feign disillusion and claim disagreement. Yet, due to implicit or subconscious bias underneath is adherence to rape cultures rules and values. People disagree with rape myths when measured but then support that alcohol, loose women, and stupidity cause rape. Few, if any, believed that rape is characterized by strangers and dark allies but also were quick to note that slut shaming and victim blaming are the aftermaths of disclosing stories of sexual assault or hearing about these stories.

Students, faculty, and staff all built the idea that stereotypes of safer universities exist: those schools who are not known as party schools, sport schools, or Greek life schools are safe from the harm of sexual assault. No one believed that schools were free of sexual assault and rape but that certain types – private, small, not division 1 or ivy league, religious-based – were safer. This misconception was found throughout the campus and even when faculty, students, and staff opposed rape myths, many adhered to the misconception of drinking and debauchery creating rape. Further, it is a concern that those who disagree with rape myths and support feminism still hold ideas and conceptions of conservative sex roles and behaviors to support rape culture ideologies. Thus, the misconstruction of the causes of sexual assault, including unruly male populations at parties, connects to false safety and a lack of concern about these universities.

If the university life is illustrated as carefree and safe, money and resources do not need to be placed in programming about sexual assaults, rape myths, bystander intervention, and consent. This is not only a concern at the university as it is a smaller social group within the large social context of the United States, but universities must address what this means for their student and employee community.

References

Armstrong, R. L. (1987). The midpoint on a five-point Likert-type scale. *Perceptual and Motor Skills, 64*, 359–362.
Albaum, G. (1997). The Likert scale revisited. *Market Research Society Journal, 39*, 1–21.
Bowie, S. I., Silverman, D. C., Kalick, S. M., & Edbril, S. D. (1990). Blitz rape and confidence rape: Implications for clinical intervention. *American Journal of Psychotherapy, 44*, 180–188.
Brewer, V. E., & Smith, M. D. (1995). Gender inequality and rates of female homicide victimization across US cities. *Journal of Research in Crime and Delinquency, 32*, 175–190.
Brow, S. (1975). *Against our will*. Fawcett.
Burt, M. R. (1980). Cultural myths and supports for rape. *Journal of Personality and Social Psychology, 2*, 217–230.
Casey, G. (2020). *After #metoo: Feminism, patriarchy, toxic masculinity and sundry delights*. Ingram Book Company.
Clay-Warner, J., & McMahon-Howard, J. (2009). Rape reporting: "Classic rape" and the behavior of law. *Violence and Victims, 24*, 723–743.
Cohen, C. (2014). *Male rape is a feminist issue: Feminism, governmentality and male rape*. Springer.
Conaghan, J., & Russell, Y. (2014). Rape myths, law, and feminist research: 'Myths about myths'?. *Feminist Legal Studies, 22*, 25–48.
Creswell, J. W. (1999). Mixed-method research: Introduction and application. In Cizek, G. J (Ed.) *Handbook of educational policy* (pp. 455–472). Academic Press.
Creswell, J. W., & Creswell, J. D. (2017). *Research design: Qualitative, quantitative, and mixed methods approaches*. Sage publications.
Croasmun, J. T., & Ostrom, L. (2011). Using Likert-type scales in the social sciences. *Journal of Adult Education, 40*, 19–22.
Dick, K., & Ziering, A. (2016). Brewer, V. E., & Smith, M. D. (1995). Gender inequality and rates of female homicide victimization across US cities. *Journal of Research in Crime and Delinquency, 32*(2), 175–190.
Dillman, D. A., Smyth, J. D., & Christian, L. M. (2014). *Internet, phone, mail, and mixed-mode surveys: The tailored design method*. John Wiley & Sons.
Echabe, A. E. (2010). Role identities versus social identities: Masculinity, femininity, instrumentality and communality. *Asian Journal of Social Psychology, 13*, 30–43.
Edwards, M. L., & Smith, B. C. (2014). The effects of the neutral response option on the extremeness of participant responses. *Journal of Undergraduate Scholarship, 6*, 30.

Farmer, G. L., & McMahon, S. (2005). Scale for the identification of acquaintance rape attitudes: Reliability and factorial invariance. *Journal of the Human Behavior and the Social Environment, 1*, 213—235.

Fisher, B. S., Daigle, L. E., & Cullen, F. T. (2010). *Unsafe in the Ivory Tower*. Sage.

Ford, C. (2019). *Boys will be boys: Power, patriarchy and toxic masculinity*. Simon and Schuster.

Ford, C. (2016). *Fight like a girl*. One world Publications.

Ford, L. (2018). *Women and politics: The pursuit of equality*. Routledge.

Freitas, D. (2018). *Consent on campus*. Oxford University Press.

Guy, R. F., & Norvell, M. (1977). The neutral point on a Likert scale. *The Journal of Psychology, 95*, 199–204.

Hawkins, D. I., & Coney, K. A. (1981). Uninformed response error in survey research. *Journal of marketing research, 18*, 370–374.

Higgins, L. A., & Silver, B. R. (Eds.). (1991). *Rape and representation*. Columbia University Press.

Hinck, S., & Thomas, R. W. (1999). Rape myth acceptance in college students: How far have we come? *Sex Roles, 40*, 815–832.

Kindlon, D. (2006). *Alpha girls: Understanding the new American girl and how she is changing the world*. Rodale.

Kipnis, L. (2017). *Unwanted advances*. Harper Collins.

Klein, E. (2020). *Why we're polarized*. Avid Reader Press.

Krakauer, J. (2016). *Missoula: Rape and the justice system in a college town*. Anchor.

Kruttschnitt, C., Kalsbeek, W. D., & House, C. C. (Eds.). (2014). *Estimating the incidence of rape and sexual assault*. National Research Council of the National Academies.

Lavigne, P., & Schlabach, M. (2017). *Violated: Exposing Rape at Baylor University Amid College Football's Sexual Assault Crisis*. Center Street.

Lonsway, K. A., & Fitzgerald, L. F. (1995). Attitudinal antecedents of rape myth acceptance: A theoretical and empirical reexamination. *Journal of Personality & Social Psychology, 68*, 704–711.

Lonsway, K. A., & Fitzgerald, L. F. (1994). Rape myths: In review. *Psychology of Women Quarterly, 18*, 133.

Mac Donald, H. (2018). *The diversity delusion: How race and gender pandering corrupt the university and undermine our culture*. St. Martin's Griffin.

McMahon, S., & Farmer, G. L. (2011). An updated measure for assessing subtle rape myths. *Social work research, 35*, 71–81.

Miller, C. (2019). *Know my name: A memoir*. Penguin Books.

Murphy, P. F. (Ed.). (2004). *Feminism & masculinities*. Oxford University Press.

Payne, D. A., Lonsway, K. A., & Fitzgerald, L. F. (1999). Rape myth acceptance: Exploration of its structure and its measurement using the Illinois rape myth acceptance sale. *Journal of Research in Personality, 33*, 27–68.

Patterson, J. (2016). *Queering sexual violence: Radical voices from within the anti-violence movement*. Riverdale Avenue Books.

Phillips, N. D. (2017). *Beyond blurred lines*. Rowman & Littlefield.

Scarce, M. (2008). *Male on male rape: The hidden toll of stigma and shame*. Basic Books.

Spruill, M. J. (2017). *Divided we stand: The battle over women's rights and family values that polarized American politics*. Bloomsbury.

Suarez, E., & Gadalla, T. M. (2010). Stop blaming the victim: A meta-analysis on rape myths. *Journal of interpersonal violence, 25*, 2010–2035.

3
DECONSTRUCTING STUDENT CONFUSION AND BEWILDERMENT

Ignorance surrounding sexual assault and rape myths cannot be ignored. Ignorance allows for disavowing tragedy to limit discontentment with society. Justifications and excuses can be hung from the hook of ignorance because if it is not known, then an action, behavior, value, or belief cannot be one's fault. Ignorance might be blissful for some, but it is misery for others. Definitionally, ignorance is not knowing something or not being privileged to know reality. Ignorance is not being dumb or unintelligent – it is simply not knowing what you do not know.

Ignorance works in various ways for rape myths, rape culture, and sexual assault. Obliviousness allows for many of the rape myths to exist in the labels used to measure them. *She asked for it*. Ignorance. *He didn't know it was rape*. Ignorance. *He didn't mean to do it*. Ignorance. *She lied*. Ignorance. Rape culture is the beliefs, perceptions, and attitudes that allow male aggression to control females in patriarchal societies, thus enabling the precursors and foundations of rape to be trivialized. Ignorance.

Ignorance conjures a society that does not have to recognize realities about sexual assaults. It is not that people view sexual assaults and rape as preferred activities or that the majority of people are engaging in rape willy-nilly; in fact, statistics show otherwise (Kruttschnitt, Kalsbeek, & House, 2014). Only about 6% of males are rapists and less represent those who engage in more serious extremely physically harmful rapes that fill media stories. Concerningly and connected to rape culture, about 40% of men state that if they could get away with sexual assaults, they would do so. This itself is a problem that demonstrates rape cultures existence in society. Somewhere in this mixture is the moral fiber, criminal conviction, and an inability to cause harm to another human that keeps beliefs in check with the values of wrongness. The ignorance of sexual assault is a bit uglier and perhaps more subtle.

Most people who are victims of sexual assault are attacked by people they know or at least feel comfortable enough with or entered a situation willingly (Kruttschnitt, Kalsbeek, & House, 2014; Parrot & Bechhofer, 1991; Raphael, 2013). Most commonly, rapes in college are acquaintance or date or party rapes and viewed as hookups gone wrong. These sexual assaults are still based on opportunity but different than the lurking stranger, assaults and rapes are engaged in by those we know. Why is this? Why do people engage in behaviors not valued in our society and when asked state they are against? What allows for this disjunction of behavior and attitudes? Why do dispel attitudes seem to be against rape myths and rape culture but engage in rape? Why are so many people feminists but trivialize sexual assault? Defensible IGNORANCE!

Ignorance is not only not knowing; it is a level of cognitive dissonance or the inability to recognize information as facts. A person can separate themselves and purposely choose not to believe something that is indeed real. We can use our opinions and beliefs about a subject to never open up to other versions of reality. It is difficult to see the process of where one does not believe in rape myths but then slut shames a woman who showed too much skin, drank too much alcohol, danced with too many men, kissed someone, and reported a sexual assault the next afternoon; yet, this happens a lot (for instance, Almazan & Bain, 2015; Hackman, Pember, Wilkerson, Burton, & Usdan, 2017). Humans have the ability to separate the horribleness of rape as an action and its stereotypical socialized supported causes as rationales. In this vein, it is not as the saying goes; ignorance is not bliss when it comes to sexual assault and rape.

Although ignorance is not stupidity or unintelligence, there is a need to look outside of yourself and conditioned beliefs to see the world differently. This is sometimes called viewing the world through the eyes of others, or sociological imagination. It means determining what needs to be learned from the vastness of personal and vicarious experiences through your history and the society and culture you live in (Mills, 2000). People interpret the world around them through the lenses brains are accustomed to using. Without the ability to dream of the unknowable, humankind would never progress.

One issue with rapes and sexual assaults is that it does not impact everyone personally to the same degree of harshness. It happening to you or your sister or best friend is different than hearing about a classmate from your introduction to chemistry class being raped or hearing about a stranger much on the news. Some can say, "I don't know anyone who has been raped"; however, if saying this in a room of women (and men), chances are you do. People are allowed ignorance in this society about sexual assault and rape because stories are not encouraged to be shared. People hide their stories under stigma, shame, and a sense of duty.

Sexual assault stories are not shared for many reasons but the most compelling might be that people do not believe victims of rape. This is especially when the assault scenario does not fulfill our version of "real" rape (Freedman, 2013; Gay, 2018; Mac Donald, 2018; Nass, 1977). The lack of a blitz rape or "real"/"classical" rape adds to the shame and stigma felt by a victim. The assault brings one level of pain but the decision to report the incident to family, friends, therapists, law enforcement, and campus authorities creates fear in wondering about the response. Many do not tell others because of the growth in shame via victim blaming they think will follow.

As learned through a video used in focus groups, women raped at the university shared their horrific accounts of what the college community did in the aftermaths of rape. The rapes were horrific in their own accords, but the rape culture destroyed them afterward. These women were ostracized, cut out from friends, and pushed away from their athletic teams. People showed utter hatred as they spat on them, threw food on them, refused to sit by them during meals or in classes, and slut shamed intensely in public, on social media, and written on their dormitory doors. Both students from the video withdrew from the university at the end of semester and changed campuses. The restraining orders and changes in dormitory rooms were not enough to protect them from the continued mocking and threats by strangers and so-called friends. One of the women even had video documentation of the event shown via social media by the accuser – the verdict from the campus community and her close friends was that she enjoyed the attention and blamed him for making her a slut after she sobered up.

This is the rape culture at work (Phillips, 2017; Richards & Marcum, 2015). Do not share. We are allowed ignorance. Do not report. We do not need to know. Do not tell your family. We can live without it bothering us. Do not tell your next boyfriend or girlfriend. They do not need to be bothered with this knowledge. Hold it deep, so the stigma and shame clutch on. The rape culture does not allow healing to occur because it manifested a catastrophic culture prone to ignoring our ignorance about rape and sexual assault.

An interviewee in study 14 shared her story that shows blurred lines and an inability to fight off a boyfriend rapist after declaring how many times she has been raped and assaulted:

> I've been assaulted many times. While staying on campus in one I was living on campus and it was someone who went to school here. Another time my boyfriend at the time in the scenario dislocated my hip yeah my freshman year. At 16, one of my fellow classmates in my high school and then when I was five my female teacher and then two of the male students assaulted me. [Researcher: let's focus on the boyfriend scenario first] We had lost her virginity with each other. We've been dating for about four or five months at a time and I had severe depression at the time. When I get in that state I'm kind of like 'well I don't want anything, I don't want to you.' You can sit next to me and we can chat. We can do those things. Historically in my life I have been very open about that with other friends and my current fiancé is totally chill with it. Like when those things happened [the prior assaults] and I was like you can come over these nights but I'm not gonna do anything I don't want because this is how it is. If you come over to my dorm, we can hang out, I don't want to do anything [sexual]. He said

that he was fine with it and then every few moments he would try to begin something. Each time it would begin with us cuddling and he would kind a get on top of me and start doing things that I would say stop, physically hit him, and yell. So, I wasn't necessarily as like emotionally strong as I have been in the past and I just would be like fine, whatever. But I was in such a state I wasn't in the kind of scenario that I was used to emotionally or mentally. It happened physically fighting him off three different times with me eventually giving up.

Here was a woman who was raped as a young child and again as a high schooler by people she should have been able to trust. These assaulters and rapists included her stepfather, her teacher, her friend, and her boyfriend. These are all assaults the authorities do not know about. Some friends and her current fiancé know her sexual assault history. Her mother is estranged because she did not want to see all the hurt being caused in her daughter's life. These date rapes and acquaintance rapes started as coercion, demonstrated a lack of consent, and ended in despair. Later in the interview, she commented that the boyfriends never saw what they did as rape and did not understand why she eventually left them. It took strength and bravery to end these relationships because she wanted love and companionship. The rape culture did not show these other people in her life an appropriate way to form love without taking control and power.

Their stories are not unique – you can find similar stories in most rape victimization books written. In *The Things we didn't talk about when I was a girl* (Vanasco, 2019), they discussed the author's past and pain from sexual assaults and rapes. This memoir details her account years later when she reconnects with one of her assaulters. They were friends at the time of the non-consensual fingering and masturbation. They stayed friends for a time until there was a natural sliding away. She details other assaults by trusted people and how these men, a teacher, an advisor, a friend, some boyfriends, and an almost stranger, took what they wanted without hearing her.

In *Know my Name* (Miller, 2019), Channel talks about how Brock's family, school, and criminal justice system chastised her for ruining his youthful life and prospects in swimming and career. In *Violated* (Lavigne & Shlabach, 2017), numerous women were humiliated for reporting rape allegations to the university and police departments because of the downfall it would lead to the pristine football team and the money that comes with the team. Similar with *Missoula* (Krakauer, 2016), numerous women victims with various accusations against athletes were ridiculed for sharing their story and blamed for bringing turmoil to the city and university. This does not only occur in the university. Society is filled with countless victims who decided to come forward only to be scorned for her gull at blaming a man of such an awful deed.

A *Woman Scorned* (Sanday, 1996) and *Beyond Blurred* Lines (Phillips, 2017) shared many of these stories of women trying to have their story heard and the powerful in society mocking their voice. These books detailed events of sexual assault followed by hatred of selves and others. Identities alter in the aftermath of assaults due to shame and stigma felt and the pressure of holding onto a life-destroying secret. It is the rape culture that delivers additional pain, the inability to focus on treatment in a culture that demands victim blaming and hatred. For example, the reporting effort in *Justice on Trial* (Hemingway & Severino, 2019) where Dr. Blassey Ford explains to a senate committee the sexual assault of accused Justice Kavanaugh while she was in high school and him in college. Half of the world seemed with him, while the other half supported her and were more enraged about his due process rights and affronts to his esteem than finding the truth behind the accusations. All of this and more result in victims being afraid to come forward because the internal shame might be less than the external shame hovering over a person from the rape culture.

I hope at this point, you are still following along and trying to make sense of all this. It is hard; I am still confused after working on this topic for nearly six years and being an official card-carrying doctor in criminology (criminologist) for nearly ten years. This includes prior work in criminal justice and sociology that earned me a bachelor's degree and the subsequent work in criminal justice (and again sociology) that earned me a master's degree in criminal justice. Additionally, my experience includes the jobs and internships where I worked alongside judges, case managers, police officers, social workers, counselors, prosecutors, defense attorneys, researchers, academics, and the clientele. In these positions, I spoke with people who would be defined as criminals, prostitutes, rapists, drug offenders, drug users, violent offenders, first-time offenders, career criminals, murderers, victims, witnesses, and everywhere in between. I have seen due process and justice fought about, meddled with, and handed out. It is created and built by ordinary procedures every day. I have engaged in research projects about theories, policies, and procedures in the juvenile justice system, municipal courts, jails, prisons, and university. I have interviewed and surveyed social workers, students, faculty, staff, juvenile justice counselors, judges, attorneys, wardens, sheriffs, and women who have been in prison to learn and grow. There are still many questions and a lack of answers. Confusion still abounds; inquiry and honest reflection are enough.

People want to be good. People wanted to be liked by our society and its rules (Durkheim, 1897/1961; 1933). People do not want to make bad decisions that alter their lives and the lives of those whom they harmed. People want to fight for justice and due process. People want to be morally correct. People want truth, love, empathy, and compassion. Sadly, the rules of life, its norms, values, and beliefs are difficult to navigate. We struggle seeking truth and reality over opinion and personal experiences; this is how humans are programmed. We have a hard time hearing science over discontent, opinions, and confusion. It is difficult to accept that learning takes courage and chaos. Comprehending rape myths and rape culture as well as their influence on our personal and social lives is cumbersome. This is why there is so much need to discover past confusion and bewilderment.

We have to take it upon ourselves to move past the nastiness and pain of the topic. It is not something I ever thought I would research, discuss openly, and teach freshman about, but here I am. It takes time to overcome the fear of ignorance in the pursuit of knowledge especially in a topic we are taught (though the rape culture) to not discuss or deliberate over. I have read books I wanted to throw across the room. I read books that hurt my soul and brain as I wholeheartedly disagreed with their premise. I have read books I needed to put down over anger, sadness, sorrow, empathy, and love. I have cried during many books sometimes due to sadness, more often due to anger. This does not include the studies I have done with people in my community that has bolstered my heart and moved me to tears. This topic of sexual assault, rape, violence, victimhood, survivorship, rape myths, and rape culture is not easy. Take your time – it's the pursuit that matters not the length of time it takes you to get somewhere new.

Data

This chapter explores student perceptions of definitions and the difficulty in processing from data collected. Quantitative data supported student perceiving the campus as a safe environment not to be feared where sexual assault is not a problem. Students pronounced that the campus engaged in enough tactics for student protection against violence, including the violence of sexual assault. Even though most students disagreed with the items and scales of Illinois Rape Myth Acceptance (IRMA) scale, concerns became apparent in interviews about their attitudes surrounding myths and rape culture.

Although the numbers from surveys discussed in Chapter 2 were interpreted, somewhat straightforward questions arose about what the numbers could actually mean. The interpretation of the numbers alongside interviews and other researchers' work is found in Chapter 2. As discussed there, there is concern about the neutral category and its interpretation means when students, faculty, and staff responded to IRMA statements by choosing to sit on the fence. This created wonderment about reliance on numbers that might be hiding, hence the interviews.

Two sets of interviews were completed with seven different women. Interviews were open to all but only women came to their appointments. Five men signed up for interviews in study 8 but did not come even after follow-up requests. The second set of interviews from study 14 were completed by women victims or survivors. Bystanders were signed up but due to Covid-19, the university closed all in-person activities, including research. Most of the researchers in this chapter are from study 8 and noted if otherwise.

The interviews in study 8 with seven women showed that students might not notice all aspects of university life and might not have an ability to see what should be feared or observed. If you do not have experience with sexual assault, you might not know to look for it or want to see it (remember the slogan of ignorance – cognitive dissonance). The interviews suggested that consent, sexual assault, rape, and rape myths are messy, chaotic, and confusing. Many students started their answers initially with "I never thought about that" and I wonder if they now do. Without exposure to terminology or the time to think clearly about topics, humans often do not take the chance; it's a reason we have college.

Overall, interviews suggested that students did not know full definitions of sexual assault or how to build and practice positive consent. Hence, lower-level assaults such as fondling were remarked as drunken mistakes on both parties where consent was unclear and could not have been an assault. This diminishes clarity about when sexual assaults occur and limits what students perceive as real, noteworthy assaults. The confusion leads to a misinterpretation of rape myths and how rape myths impact these students' lives. Surrounding the bewilderment of sexual assault and consent were beliefs of traditional, conservative sex roles so that her sexual actions lead to him going too far. Victim blaming was apparent in most of the studies conducted making me question how female empowerment connects to suitable definitions of sexual behaviors.

From the quantitative studies, most students did not agree with most rape myths although some students did with some of them. Of concern were the items that connected with the scales of *he didn't mean to* and *she lied*. Surveys also provided information that students were supportive of feminism, limited progressive sex roles, positive consent practices, and traditional sexual behaviors. The interviews were to help provide stories exploring these topics and gain depth. What the interviews did was demonstrate the murkiness of these topics and the unsureness students have in these topics.

Definitions that are important to the study of rape myths and rape culture are not always easy to grasp (Bevacqua, 2000; Burt, 1980; Edwards, Turchik, Dardis, Reynolds & Gidyez, 2011; Freedman, 2013; Phillips, 2017). They can change throughout time and between jurisdictions. For instance, the definition from the FBI that dictates law enforcement actions in reporting official statistics stated that rape needed to be forcible and penetration usually of the vagina by a penis. In 2013, the FBI removed the requirement of the assault being a physically forceful action. Research showed that some people fight and flee but others freeze; many victims do not do anything out of fear, so the actions and assault are not necessarily forceful. Additionally, jurisdictions such as states have different definitions. Thus, you can engage in the same assaultive behavior in two different states and be a rapist in only one of them. For instance, in California, laws used to claim penetration needed to be by a penis, not an object or finger, to be considered rape. This is why the sexual assault of Chanel Miller by Brock Turner is not rape; California has since changed its laws to make any type of penetration into the vagina or anus without consent rape. This difficulty in law to similarly define rape and assault is perhaps a reason for confusion in personal definitions of these actions. These basic attributes are known but the nuances were fuzzy.

Study 8 gained an appreciation from the previous quantitative studies with students. Interview data was directly about rape myths, rape culture, consent, definitions of sexual assault and rape, and perceptions of university life in connection to fear and safety. The question guide is in Appendix B. Students, one female and two males, aided with the data collection but the female student and researcher were present always. Participants were able to decide whom they wanted to interview with, and informed voluntary consent was explained. In one interview, the participant spoke of a personal sexual assault story at the end of the formal interview. At this time, the recording was turned off and we spoke with her about the incident as she chose.

The interviews included various questions to make the person at ease. If students were not connecting well to the student interviewers, they would change tactics and start to talk about their friend's beliefs or their friend's actions, as sometimes it is easier to cloud answers from those you know. We could follow up by asking, well, what do you think about that. This allowed us to see the perceptions students held about their friends' ideas and the student's ideas connected to their perceptions. After a time in the interviews, usually once the students started detailing their definitions of constructs, students were given the definitions we used. See Figure 3.1. This provided students a chance to compare how their personal definitions and thoughts connected with actual definitions used in law. Overall, students' ideas characterized the general continuum of sexual assault and realized that rape was penetration, but other concepts such as consent, rape myths, and rape culture were less clear.

Sexual assault is *any type of sexual contact or behavior that occurs without the explicit consent of the recipient. Sexual assault is basically an umbrella term that includes sexual activities such as rape, fondling, and attempted rape.*
United States Department. of Justice

Rape is *penetration, no matter how slight, of the vagina or anus with any body part or object, or oral penetration by a sex organ of another person, without the consent of the victim. Attempts or assaults to commit rape are also included; however, statutory rape and incest are excluded*
Federal Bureau of Investigation

Rape myths are the *attitudes and beliefs that are generally false but are widely and persistently held, and that serve to deny and justify male sexual aggression against women.*
Lonsway & Fitzgerald, 1994, p.134

Rape culture is the shared attitudes, behaviors, and beliefs that create the normalization and trivialization of sexual assaults including rape and lends itself to victim blaming.

FIGURE 3.1 Definitions used in studies.

Sexual assault and rape – Students had a difficult time recognizing the lower end of the sexual assault continuum. Remember lower end does not equate with perceptions and impact of these assaults; it is a way to categorize and discuss sexual assaults. A butt grab, forced kiss, or penis in the face can still impact people negatively and change trajectories of life akin to fingering and sex without consent. Students were able to discern the difference between rape and sexual assault; some were uncertain that sexual assaults included rape.

Students in surveys were asked to link their level of agreement to added item 23 of IRMA which read "only females can be victims of sexual assault and rape." From item 23, student participants (study 6 $\mu = 3.91$; study 9 $\mu = 3.87$; study 10 $\mu = 3.89$; study 13 $\mu = 3.83$; and study 7 that held a neutral category $\mu = 4.79$) understood one definitional change of rape – that men can be assaulted and raped; it is not just a female crime. This is one definitional item that connects to the it wasn't really rape scale that most studies showed high disagreement in the individual items and the scale. This is a generational positive that would not be seen traditionally.

Students also discerned the difference between sexual harassment and sexual assault. For instance,

> I think that to define it, it would be an extreme form of a sexual advance, different than sexual harassment because that can either be like touching or like verbal use of [inappropriate language and hurtful comments]... that type of thing. So, I automatically think of rape for when I think of sexual assault, that's just me.

This woman was able to separate harassment from assault but equated assault with rape, and rape only. Another woman declared after some deliberation in a careful choice of words,

> Harassment is usually verbal and then assault as far as I'm aware is usually physical in nature. Sexual harassment could be catcalling, and sexual assault could be inappropriately groping someone at a concert, there's like a whole spectrum of invasiveness of that contact.

Appropriately, this student divided harassment from assault as the verbal versus physical attention and attacked on another. A third female student was able to notice that regardless of an action being harassment or assault, both cause harm to a person's emotional well-being.

> If someone were to grab someone inappropriately, or say inappropriate things, I mean there's a wide spectrum of what it means – there's different names for different things but just like anything that is inappropriate and causes harm to another person.

These statements demonstrate the fogginess of the terms and that without a lot of education and change to discuss these topics, young adults are left hanging. When discussing these definitions, most of the women confessed that they knew of the terms but did not talk openly about the terms with anyone: not family, not friends, not boyfriends or girlfriends, not teachers or professors, not anyone. This means that my interview was one of the first, if not the first, time they were allowed to think and provide their opinions about these topics and definitions. Before any answer, there was often trepidation like they wanted to provide the right answer and did not want to say the wrong thing to be offensive. I think this is what we have taught our women and young adults; these topics are taboo and confusing, so we do not even try to figure it out. This is a disservice to our society, culture, and identities.

It is positive that women students could differentiate harassment from assault. However, as eluded to in the first quote, the subtle nuances of sexual assault were not easily distinguished. Rape was the same to many as sexual assault and it took time to get students to discuss its continuum nature and how kissing can be assault. This differentiation occurred often after the definitions were shown and discussed during the interview.

Two quotations illustrate this effort in creating a working definition. First,

> If someone – I'm not going to use gender – if someone is trying to have sex with someone and they're not consenting to it, they don't want to do it, that's sexual assault or any time of action that is revolved around sex.

Like the original quotation in the sexual harassment definition, this woman was unable to see sexual assault beyond sex. When questioned further, she was unable to state that assault could include actions other than sex. Forcible kissing and grabbing was not assault to her. When we conversed with these women, we did not provide examples or controlled the conversation; we let their brains work through the questions and statements we made. Even after providing the definitions of sexual assault and rape, she was unable to see assault as anything less than rape. This is common in rape culture; we minimize trauma to being raped and only "real" rape by a stranger in a dark alley with lots of physical bruises and brokenness counts as trauma incidents. Some inaccurately presume that party or date or acquaintance rapes are just missteps and not trauma-building assaults (Burt, 1991; Freedman, 2013; Kipnis, 2017; Mac Donald, 2019). This disconnect causes additional shame for the emotions felt about being assaulted.

The second set of female students were able to discern that rape is part of sexual assault and lots of non-consensual activities can fall under the term sexual assault.

> So I think sexual assault is… when it can be male or female either ends up being a victim either male or female can end up being taken advantage of in a way that is non-consensual and that the other perpetrator is, I guess,

taking advantage of that person. So like an example I would say like... for example if a girl is out at a bar drinking and hanging out with her friends and then a guy comes along and like kind of harassing her, and then ends up touching her in an inappropriate way, and she's like "No. Stop. I don't want to be around you" and he continues pursuing, doing whatever he wants regardless of what she would be saying.

These women provided definitions through situations and examples. This created illustrations of the actions and descriptions of sexual assault to connect to definitions. In this instance, the student discussed the assault as starting smaller and leading up to larger actions while a man refused to listen to a woman. The inappropriate touching was a common theme among the interviews who noted that sexual assault was more than rape. In this example, you can also see rape myths at work – as the situation includes drinking at a bar with a male who is close to a stranger or what he sees as a hookup possibility. You can also see the blurred lines of consent as he makes a move and then she keeps trying to move away – this thread is a common situation for sexual coercion, assault, and rape.

Consent – Most of the studies had a question with the IRMA rape myth items that asked people *if consent is given once, consent for sex is always there*. There was a quick one-item question to judge perceptions about consent and its worth in sexual relationships in added item 24 of the IRMA scale. This item stated, "if consent is given one, consent for sex is always present." This is false; per law and to stay clear of sexual assault, consent should be given each time a sexual act occurs from a kiss to sex. Consent often becomes implicit between long-standing relationships or even short-term connections and is not always verbal. However, in sexual experiences, do you want someone to simply go along or do you want excitement, including a pronounced YES (Freitas, 2018; Friedman & Valenti, 2008; Grigoriadis, 2017)! From item 24, student participants (study 6 μ = 3.82; study 9 μ = 3.72; study 10 μ = 3.83; study 13 μ = 3.69; and study 7 that held a neutral category μ = 4.65) were in favor of appropriate and positive consent practices, which differentiated from the interviews were most demonstrated about consent in practice.

At one point during data collection and studies, the university hung posters stating that verbal consent was obtained in at least 80% of all sexual connections. This was from a university conducted survey of students. For the research, study 9 completed at the same university held a scale for measuring the use and practice of consent. Consent practices were measured through a scale with 18 individual items. The scale is found in Appendix 3. Items included phrases such as "I think that verbally asking for sexual consent is awkward" and "I feel confident that I could ask for consent from a new sexual partner." This scale shows how much participants feel able to seek consent openly and if they actually do so. This study had a scale range of 0–42 with a possible range of 0–54 as measured from strongly disagree to strongly agree of 0–3 on the individual items. The mean/average was 20.25 with a median and mode of 22. The midpoint of the range is 27 with 88%

of the sample responses being at or below 27. This means that students in this sample have a hard time practicing positive consent and that perhaps the 80% verbal consent rate might be inflated. Students know that they should be asking and sometimes surveys gather attitudes and ideals not practices. Because from the interviews, this high rate of verbal consent does not appear to be occurring.

The interviews, instead, showcased the confusion and bewilderment of consent practices during sexual behaviors. Students interviewed understood that consent is to be spoken but that the action requestion consent is weird and seems like unchartered territory. The asking for and proclaiming consent often does not happen as consent becomes an implicit process. Also, that if someone does not say no (perhaps many times), then yes becomes the implied narrative, which is against what many of these students have been taught through college trainings and possible health classes in high school (Freitas, 2018; Grigoriadis, 2017; Kindlow, 2006).

For instance, students admitted that trying to work consent into the weekend hookup is awkward and not often noticed as happening.

> I think in the ideal world, Oh, not giving consent is saying no. But in reality, on the weekend how many times are you out and someone is like 'Oh, can I kiss you?' So, I think a lot of times it's not being asked consent, it's like having the courage to step up and say 'Hey, no, I am not okay with the way you are treating me.' … I think that people if they're the abuser or something like that you might think 'Oh well she didn't say no. Just because I didn't ask, she didn't say no either.' Where the victim could say 'Well, he/she didn't ask' so it's like you can blame the other person for not asking or not stepping up regardless of either situation.

The lack of consent is noted as way into sexual assault and rape.

The looseness of consent is also part of the hookup culture. The weekend plans for fun can include desire of sex with semi-known individuals. When people are struggling to learn about appropriate sexual desires and actions and how to navigate these scenarios with consent, it becomes harder if the event includes alcohol and semi-strangers (Gay, 2018; Johnston, 2013; Kipnis, 2017; Wade, 2017). To illustrate further,

> I do think that you can have strong consenting, you just have to be aware of yourself to truly like be consenting in the hook up culture. If you want to participate and have like tons of people who were like 'I've never engage in anything that didn't make me feel comfortable' then consent is so very important, especially when you have a hypersexual culture that encourages these things.

In truth, consent is a desired part of sexual relationships and most people do not want to assault others. Yet, the murkiness of situations and people without strong voices makes these practices hard to demonstrate in clear-cut patterns. Social anxiety, awkwardness, and shyness can evolve into ignored sexual desires as much as coercion and engagement in acts you do not want to participate in. The hookup and rape culture make it assumed that everyone is engaging in binge drinking and sexual conquests; this is simply not true (Ford, 2019; Grigoriadis, 2017). Yet, the pressure to perform exists.

Stable connections and sexual relationships still abide in this environment. Not everyone connects to the hookup culture; some still desire traditional relationships. Even in these, consent might be discussed but problems exist in the culture. Consent is a learning process that relationships can work on, but the pressure is high to make it a laughable matter.

> I think it depends on the relationship. Consent happens like for me and my boyfriend we talk about it and then kind of like in the moment like if he thinks he wants to do something and then he'll ask. We are then completely on the same page because he knows how feel and what we want as a couple. But he's a joke to others. He treats me like a person, but friends make fun of us. Instead they see it as a joke. Like she's your age so there is your consent. They don't want relationships, they want sex and see consent as that cut and dry.

In this environment, it is hard to work for consent practices that work within a relationship especially when other relationships or connections might have had other rules. She demonstrates the need to ask and be careful to address the feelings and desires of both people in the relationship. However, she does not see this as the norm on the university campus.

From these examples, you can almost see rape myths and rape culture at work in the mind of these female students. First, someone needs the bravery to ask for consent in the simple actions of kissing and touching (e.g. Can I kiss you?). Second, someone must find the courage to respond honestly about their needs and wants in the situation (e.g. Yes, you can kiss me, but keep your hands to yourself). Third, if either person goes against wishes of sexual connection, you must hold the ability to say so (e.g. Stop that!). Fourth, if none of this happens and no one speaks up, it is often assumed implicit consent. Fifth, technically, if one of the parties did not want the sexual action and did not have the skills to state so during the interaction, it is sexual assault regardless of implicit assumed consent. This fifth part is hard for some people in the rape culture to understand and accept because if you did not say no and went along with it, obviously you wanted the sexual actions to happen.

Not always, sometimes it is because a person is too scared or too nervous or too overwhelmed to do anything (Gay, 2018; Nass, 1977; Vanasco, 2019). It is not in everyone's ability to run or punch or scream; some people freeze and do nothing. In a society where hookups and rape culture help fuel our socialization and norms of sexual encounters, this is troublesome. Without verbal consent,

90 Student confusion

there is no consent. Without true consent, it is sexual assault. Yet, the rape culture does not allow us to think this way – without no, we can go ahead especially in a male-driven sexual encounter – it is their right and ability to coerce others; or so we are taught.

Here are two sexual assault scenarios from study 14 interviews that show how consent practices are ignored and confusing:

Story 1 – *Last February, I was 18. I was new to like sex. I don't know like what to expect. It was only my second time having sex with first time being a couple weeks prior from that. I wasn't sure what to do and I don't really know it was like. Both events were a random like on tinder. With those people like I told by others what not to be like, like not too demanding or weird. Don't demand things or think they will care for your feelings. Just go with the flow or whatever and I wasn't educated on like what's OK [sexually] and what's not OK. So, I was mad.*

I went to this random person's house. It was just a bizarre situation and then yeah then we went to his room and I was kind of psyched. It all progressed and then it was all consensual and then he kept asking me if you could take off the condom and I was like no. I told him I would stop if it took it off. Like I really don't want you to and I said it many times because it kept repeatedly asking me that. Several times I was like no, I don't do that, and I don't want you to do that now. We were both under the influence but like not like extremely gone. I was still very much in my right mind. Then he like got up and took his condom off and then continued [to have sex with me] and I liked it until I realized after what he did.

But at time I thought that this was completely normal. I thought that was OK, and I had weird expectations. I didn't really think anything of it when I left. I felt uneasy but I was like whatever, it is done with and I never have to see him again. A couple weeks later though I saw some friends. I told them what happened, and they were like that's not OK; like that's kind of sexual assault. I then was like talking to my therapist about it and she agreed with my friends. So, from now I just got a learn from it. That people do these things, that it is a thing and I know hoe now to leave. As a follow-up, she told me about the consent process she alluded to before the situation turned to assault. *"It was just kind of implicit; there was no verbal anything."*

In this story, the woman did not realize that verbal consent was a positive experience. She was still learning how to have sex and meet her sexual desires. She did not realize that people would take advantage of you during the experience; when it appeared, consent existed. She realized that some would not consider this assault, same as she did not at first. She wanted sex but also wanted a condom; sex without a condom did not have consent. Although she verbally told him this, she admits to not fighting it off. She carried blame with her for being naïve but believed that she would never let it happen again. As the rape culture informs, this was her fault not his.

Story 2 – *It [sexual assault and rape] actually happened to me twice from different guys. First, it was my freshman year in high school. My parents were getting divorced that my parents, so I guess I was just going through a lot since that was going on. I had a lot going on always, so I never really had free time for myself. I had to be busy, my parents liked that. I guess I was just really sad and needed something else. So, I started dating a family friend.*

It happened really fast because I told him I was going on he was understanding. He had invited me over this one time to his house so I could leave mine because I had homework to do. When I went over my mother and father were fine with it because he is like family and everything was OK. I'm now like I was only a freshman in high school; I know it's it is pretty like stupid to say 'oh you know you should've known I guess it is not true but it feels like it is.'

So, I went to his room. He said 'I'm gonna put a movie on' and 'I'm like OK that's fine.' It was during summer so I had shorts on and he's all like if you want to you can get more comfortable. I'm like no, like I'm already comfortable, what more can I do. I mean I was fine, we just met. So, it felt like I said a thousand times no it's fine and he keeps saying 'come on come on' and I was like no it's fine. And he's like come on you're hot, don't you like me? I'm like no it's fine. So, then we were laying down and he was fine. But then all of a sudden it became really awkward and he got on top of me. I was like what are you doing and he's like oh what do you mean what are you doing. Then, he was just like come on and I was like no it's fine. I really like you and but please get off me. And then he was like no.

I tried to push him off, but he said something like you know you want me to do this. I do like you but get off. And then he started pushing, like he got my hands and legs. I told him to stop playing like this. I'm on my phone, you really need to get off. He grabbed my hand again and threw my phone. I started yelling. He said I thought you like yelling and screaming so I will keep going. I'm like dude just get off, and he wouldn't get up, and he just kept holding me down and then like when he was holding me down he said please don't hate me. I just like kind of like stared off while he was doing it and I just cried, and I thought like maybe if he saw me crying he would stop. He didn't. So, he did his thing and I got dressed. I remember thinking I was like I just lost my virginity. I just ran outside but I couldn't drive yet. I didn't want him to drive me so 20 minutes to my house, so I just walked, and I was crying the whole time.

What a senseless way to be introduced to sexual behaviors and conquests (Brownmiller, 1975; Nass, 1977; Vanasco, 2019). She came from a highly religious family who believed in virginity and its specialness. She could not tell her family. When she asked friends, they told her that it was normal, and he was a good guy. It was implied that she was second-guessing her behavior because her father would be mad if he found out. It was not until college when she met some other friends where she could actualize the rape for what it was and that it was not her fault.

This links to misunderstanding about sexual assault and who engages in the behaviors. Most attacks are not from strangers lurking in the bushes ready to pounce and physically attack a woman to rape them. Most attacks are milder and from those we know. It is the lack of consent that makes a sexual action turn into an assault, not who is doing the behavior. For illustration from a woman student interviewee,

> I think most people when they think of assault and rape they think of someone forcing themselves on them, physical, physical activity, but I also think there is a huge under talked about underrepresented section of assault

> and rape victims – like it was someone they knew or it was a relationship and because they didn't know how to consent or they didn't consent and because they're in a relationship they don't know how to handle it and I think that definitely here on campus that would be the majority of the things that would happen because I think most people know you shouldn't go and hurt somebody.

Even though we know not to hurt people, this consent confusion lends itself to the he did not mean to myth that we succumb to. If only he understood how consent worked, he would not have assaulted his girlfriend. Myths and connected beliefs are not an excuse; the behavior that we trivialize and ignore was an assault. Thus, we learn to ignore rules of consent and not trust perceptions of assault.

Consequently, the rape culture itself lends to more assaults because we fail to teach people appropriate consent practices. We do not speak about normal sex routinely so that all topics connected, especially rape, become taboo. It is awkward and nerve-wracking to have these conversations with our children, students, friends, and partners much less with those we hookup with. A student explained:

> I think we also don't like to ask hard questions in our culture. Nobody wants to ask someone 'Can I have sex with you?' That's kind of awkward – even if that's what needs to happen – if you're in the moment and you're both intoxicated and it just happens how do you address it without asking a question you don't want to ask, and you may not know how the other person is feeling. And just because you didn't see it as assault doesn't mean I didn't see it as assault. I think that's when it gets really blurry, but the only way to make it not blurry is to ask people questions they don't want to ask.

People do not know how to behave in these encounters as they might be newer to sex and without social scripts. Without these quick connections, people have to work harder to understand the person they are with. Without this understanding, consent and other practices are tougher to accomplish without feeling weird. We must work on this as a society and individual to appreciate this practice.

Another woman sums this predicament up nicely but confusingly,

> I think some people that if they don't say no that means yes, especially with the whole like 'no means no' that everybody says so what does nothing mean? You didn't say 'nothing means no' just 'no means no'. So, I think that is often times the defense that people use.

This defense she is referring to is the justification of why someone would engage in sexual assault. It is akin to the *it wasn't really rape* or *he didn't mean to* rape myth scale constructs. If he did not seek consent and did not hear a no or was not pushed away, then what he was doing was allowable. If he did seek consent, was not pushed away, but did not hear an affirmative yes, his actions were still permissible, and acceptable. This is how the rape culture allows sexual behavior to occur. He did not mean to engage in sexual assault because how was he to know he should receive a verbal yes after asking for consent. It wasn't really rape because no one forced him away or fought him off. This is the practice of consent when rape myths and rape culture are allowed to thrive.

A female student was able to see this discernment but wrestled with the need for clear verbal consent.

> I don't think that there is it's a very clear verbal consent. I know that the school stresses a lot about the verbal part of it. I don't necessarily think that it's needed in every case, but at the same time it's like in terms of if someone was going to accuse someone of something then like they have the verbal part of it and I think that is the most strong version of it because then there is no like misreading anything so.

This is a concern with consent (Freitas, 2018); it is difficult to navigate the pathways of relationships and sexual connections or hookups gracefully. The identities we hold to play our parts are connected to socialization, gender roles, sex roles, sexual behavior traditions, rape culture, and so many unknown normed behaviors as we are becoming adults (Ford, 2016; Kindlow; 2006; Murphy, 2004; Vanasco, 2019). These books exemplify the paths of learning how to be sexually brave within the confines of tradition and socialization.

Men are to control any sexual situation; it is their role to be the aggressor to take control. Women play meek and need to be coerced into wanting sexual connection. Men hold the hierarchal power in this group dynamic (a group is any interpersonal connection with two or more people moving toward a general goal). Women hold less authority, although they are tasked with saying yes or no to the sexual hookup. Per expectation states theory and situated identity theory, this role play is common and assumed. It is so customary; there is a Christmas song about this dance and ritual: "baby it's cold outside." It details the ritual of coercion and consent in song form. As women, it is known that we have the ability to say yes or no to the requests but the requests do not often come verbally and it is difficult to fight off a larger more physically and socially powerful male in a situation where comfortability and assuredness do not exist.

Things we didn't talk about when I was a girl (Vanasco, 2019) showcases this rite of passage into sexual encounters delicately with humanness. Her sexual assaults, including rape, were times where consent was not given but her frozenness and lack of ability to scream stop or to push the man away or to punch him in the face perhaps allowed the man to assume his actions were allowable. Not that when you are passed out drunk or pinned down to a bed should ever be taken as consent. Vanasco reminisces and wonders if her passivity and reverence to men caused her to be sexually assaulted. What was it about her that made men, including teachers, friends, and strangers, take advantage of her? This personal shame and victim blame runs through the world of rape culture and rape myths. The sketchy path of consent in gender and sex norms creates confusion and tension prior, during, and after sexual assaults. If everyone just assumed you needed a strong YES to sexual actions, would sexual assaults be lessened? It certainly would allow victimized people to know that they were victimized and stand on the shoulders of those similar to them. This is where you need to look up the tea video about consent – it serves the point made well.

Rape myths – Shrewder answers were provided when female interviewees were asked about the causes of sexual assault and rape. This seems to be something people wrestle with, think about, and perhaps even talk about. Women have a regard for this as we are taught since youth how to protect ourselves from others through beliefs of just say no, stranger danger, and idioms of men protecting their dating daughter with rifles and strength. Females are taught self-defense, how to dress appropriately (aka not slutty), where to go (aka not along with strange men), what to do (aka do not drink or party too much), and what behavior to constrain (aka anything and everything sexual). This is all the rape culture fitting into rape myths and packaged beliefs. If we can keep our girls and women safe, rapes will not happen to them; we forget if you teach boys and men to not rape, it will not happen.

Women tended to agree with Brownmiller (1975) about rape being beholden to the power, control, and prestige of men in our society and culture. For instance,

> I think that that is a very convoluted matter. I think that a lot of times its desire for like dominance or power or like revenge. There's human behavior is very complex, as a psychology major, I know that, there's a lot of I guess motivation behind why someone would want to take advantage of someone in such a profound intimate intense way. But I would say usually it would have to do with power or control or revenge.

Another woman proposed,

> Often times I think it's because somebody wants something, and they think that they are entitled to it and they don't take the other person into consideration. It often does happen with alcohol involved, but it can happen without it and just somebody wants something so badly that, I guess, their willing to put aside the other person wants or desires and just only go for what they want. Yeah. I guess also kind of media kind of has a huge influence in that.

Both of these women speak of the inability to understand why someone would want to do this, why hurt someone just because you can. It is attributed by both women to be due to control, power, and even revenge.

This is part of the privilege men inherit through socialization in a patriarchal system. Men are able to take what they want when they want it – this includes sex. The cultural belief is that men deserve sex and have the right to be offended when women say no. Masculinity is tied to sexual conquests and male identities are tied to not being a virgin as sexual coercion becomes excusable; sexual coercion is the norm because it is how you get women to do what you want. The rape culture whispers if coercion does not work, assaults do, and do not worry because you will not be caught as she will not be believed. Then, these actions are not held accountable, women are too afraid to speak up from fear of shame and stigma, while the men are high fived by their bros for getting in her pants. Rape culture allows for this to continue because we are stuck in a cycle of not appreciating or respecting sexual desire and autonomy.

Another message in these statements is the place of alcohol and drugs as a causation tool. Even the faculty and staff-focused groups discussed this as to why their university should be safer: a lack of parties, fraternities, and big ten athletics. These ideals, however, represent rape myth ignorance and byproducts of rape culture. When asked about causal reasons for assaults, a female student declared:

> I would think alcohol, number one, I think that regardless of gender when people are under the influence there is an increased probability that rape or assault could occur. I think maybe that maybe – I guess drugs could have an impact or even just being at a small school guys know that there is four girls for every one guy – so like some of them might have this stigma of 'oh there's four girls for me'.

This quotation illustrates a link between men obtaining what they think they deserve through the perceived power that comes with the consumption of alcohol and other drugs. The drinking becomes a catalyst. I only did that because I was drinking or smoking; I was under the influence – the whiskey and beer did it, not me. She was wasted too; she wanted it at the time.

This is the privilege of men. Men recognize that they have earned the right to have a woman and take control over the woman (Brownmiller, 1975; Ford, 2019; Mardorossian, 2002; Murphy, 2004). This society is not far enough past where women were property and considered owned by men either as wives or as daughters for the pretext of sex. Although current laws dictate that females are not property, culture and ideals still create a sense of entitlement to women and sex. The rape culture includes this entitlement and belief that *"oh there's four girls for me"*; so if I drink, I can hook up and not be concerned with consent practices or sexual assault. It is my right to grab hold of women and alcohol gives me the courage to bypass my concerns. This young adult world of hookups, and confused consent, and bewildered definitions allows men to work their way through inappropriate behaviors that are then trivialized. This can lead to the myth of he didn't mean to.

This ability by men and women to cross lives without emotional attachment has become normed (Ford, 2016; 2019; Grigoriadis, 2017; Johnston, 2013; Kindlow, 2006; Wade, 2017). Binge drinking in men and women provide them with liquid liberation from the shackles of life and thought. Their rational thinking can be limited and dive into the world of desires and needs. One danger is that if you have drank too much, consent cannot be given. Another is that perhaps you have drank enough to not care if consent is earned. It is not the drinking that causes rapes, but it allows for a feeling of freedom that people are willing to take advantage of.

One of the female students tried to explain that sometimes sexual assaults just happen due to miscommunication. This miscommunication is really a lack of listening and understanding verbal and non-verbal cues. It is an inability to read a situation to determine if the person you are sexually engaged with is really into the actions or just playing along.

> I think it again depends on the situation because for like the example of the if your taking like a guy and a girl, and the girl not giving verbal consent then they could read the situation wrong if the woman uncomfortable and didn't voice it then, you know although he was doing it at the same time she wasn't, you know that may have changed things and that's in this particular situation.

If the man can hear the woman scream "no," "stop," "don't," or pushed him physically away, perhaps he would understand the clue and interpret a lack of consent. Consent becomes fuzzy especially when it is provided physically and not sought verbally. It is clear that this interviewee was fighting for the myth; she supported it; if consent is unclear, it is not his fault for raping her – it might be hers.

Victim blaming is a common rape myth byproduct of the rape culture. Rape culture has created a structure where if the woman speaks up against a sexual assault and admits to being victimized, many conclude that she must have done something wrong. This is one reason so many programs and anti-rape efforts are aimed at women. Women and girls must be educated in self-defense, including the ability to fight off a predator and to not put one in sexual assault situations. As one student commented:

> Like I think it's so much easier to say that it was everybody else's fault for what they were doing and so if you say 'I'm not getting drunk, it's not going to happen to me' [or] 'It was your fault because you were getting drunk' then it makes it your fault… it puts a separation between you and whoever it's happening to.

Victim blaming allows polarity; it provides an us versus them in a shelter of safety. If rape is caused by the victim and I do not do the stupid things that lead to rape, I will be safe. If I do not go to parties, if I do not drink, if I do not walk alone, if I dress conservatively and do not show my cleavage, if I do not kiss random (or any) men, if I do not allow myself in a room with a man, or any other various variety of this statement.

We move to blame the victim because it is easier to understand a person's poor decisions than to blame the larger structure of society that does not hold people accountable nor is willing to teach appropriate sexual practices. It is taught that rape exists, do not let it happen to you (Grigoriadis, 2017; Mac Donald, 2019). This is similar to the explanation that locking doors completely prevents burglary – it does not. We teach women to cover up and reel in their emotional and physical desires, while men can let it all hang out except for real emotions of course. As a woman, you know what you are supposed to do and not do because of your sex and gender. The roles and rules are distinct from the roles and rules that control men. When it comes to sexual assault and rape, the values, beliefs, and norms protect male perpetrators while harming potential female victims. Blaming the victim means that more aggressors are not recognized or caught which allows them to harm more victims. If victims do not speak out, the next victims are not safe to speak up either because of rape culture's shackles (Gay, 2018; Grigoriadis, 2017; Kantor & Twohey, 2020).

Even though the women all stated that the blame was ultimately on the rapist, the struggle in their explanations was real. For instance,

> it's always someone else who has their own issue, like it's a power thing, I don't know what's going on in the mind of a rapist or someone who assaults someone else, but it's always one hundred percent on the person who commits the crime, it's always on the person who made the decision to harm someone else.

This was stated by the same woman as the prior quotation that being drunk offers an excuse to both the perpetrator and prey or aggressor and victim. It is hard to rectify that the behavior of rape and sexual assault is wrong versus the victim's supposed role in her victimization. Note that this role in victimization is a socially proscribed artificial reality; it is a construction of the rape culture and by no means correct. Rapists and assaulters are always to blame, not their victims, ever.

Another aspect of the rape myths that connections with victim blame is the myth of she lied. Although this was found to be agreeable in the survey scales, these seven women did not talk about this myth directly. There was no mention of women lying about rape to gain control over a situation or because they regretted having sex and now wanted her virginal disposition to be saved. This particular myth did not seem to connect well to the women in the interviews.

The real rape myth was alive for at least one of the women. Most of the women talked about the continuum of sexual assault and how there are various forms of assault that can lead up to rape and even rape itself can occur in various degrees and designs. Yet, one of the women who also had a hard time connecting with the definitions of sexual assault could see rape in only its most horrific form (similar to Mac Donald, 2018). Rape was the stereotypical nightmare or what is known as the blitz rape or what some people term "real" rape. This links to the *it wasn't really rape* myth that showed little agreeableness in the quantitative survey; hence, why only one of the women discussed it. It appears that there is low viability in this myth among this generation and most recognize the various degrees and manners of rape, including acquaintance rape and date rape or statutory rape, including pedophilia.

The woman had a difficult time seeing rape as anything other than a situation where the victim and perpetrator physically fought against and for the rape. That screaming, hitting, holding, and a lack of freedom occurred. She stated,

> if one of my friends was telling my friend group 'I was raped by my boyfriend or really good friend, but I didn't say no, or it felt normal' or things like that I think we would all be like... you know... friends would be like 'You're saying you just got raped but I don't classify that as rape myself'.

She is a disbeliever of the various scenarios of sexual assaults and is a product of the rape culture, and although she was the only one in this study, she is not alone.

This is at the heart of why many women and presumably men feel unjustified in their reactions to various sexual assault situations. Vanasco (2019) discusses this throughout her book and ponders why the non-consensual fingering by a close friend, the touching of her by a high school advisor, and other sexual assaults in her life did not leave her more angry and resentful but instead afraid of what it could do to the man if she told. She believed that her assaults were not as harmful as real rape and did not deserve her shame nor actions by law enforcement. She never disclosed the sexual assault of her long-time family friend because of the pain it would cause his family and her own; she was more worried about his life than protecting her own worth. Again, in the Justice Kavanaugh hearings with the allegations brought forth by Dr. Blassey Ford, since it was "just" an assault and possibly an attempted rape, she was not sure that it really mattered. Even though the (alleged – not proven in court) assault traumatized her throughout her life, she did not think it deserved to harm Kavanaugh's life leaving it to the senate commission to determine the worth of the allegation (Hemingway & Severino, 2019; Kantor & Twohey, 2019; Pogrebin & Kelly, 2019).

As the book *She Said* (Kantor & Twohey, 2019) dictates, so many women fall victim to the rape culture because she does not see her victimization as matter as it was not real rape. Sometimes, this is because it was a sexual assault and not rape. Sometimes, it falls under the category of harassment or coercion and not assault. Either way, these are mechanisms to get women to do things they have no interest in doing. Sex is a byproduct of control and power often used in the rape culture by men who are acquainted with their victims and not willing to out the man for many reasons.

To push past these ideologies and paradigms, all the women must speak out. This was noted by Kantor and Twohey (2019) but this was also a purpose of the #metoo movement. As created in *#metoo and the Politics of Social Change* (Fileborn & Loney-Howes, 2019), #metoo should be a catalyst for reform. It should connect with feminism movements in finding voices and freedom from the world created by men. It is not simple to create social change and movements but if enough women speak up and shout their stories, more come forward. It creates widespread awareness that politics finds hard to ignore. Women must become part of the agenda to change the rape culture. It is not about demonizing men; it is about reclaiming power for a stronger and more fit society. It is about recognizing the many faces and colors of sexual assault to bring about equity.

However, these visions are not shared by all. Some spend time testifying that this type of feminism has lost its ways and it is time to move onto other ideals (Casey, 2020). Men do not need to be free for emotions and females do not need freedom to make their lives more like men. All of this is a created reality to shame men and power. Rape culture and toxic masculinity do not exist and thus do not need to be fixed. Females are equal enough and just want something to complain about; this is part of the new culture – unhappy women. These arguments are roughly won by those stuck in the past of conservative, traditional ideals.

Further, as declared by Johnson and Taylor Jr. (2017) in *The Campus Rape Frenzy* and Mac Donald (2018) in *The Diversity Delusion*, many events must come together for a rape to be considered a real rape, one that would be held up in the court of law and lead to a conviction; anything else is simply not rape. To represent, if a woman does not come forward about the allegations, it was not real rape. If penetration and forcible physical action did not take place, it was not real rape. If it was correction that led to a sliding of consent practices, it was not real rape. If it did not leave you bruised and bloodied, it was not real rape. If the alleged victim was supposedly raped by a boyfriend, husband, co-worker, or friend, it probably was not rape. In short, anything less than the worst-case scenario is not rape and women should not feel propelled to report the action. Sadly, these ideals are pieces of the rape culture.

This is a complicated process where one must move past ignorance and trainings of our culture to move into a position to see why women believe in rape myths but also deserve to speak out against their own or others' victimization whether it be from harassment, coercion, assault, or rape. As an interviewee articulated,

> it's kind of a complicated question I feel like, because… so for what causes it I feel like in some cases it could be a lack of respect for the person, in other cases I think for rape as well there could be cases where someone doesn't, isn't, how do I phrase this. Like doesn't necessarily like, can't give verbal consent, because either their like scared or something like that. Which some people would determine as rape, because it was unwanted even though it wasn't like a verbal yes. I know that I don't know of a lot

of people that verbally say yes, I guess if there is a lack of that and a person could read the situation wrong in some cases it could lead to that being categorized as rape, however, I do one-hundred percent believe that there are people that unfortunately do say no and then that happens.

She understood, without perhaps realizing, the context of rape myths and sexual assault. There are too many nuances to claim that one action is real rape and the other is not. Definitionally, some behaviors are instead assaults, coercion, or harassment; not every action is penetration and thus does not constitute rape.

However, the pain involved in these actions and the lifelong processes women victims must go through show the strength of all these incidences. Perception and internalization of the pain are real and must be treated as such in society. Empathy and compassion are necessary as well as a social construction that places these victimizations as worthwhile. It takes many voices to overthrow a paradigm; many women must speak at once for people to notice that the change is coming. Ignorance simply is not allowed anymore; it is time to be woken.

Feminism – Feminism, the belief in equity among sexes and genders, was confirmed in the surveys competed at the university. Most (almost all) students, faculty, and staff declared their agreement with feminism. What was not figured out in the surveys was how people saw this connected to rape myths, sexual assaults, and rape culture. The first interview did bring about one idea that exemplifies the complicated nature of feminism, the women's movement, and moving forward in a new territory with newer norms, values, and beliefs related to ruling one's sexual desire as a female.

> "Girls you have to be strong, you have to be powerful and show that you can do things people don't think you can do!" So sometimes you – okay, if I'm going to be strong I'm not going to stand up to you and tell you no – that's one side – I can handle this, I'm strong enough to deal with how you're treating me without telling you or going to authorities about it because I can deal with it on my own. I think that's one of the things.

This showcases the debate and double-sided ways females must perform. We have to be strong but gentle, lovable but take no garbage, powerful but docile – the normed personalities and identities of women are still convoluted.

As presented in *Alpha Girls* and *Blurred Lines*, girls and woman have a challenge of accepting all these new norms but not stepping out of bounds too much to warrant excessive disapproval by society, men, friends, and families. The traditional sex and gender norms and the corresponding sexual behaviors are dissipating from more conservative roles to liberal ideologies. Women are allowed to make their desires come true with the realization that rape and sexual assault is still a disproportionate reality of life. The surveys supported this ideology shift as well; the students were less socially conservative when it came to gender roles and sexual behaviors; politically, they were split evenly. As argued in *Blurred*

Lines, we are sitting at the forefront of a paradigm shift for girls and women; it is time to relish sexual desires and freedom. However, this freedom is still hard won even with support for the hookup culture.

In the second interview, women victims and survivors were asked directly about how they saw the connection between feminism, femininity, masculinity, and the concepts of this book. A disconnect was apparent. They saw their ability for freedom in choice and action but constrained by family socialization patterns of what it means to be a nice girl to a good man in a society where slut shaming and being called a whore are still very real. They easily and quickly identified the struggles of relationships and friendships in learning how to be sexually active and not fall victim to sexual coercion while wanting to be loved or just wanting a hookup. The battles between one (or many) night stands did not seem to differ between relationships; the norms and standards were difficult to follow, consent was hard to work through, and wanting to keep things acceptable and friendly was a huge task.

The interviewees agreed that the roles of female and male were part of the sexual assault and rape culture concerns. That females had more freedom to be their true selves sexually, emotionally, and physically. Males still had so many lines to stand behind with their emotions and behaviors; they still had to be strong, angry, stoic, and manly. Men still were not able to show their true selves to the public much less women who they wanted to have sex with. This was seen as a rationale for sexual coercion, harassment, assaults, and rape.

The female students thought that sexual coercion was still very connected to their femininity and beliefs of the docile female who can be conquered in the bedroom. Many of the stories of rape and sexual assault started with partners talking them into it out of love, devotion, payment, and requirement. Those in relationships were told so often the typical "if you loved me" you would have sex with me. Some men told the women you owe it to me out of love, paying for dinner, or just being a boyfriend. In hookups, men told the women that it was their duty and whole purpose for being together so they could not say no. Although women want to move forward, there appears to be events and beliefs holding them back.

Summary

The topics of this chapter, rape myths, rape culture, sexual assault, and rape have eluded societies for centuries. The terms are not easily created nor developed in personal or social lives. There is discontentment in how rape culture is viewed in university lives by researchers, academics, administrators, faculty, staff, and student. There is real pain on all sides of these issues. People feel attacked when rape culture and patriarchy are damned; people are attacked during sexual assaults and in the aftermath by those who love them but dole out shame and stigma because victim blaming is a cultural trait.

Our society and culture through its social institutions have a hard time progressing and acknowledging through the views of us versus them. It is hard to use one's sociological imagination to see the other in our lives. Without seeing the world through its history and social functions, there is little catalyst for change. We are too stuck in ignorance. We are set to distrust those who see the world differently from us or who are different from us. A bunch of feminists yelling at men for their privilege power is met with backlash and hatred. Especially when it is not the middle ground being sought, it is freedom from controlling thoughts and ways that limit everyone's full potential. Although plenty argue that no one is suffering from the rape culture, it appears many are. Take a moment to ponder the people in your life and how their experiences could be different with a shared view of humility, love, and compassion instead of power, greed, and control. This is the life sought and the cultural change needed; perhaps we all need to listen to Katy Perry "you're gonna hear me roar."

References

Almazan, V. A., & Bain, S. F. (2015). College Students' Perceptions of Slut-Shaming Discourse on Campus. *Research in Higher Education Journal, 28*, 1–9.
Bevacqua, M. (2000). *Rape on the public agenda*. Northeastern University Press.
Brownmiller, S. (1975). *Against our will*. Fawcett.
Burt, M. R. (1991). Rape myth and acquaintance rape. In A. Parrot & L. Bechhofer (Eds.), *Acquaintance rape: The hidden crime* (pp. 327–340). John Wiley.
Burt, M. R. (1980). Cultural myths and supports for rape. *Journal of Personality and Social Psychology, 2*, 217–230.
Casey, G. (2020). *After #metoo: Feminism, patriarchy, toxic masculinity and sundry cultural delights*. Imprint Academic.
Durkheim, E. (1961). *Suicide*. Glencoe.
Durkheim, E. (1933). *The division of labor*. Trans. G. Simpson. Macmillan.
Edwards, K. M., Turchik, J. A., Dardis, C. M., Reynolds, N., & Gidyez, C. A. (2011). Rape myths: History, individual and institutional-level presence, and implications for change. *Sex Roles, 65*, 761–773. doi:10.1007/s11199-011-9943-2
Fileborn, B., & Loney-Howes, R. (Eds.). (2019). *# MeToo and the politics of social change*. Springer Nature.
Ford, C. (2019). *Boys will be boys: Power, patriarchy and toxic masculinity*. Simon and Schuster.
Ford, C. (2016). *Fight like a girl*. One world Publications.
Freedman, E. B. (2013). *Redefining rape*. Harvard University Press.
Freitas, D. (2018). *Consent on campus*. Oxford University Press.
Friedman, J., & Valenti, J. (2008). *Yes means yes*. Seal Press.
Gay, R. (Ed.). (2018). *Not that bad*. Harper Perennial.
Grigoriadis, V. (2017). *Blurred lines: Rethinking sex, power, and consent on campus*. Houghton Mifflin Harcourt.
Hackman, C. L., Pember, S. E., Wilkerson, A. H., Burton, W., & Usdan, S. L. (2017). Slut-shaming and victim-blaming: A qualitative investigation of undergraduate students' perceptions of sexual violence. *Sex education, 17*, 697–711.
Hemingway, M., & Severino, C. (2019). *Justice on trial: Kavanaugh confirmation and the future of the supreme court*. Regnery Publishing.
Johnson, K. C., & Taylor Jr., S. (2017). *The campus rape frenzy: The attack on due process at America's universities*. Encounter Books.

Johnston, A. D. (2013). *Drink*. Harper Wave.
Kantor, J., & Twohey, M. (2019). *She said: Breaking the sexual harassment story that helped ignite a movement*. Penguin Books.
Kindlow, D. (2006). *Alpha girls: Understanding the new American girl and how she is changing the world*. Rodale.
Kipnis, L. (2017). *Unwanted advances: Sexual paranoia comes to campus*. Harper Collins.
Krakauer, J. (2016). *Missoula: Rape and the justice system in a college town*. Anchor.
Kruttschnitt, C., Kalsbeek, W. D., & House, C. C. (Eds.) (2014). Panel on Measuring Rape and Sexual Assault in Bureau of Justice Household Surveys, Washington, D.C.: The National Academies Press.
Lavigne, P., & Schlabach, M. (2017). *Violated: Exposing rape at Baylor University amid college football's sexual assault crisis*. Center Street.
Mac Donald, H. (2018). *The diversity delusion: How race and gender pandering corrupt the university and undermine our culture*. St. Martin's Griffin.
Mardorossian, C. M. (2002). Toward a new feminist theory of rape. *Signs: Journal of Women in Culture and Society, 27*(3), 743–775.
Miller, C. (2019). *Know my name: A memoir*. Penguin Books.
Mills, C. W. (2000). *The sociological imagination*. Oxford University Press.
Murphy, P. F. (Ed.). (2004). *Feminism & masculinities*. Oxford University Press.
Nass, D. R. (1977). *The rape victim*. Dubuque, IA: Kendall/Hunt.
Parrot, A., & Bechhofer, L. (Eds.). (1991). *Acquaintance rape: The hidden crime* (Vol. 157). Wiley.
Phillips, N. D. (2017). *Beyond blurred lines*. Rowman & Littlefield.
Pogrebin, R. & Kelly, K. (2019). *The education of Brett Kavanaugh: An investigation*. Portfolio.
Raphael, J. (2013). *Rape is rape: How denial, distortion, and victim blaming are fueling a hidden acquaintance rape crisis*. Chicago Review Press.
Richards, T. N., & Marcum, C. D. (Eds.). (2014). *Sexual victimization: Then and now*. SAGE Publications.
Sanday, P. R. (1997). *A woman scorned: Acquaintance rape on trial*. Univ of California Press.
Vanasco, J. (2019). *Things we didn't talk about when I was a girl: A memoir*. Tin House Books.
Wade, L. (2017). *American hookup: The new culture of sex on campus*. WW Norton & Company.

4

CREATING IDENTITY IN ROLES, STATUSES, AND CHARACTERISTICS

We manifest our personas to others using guidelines of symbolic interactionism. We are individuals connected to each other through society and culture. Humans are not beings defined as separate entities; we are enmeshed with each other and defined by those we know and connect to the most. These identities change throughout our personal lives but also as a cultural experience over time. Social identities are a product of society, its institutions, and selves.

Remember, socialization is the process where we learn our values, beliefs, and normed actions. Socialization occurs throughout our lifespan, but the main foundations are laid during our first six to eight years in learning how to be a person. The building blocks include parents, guardians, grandparents, other family, friends, teachers, religious leaders, employers, coaches, instructors, and anyone else you can think of that impacted your life either small or large for good or bad.

Many theories suggest that the relationships we build create who we are. Earlier in the book, I suggested two symbolic interactionist theories of situated identity and expectation states to help explain the decisions we make in our groups. Groups can be considered a collaboration of two or more people coming together for a joint purpose or goal. Both theories taken together suggest that people want to impress the people we like. We build connections based upon similar interests and use stereotypical knowledge of traits and hierarchies to make quick decisions about what we think others would do, what we should do, and then what we do.

These theories are not suggesting that people rape because friends and teammates believe that rape is a good thing; in fact, most think rape is horrid, bad, a sinful action, something that is not to be done. A critique of rape culture exists that is a misinterpretation of the rape culture. It suggests that rape culture is the fostering and creating of rapists; it claims falsely that rape culture turns us into rapists because we live in a society that is fond of rape (Johnson & Taylor, 2017; Kipnis, 2017; Mac Donald, 2018). Rape culture is not advocating the behavior of rape but rather that society and culture produce beliefs about rape that diminishes it by ignoring, distrusting, and disbelieving victim stories. Rape culture purports the ignorance of sexual assault and rape and disallows appropriate community responses.

Consequently, rape culture becomes our societal ideology. It is a framework that builds identities and social constructions of behaviors. When combined with rape myths, rape culture forms a pathway to excuse rape and sexual assault through victim blaming and an inability to view its truths. Thus, when in social groups such as athletic teams, fraternities or sororities, clubs, and friendships, we use rape myths to guide conversations and expectations of behaviors. It creates appropriate places for rape jokes, locker room talk, sexual coercion, and binge drinking fueled hookups. It allows people to go unchecked for sexist, misogynistic, patriarchal, (female) virgin ideation, and unrealistic sexual comments and experiences.

True Gentlemen by Hechinger (2017) case studied a fraternity to show the dichotomy of their lives and socialization. On the one hand, the university men learned how to be socialites and kind men during the day in official fraternity retreats. At night during raving parties, the brothers absorbed rape culture and myths. The book decreed that in most fraternities, especially those at large institutions, sexual assaults were expected during parties and dates with their men; sexual assaults or at least coercion and conquests might even be required of pledges.

Of athletes in the book *Beer and Circus* (Sperber, 2000), it is assumed that no is never heard and that athletes were given special permission to engage in sexual assault. They will never be caught or dealt with by college administration as sports are imperative to the large landscape of the campus and its budgets. Large institutions were beholden to sports for money, fandom, and students. Sperber (2000) argued, using quotes from various university presidents and coaches, that rape becomes part of the college experience if you want to party with the big boys. *In Out of Bounds,* Benedict (2004) concurs with this image of sports and writes about its continuance in the NBA; the professional athletes have been conditioned to have women do their will and when the women do not, the men will conquer through assaults and rape. Like universities, this becomes a backdrop to sports as most men are never caught criminally and might even pay off these crimes civilly.

The author of *Man Made* (Stein, 2012) assembled a quest to do all the things that make manly men manly but refused to engage in sexual assault. He suggested that if a man wants to prove masculinity to the world around him, sexual assault in various forms is one clear means to do so. Let that sink in one more time – to demonstrate you are a true man in this culture, you must sexually assault a female; thankfully, the author and many other men refuse to do so.

This aggression over women (and other men) is part of our general society (Murphy, 2004). Chu and Gilligan (2014) in *When Boys become* BOYS argued that aggressive or stoic or toxic masculinity is part of boys' young socialization.

There is a path taken by many boys between the ages of 5–8 that ends the empathic, crying, nurturing child to become a boy who cannot show his full range of emotions and is limited to acceptable forms of male displays. This is seen in aggression, anger, stoicism, and toughness. In *The man they wanted be to be* (Sexton, 2019), the author digested his life through the gaze of research and journalism. He confronted his past through familial connections after the death of his father. He never felt that he fit in with his family and was often punished for being too soft, too timid, too quiet, and not interested enough in manly endeavors like sports and boy scouts. The author looked at his uncles, dad, cousins, and other men in his town to note how masculinity torn them internally down at times leading to depression and suicide. How the need to show aggression, anger, and other manly traits limits the range of emotions boys and men can show. This internal struggle can destroy life as it almost did to the author before he escaped to find his wholistic self.

Similarly, Ford (2018) in *Boys will be Boys* digests the condition of boys to become men. Men who are not allowed to be girly or show any feminine traits, men who do not engage in household tasks and rule the house, and men who can use their power in so many ways, including sexual assault and rape. Men and women both face gender oppression limiting the way to express oneself based on short-sighted versions of suitable biological traits of penises and vaginas. She is not blaming men for the woes of the society and culture. She is not claiming that men are the problem – culture is the problem. For men to become complete humans, the rape culture must be cleared so that all can have fresh starts and less relationships developed through power taxonomies.

Our culture does not allow men to become their true selves until it is too late as men are rewarded for aggression, but not other emotions such as empathy and compassion. Men learn that it is a proper practice to subjugate women. Men know women will not always call them on their faults because it is not to be done or allowed. In a world of patriarchal privilege, men have the upper hand in showing control, but all are at a loss until everyone gains the power of self.

This is a call of feminism. The version is used in my studies. The most simplistic human-loving way to define it – equality and really, equity. Identity is powerful – what one feels he or she or they can show in their life matters. Can I have long hair? Can I wear a dress? Can I hug someone in public? Can I cry at work? Can I love my child openly without question? Can I accept myself if a hookup turns me down? Identity allows us to see possibilities in the world in how respect is gained. These various books among others about masculinity, athletes, and fraternities are showing how limited this traditional, conservative version of manhood can be. Locker room talk not only leads to sexual assault and harming of women, but it also troubles men.

As stated by Gloria Steinem, "We've begun to raise daughters more like sons… but few have the courage to raise our sons more like our daughters." This statement addresses part of the rationale for feminism but also the need to reduce patriarchal, misogynistic, toxic maleness. The privilege of men is palpable, and most women will speak to it as the age into experiences such as careers, motherhood, and of course balancing the two (Ford, 2016; 2018). Although some equity is found in these homelife landscapes, women have gained an edge in being able to find themselves. Men often are stuck in the traditional sex roles view of identity. Equity is best for all.

Many books demonstrate the rules and rituals tolerable in a rape culture – one that allows male aggression to thrive and female meekness to persist. When boys and men are socialized to not be themselves and only shown a culturally accepted identity, it fosters the rape culture. *Alpha Girls* (Kindlon, 2006) expressed that the younger female adult generations of today view themselves as strong, smart, undeterred, equal, powerful, and privileged. These girls did not view feminism as a need because equality has been won and they are able to fight for themselves and rise with (and sometimes above) boys/men. These girls did not question glass ceilings because they saw themselves smashing through them without a thought or obstacle. They did not view future homelife as anything but equal in splitting household duties because why would they have a partner who would not share diaper duty and kitchen cleaning. Yet, these are generationally the women in my research. *Alpha Girls* quotations often sounded like the women in my courses or in these interviews – they cannot fathom a world where they are not taken seriously and able to accomplish anything they set their mind to. Similarly, when shown statistics of inequality between the sexes, shoulders are shrugged, and it is blamed on the older people because that will not be our generation. Without purposive change, it will be this generation and the next.

To illustrate in *Free Women Free Men* (Pagila, 2017) and *Unwanted Advances* (Kipnis, 2017), feminism is questioned and detained. Feminism is to blame for rape culture, sexual assault, and cultural sexist ills. It questions the very identity of alpha girls and their ability to fix any of this due to political climate and poor policy regulation from past feminists and pro-women structures. It argued that the reliance on Title IX to bring equity to campus as well as policing sexual assaults limited the role of the university; it pushed women back in bureaucratic red tape instead of freedom from it. Women and men looking outside of their selves to find protection from the university are ill-guided. Often, our social identities are not something we are willing to destroy to fight for justice in rape cases; universities add extra obstacles in questioning who we are and what happened.

Protection is not found in Title IX cases with universities (cite). Instead behind the closed doors of conduct hearings, students feel pressured to change stories, fail to be witnesses, and drop their own cases (cite to Hunting Game). Most hearings end in signing waivers to not speak about the case ever. Thus, other students, administrators, staff, and faculty do not learn of the truth beyond reported numbers for the Clery Act. In the Duke rape case, the alleged victim eventually closed her case, admitting it was a lie. In cases at Baylor University, many students brought allegations against fraternity members and athletes only to be swayed by administrators to not follow through with the cases. In Hunting Ground, many whistleblowers from prestigious universities show what administrators do to stop rape allegations at their schools. When Chanel Miller was sexually assaulted (not raped by California law) by Stanford swimming Brock Turner, the world provided him support and Stanford provided little help originally. It took the continued strength and criminal conviction of Turner for the school to enact small changes. The difference in this case was the witnesses of the assault and that Miller was not a student; she did not have to go through the Title IX process; she was able to use the State Criminal System (which was fraught with its own obstacles).

Our identities matter. How we see ourselves matter. We define ourselves in connection to our culture and social groups. If rape culture exists and cites other ideals of masculinity, toxic masculinity, hookup culture, and binge drinking, we define ourselves through that as well. For better or worse, we cannot escape our foundational identities shaped by first grade. We see ourselves through these lenses because of the endless interactions, experiences, and communication we have throughout life. Visceral connections develop to create a steadfast image of ourselves – we do not see ourselves as victims, survivors, and rapists. The studies herein show that people see themselves as positive upstanding folks – people who believe in equity and not in rape myths among other attitudes discussed below. The act of rape goes against all biological, psychological, and sociological images of self. That is what makes this so difficult – no one wants to view themselves as the other or the them – no one wants to be on the wrong side of the divide (cite see the two books about political division and divides).

College identity is as good as any place to start; in fact, many of the books I read talked about how students pick a college that matches how they see themselves. A few chapters ago, I discussed how students, faculty, and staff talked about this campus. Safe. Kind. Small. Religious. Conservative. Not a party school. Not a school based in athletics. Not a school strongly tied to Greek life. Not like those larger party schools with Division 1 athletics and a well-known fraternity row. We are kind and midwestern. We do not share those types of ideals. It is almost as if university community members were screaming the hope: WE ARE DIFFERENT.

To support these musings, student surveys asked students various questions about how they view themselves, actions they engage in, sexual behavior beliefs, consent viewpoints, group affiliations, and self-esteem. It also included self-perceptions about social-political viewpoints, feminism, femininity, masculinity, aggression, and empathy. The purpose was to expose the underlying factors of rape myth beliefs. Is there a type of person who is more likely to agree or disagree with the rape myths measured in the survey?

To note, survey statistics show large scale of how variables connect to each other. This is a macro-analysis digesting the various variables measured in connection to rape myth and then brought into the concepts of rape culture. In some ways this makes the discussion and findings reliant on stereotypes and definitions brought into the survey. It means we are looking at the large picture types of people, not a specific person. Many of the scales for variables (i.e. self-esteem, aggression, empathy) were based in psychological literature and the scales used had strong reliability and validity scores.

When using the Illinois Rape Myth Acceptance (IRMA) scale, you can see connections between variables of the rape myths and all other variables. Remember, the IRMA is technically five different measures of rape myths depending upon which individual items you are bringing together in scale form and are labeled as *total rape myth, she asked for it, he didn't mean to, it wasn't really rape,* and *she lied*. As Chapter 2 explained, the same scale was utilized for all surveys selecting the short version of IRMA as it fits on one page.

Study 3: Study 3 was the first larger study at the main university that was used to start building connections between the rape myth scales beyond programming and class standing. The sample ($n = 316$) was largely female (69%) as is the campus. The sample consisted of 60.8% lower-level students (freshman and sophomores), 23.7% athletes, 6.6% Greek life participants, and 56% other student organizations participants.

This study allowed for an examining of social identity variables through independent t-tests that can illuminate the differences between means in the rape myths because of the identity variables. Greek life, as shown in Table 4.1, was not a significant variable in changing any of the myths. This goes against a lot of stereotypes on the campus about sexual assault perceptions being different because of Greek life. If Greek life does not change perceptions of rape myths, it might be that it does not foster stronger agreement or disagreement among its members, or transversely, so much programming emphasis goes to this group; they know to disagree with the myths. It is socialized into them the attitudes they should hold.

Although athletes also receive the type of information provided to many in Greek life, Greek life hears it more. Many of the men in the sample are athletes but not necessary in Greek life; in fact, only four students were both athletes and in Greek life. Equal amounts of males and females were athletes. However, most of those in Greek life in this study were female, so this conclusion is sororities more so than fraternities, which might explain the lack of connection between rape myths and Greek life participation; sororities are often not studied.

Following other thoughts about identities, those in sports held lower means in all scales except *it wasn't really rape*. This scale throughout the various surveys and sample held the least variance and usually the most disagreement. On this campus, there is something about being an athlete that lowers scale means. The means are still in disagreement, but it means more athletes responded with neutral or agreement levels to bring the means lower. There is a culture in the sports teams that impacted rape myths. Perhaps, it is the role of sports, even for females, to be strong, aggressive, and virile. These types of beliefs connect with rape myths and victim blaming (Aronowitz, Lambert, & Davidoff, 2012; Carmody & Washington, 2001; Lanier, 2001; McMahon, 2007; Murnen & Kohlman, 2007; Szymanski, Sloan, Chrisler, & Vyse, 1993; Weiss, 2009).

Finally, the identity of sex or gender in this study reveals that females have a higher mean or that they disagree more with rape myths. This follows along with

TABLE 4.1 Independent T-tests of Scale Mean Differences for Identity Variables, Study 3

	Female		Male		Independent t-test	
	M	SD	M	SD	t	df
Total rape myth	89.931	13.698	81.461	13.382	4.993★★	295
She asked for it	24.808	4.524	22.438	4.542	4.256★★	307
He didn't mean to	23.427	4.224	21.144	4.704	4.247★★	306
It wasn't really rape	23.074	2.900	22.415	2.571	1.902★	309
She lied	18.738	4.678	15.529	4.374	5.718★★	309
	Not in Greek life		Greek life participant		Independent t-test	
	M	SD	M	SD	t	df
Total rape myth	87.152	14.0766	90.722	14.405	−1.042	295
She asked for it	24.079	4.606	24.8000	4.742	−0.675	307
He didn't mean to	22.675	4.492	23.526	4.698	−0.798	306
It wasn't really rape	22.831	2.883	23.571	1.535	−1.164	309
She lied	17.706	4.812	18.700	4.680	−0.896	309
	Not an athlete		Collegiate athlete		Independent t-test	
	M	SD	M	SD	t	df
Total rape myth	89.015	13.891	82.127	13.559	3.666★★	295
She asked for it	24.492	4.511	22.945	4.764	2.526★	307
He didn't mean to	23.319	4.419	20.922	4.254	4.254★★	306
It wasn't really rape	23.029	2.608	22.405	3.379	1.668	309
She lied	18.369	4.807	15.880	4.299	4.005★★	309

★$p \leq 0.05$; ★★ $p \leq 0.001$.

other studies as all rape myth scales were associated with higher means for females in this study. It is anticipated through socialization that females are taught to disagree with rape myths.

A caveat about these findings related to social identities and group think. Survey 8 and others check attitudes against this type of bias. Is someone answering questions on a survey because of how they think society wants them to answer? Essentially, a test of the theoretical ideas of situated identity theory and expectation states theory. Correlations existed in those studies showing that some students have a predisposition to answer survey items not necessarily how they think but how society wants them to think. It is most prevalent in the scales of *total rape myth, she lied,* and *she asked for it*. Some of these responses, although not directly tested in study 3, might be because of socialization of what we think we are supposed to believe and a reason for why in interviews and focus groups so many people speak out about victim blaming.

Study 11: Study 11 brought together identities of victim, perpetrator, and survey participant. An exploratory study uses vignettes and factorial survey analysis (see Rossi & Nock, 1982) to analyze perceived victim blameworthiness. Three scenarios were used where key characteristics of the story were changed to align with variables of study (i.e. gender) by analyzing rape scripts (Clay-Warner & McMahon-Howard, 2009; Crome & McCabe, 2001; Kahn, Mathie, & Torgler, 1994; McCaul, Veltum, Boyechko, & Crawford, 1990; Workman & Orr, 1996).

The sample ($n = 195$) was gained from student (54.4%) and faculty emails as well as social media. The samples were mostly white (95%) and female (89.7%). Many participants were not married (33.3%) but 29.7% were in a relationship and 27.7% were single with 8% divorced. The study includes 44% self-described sexual assault victims, which was not defined and answered as a yes/no question. This high victim percentage might be a result of survey response bias as those who wanted to fill out the online survey were interested and connected to the topic advertised but this might not be a concern for the data itself if the sample is taken into consideration (Berg, 2005; Dillman, Smyth, & Christian, 2014; Hendra & Hill, 2019). The participants identified themselves as feminists (91%), not masculine (55.4%), feminine (92.8), empathetic (99%), not aggressive (90.3%), and liberal (60%) through yes/no questions. For the data, you cannot infer past this sample into the general population but the data holds merit.

The purpose of study 11 was to gain an appreciation for perceived victim blameworthiness defined as did the survey participants think the victim was to blame for the sexual assault encountered in the three different scenarios. Each participant responded only to one scenario. More respondents completed scenario 2 which was used to determine connections of perceived blameworthiness to gender characteristics such as traits of masculinity and femininity. The vignettes themselves each described a blitz rape after the victim, *Alex*, left work. Alex is described as wearing a common work uniform of a polo and dress pants as well as a coat. Alex leaves work late one night and is assaulted by a stranger: hit in the head with a rock and then raped. The only difference between scenarios is the gender identity of Alex and the rapist. In Survey 1, Alex is a female raped by a male. In Survey 2, Alex is a male raped by a female. In Survey 3, Alex identifies as a non-binary person and is raped by a male. These different scenarios allowed researchers to see how sex and gender impacted participants blameworthiness in connection to the scenarios as a factorial survey analysis.

Perceived blameworthiness was a scale measured from 0 to 16, the degree the participant blamed the victim for the assault. After each scenario, there were 16 yes/no questions assessing the variable such as do you blame the victim for being assaulted, do you think the victim should have fought harder, and do you think the victim was dressed inappropriately. Independent t-tests were run with the scale to determine what identity variables connect with perceived blameworthiness. Those without statistical significance included sex, belief in feminism, or seeing oneself as feminine. There was a significant effect for masculine, $t(179) = -2.01$, $p = 0.046$, with those who see themselves as masculine

(M = 9.58, SD = 2.57) attaining higher scores than those who do not (M = 8.7, SD = 2.81). There was a significant difference due to aggression, t(179) = −1.89, p = 0.059, with those who see themselves as aggressive (M = 10.26, SD = 2.58) attaining higher scores than those who see themselves as not aggressive (M = 9.02, SD = 2.72). Thus, these masculine traits suggest that those who are more aggressive and more masculine also tend to hold victims as blameworthy.

In connection to social identity, study 11 showcases a concern with highly masculine traits and perceived victim blame. This might be why athletes and fraternities are known to be groups of sexual assault as they also contribute to ideals of "true masculinity" and "manliness" (Chu & Gilligan, 2014; Ford, 2018; Hechinger, 2017; Mansfield, 2006; Sexton, 2019). This study and those books claim that to be a man, you must hold certain beliefs and show those attitudes in public to be accepted as a man. You cannot be pathetic, weak, or emotional. You must be strong, aggressive, and in control. Part of this is acting on your sexual desires and holding women accountable for their actions. If you believe all women want you even if they say no, it was not sexual assault and they are to blame for your actions (Ford, 2018). Distinct types of people hold others responsible dissimilarly.

Another aspect of the study was trying to determine how difference rape scenarios impacted perceived blameworthiness. Each scenario had a distinct combination for gender of the victim and aggressor with other details remaining the same. The rape script was of a stranger attacking a person, Alex, at night after work. This scenario fits more stereotypical rape scripts for acceptance. In this small study, the victim mattered in how they were viewed depending on the characteristics of the viewer. This was precursory support for situated identity and expectation states theories; we make decisions based on our own in-groups and how we wish to be seen (e.g. aggressive, feminist) to that group. Decisions are based on hierarchy, the male was the most to blame, and our attributes, masculine participants blamed the victim more than any other group.

Study 9: This study did not include a neutral category in IRMA, nor any studies after this survey. It did not ask questions about athletics or Greek life as these were no longer variables of concern. The information below is from a 2019 student survey at one university; it is study 9. The survey and scales have been recreated in Appendix C.

For binary gender, students in the sample marked female at 62.1% and male at 35.2%, which is how the population on campus is divided. To note, approximately 3% marked other, transgender, or did not respond. The sample was equally dispersed among class standings of freshmen, sophomores, juniors, and seniors. The student sample lived on largely campus at 67%. Most students stated that they drank alcohol at 75%, whereas a similar percentage of 78% declared not using other illegal drugs (i.e. pot, cocaine). In this sample, 8% (or 35 students) were a victim of sexual assault and around 1% (or 3) stated that they committed a sexual assault.

Students were asked about their connection to social ideologies; the sample included social liberals (46.5%) and social conservatives (43.1%) with 11% not wanting to answer the question. The 11% who did not answer might be because they linked it to political parties and not social ideologies. Feminism was a simple yes/no question. Do you believe in feminism (meaning that women and men should be equal in all aspects of life)? Most students, 88%, responded perceived themselves as supporting the ideals of feminism.

Aggression was a pseudo measure for masculinity and what is termed toxic masculinity. It is not a perfect measure of masculinity, but aggression is developed as a male trait even from a side of evolution. Due to the nature of rape myths and rape culture, social or group aggression was measured as opposed to physical aggression. Social aggression is that a person is verbal in their aggressive tactics; it does not measure the use of physical aggression such as punches. The nine-item scale had responses of never, rarely, sometimes, and often to statements such as "My friends know that I will think less of them if they do not do what I want them to do" and " I spread rumors about a person just to be mean." The scale possible range was 0–27 with a midpoint of 13.5 of which 98.8% of the sample had numerical values at 13 or less. The range of scale responses was 0–18 with a mean/average of 3.14. Approximately 26% of the sample had a score of 0 reflecting no levels of social aggression and 52% of the sample scored 2 or lower. This sample is a low aggressive sample, which made this variable hard to use.

Empathy was a proxy measurement of femininity. Similar to aggression, it is a traditional viewpoint that in our society empathy is a female emotion. Without wanting to make the survey even longer, I used one scale for this measurement. Empathy was measured through a scale with 15 individual items, including "I am quick to spot when someone in a group is feeling awkward or uncomfortable" and "I really enjoy caring for other people." The midrange of the survey is 22.5 with a possible range of 0–45. The sample range was 8–33 with 37% of the sample at 22 or lower. The mean/average is 23.5. Most of the responses are between 21 and 25 suggesting that the students hold a midlevel of empathy.

Self-esteem measured through Rosenburg's 1964 self-esteem scale. It is a 10-item scale that determines the level of worth a person feels about themselves. Participants respond with strongly disagree, disagree, agree, or strongly agree to each statement with a possible range of 0–30. The sample range was 9–27 with a mean/average of 16.78 and 76% of the sample scored above the midpoint of 15. Most scored within the range of 15–18 with less than 5% scoring above a 20 and 4% between 9 and 12. These students hold midlevel self-esteem.

Sexual behaviors were measured through a scale linked into conservative sexual beliefs regarding sexual actions. This 10-item scale included statements such as "Masturbation is a normal sexual activity," "The primary goal of sex is to have children," and "A woman who initiates a sexual encounter will probably have sex with anyone." The possible range of this scale is 0–30 with a midpoint at 15. The sample scored between 0 and 22 with 90% of the sample scoring below 15.

This suggests that the sample of students do not perceive themselves as sexual conservatives and embrace a bit of equity in sexual relationships between men and women.

Sexual beliefs about sexual gender roles were a scale measuring the attitudes and perceptions about traditional sex roles or identities of males and females. It included 9 individual items of statements such as "it is acceptable for a woman to pay for a date" and "A woman should be a virgin when she marries." The participants selected strongly disagree to strongly agree with a possible range of 0–27 and an actual range of 3–19. The midpoint is 13.5 with 92% of the sample responding below that point. The mean/average is 9.43. The students in this study are showing their inclination to disagree with traditional sex roles.

Consent practices were measured through a scale with 18 individual items. The scale is found in Appendix C. Items included phrases such as "I think that verbally asking for sexual consent is awkward" and "I feel confident that I could ask for consent from a new sexual partner." This scale shows how much participants feel able to seek consent openly and if they actually do so. This study had a scale range of 0–42 with a possible range of 0–54 as measured from strongly disagree to strongly agree of 0–3 on the individual items. The mean/average was 20.25 with a median and mode of 22. The midpoint of the range is 27 with 88% of the sample responses being at or below 27. This means that students in this sample have a hard time practicing positive consent. It does not mean that they do not consent during sexual behaviors, but it is more focused on not saying no than declaring a yes.

We can look at the statistical analysis of study 9 in other ways to see how some identity markers link to perceptions of the *total rape myth scale*. In this study, 46 people (8.8%) were victims of sexual assault during their lives, and as victims they were more likely to disagree with the total rape myth scale. Being a victim of sexual assault had a negative relationship to the total rape myth scale, $t(527) = -1.671$, $p < 0.095$. This is significant at the 0.1 level, which is appropriate, given the lower level of variance and percentage of victims in this study.

Gender was significant with a positive connection, $t(534) = 6.846$, $p < 0.001$, where females had higher total rape myth scale scores suggesting that they disagree with the rape myth more than males. Those who believe in feminism as defined as equity had a negative correlation with the total rape myth scale, $t(542) = -4.232$, $p < 0.001$ where those who did not believe in feminism ($n = 54$) had lower mean scores in the total rape myth scale. Additionally, holding a liberal social identity was linked to a higher means in the total rape myth scale, $t(499) = -6.373$, $p < 0.001$ or that being liberal connected to more disagreement with the rape myth. Class standing was not significant in mean difference, $t(542) = 0.008$, $p < 0.994$, so that being an upper-level student or lower-level student did not impact the mean of total rape myth scale.

When OLS regression was conducted with the identity variables, the model was significant but r^2 was lower at 0.123 or the variables in the model explain

TABLE 4.2 Regression Analysis of Identity Variables in Study 9

Variable	B	SE B	β
Gender	−2.422	0.617	−0.167★★
Feminism Belief	3.886	1.275	0.132★
Social Liberal	4.148	0.777	0.231★★
Sexual Assault Victim	0.426	0.458	0.040
Class Standing	0.118	0.763	0.007

$F = 13.766$★★, $r^2 = 0.123$.
★$p \leq 0.05$, ★★$p \leq 0.001$.

about 12.3% of the variance in the *total rape myth scale*. Table 4.2 reports this regression analysis. All identity variables were significant except for class standing and victim of sexual assault. All the variables, gender, and feminism that impacted the mean difference in total rape myth scale were significant in correlating with and possibly causing the variance in total rape myth scale except for being a victim of sexual assault. This suggests that other identity markers are stronger than being a victim of sexual assault within this sample. Thus, female students who believe in feminism and other liberal ideals develop higher *total rape myth* scale scores.

The survey in 2019 did not ask questions about athletics or Greek life as I needed space in the survey and the prior surveys answered the questions well enough. Study 3 was conducted in Spring 2016. In this study, through independent t-tests that look at the differences in means due to a variable, athletics, class standing, and binary gender significantly impacted the mean of the *total rape myth scale*. Those who were not athletes held higher means in the total rape myth scale through a negative relationship, t(295) = −3.666, p < 0.001. If a student was involved with Greek life, it did not impact the mean of the total rape myth scale, t(295) = 1.042, p < 0.298. Gender held a negative connection, t(295) = −4.993, p < 0.001, so that females were more likely to disagree with rape myths. Class standing has a positive connection in total rape myth scale mean measures, t(296) = 2.819, *p* < 0.005, so that lower-level students had higher mean scores in the scale and thus disagreed with the total rape myth scale more than upper-level students.

When a regression analysis was completed with the identity variables in study 3, the significant variables stayed the same as in the independent t-tests. Class standing, gender, and athletic participation were significant predictors of the total rape myth scale measure. See Table 4.3 for the OLS regression results. The model was significant, and the variables explained roughly 13.7% of the variance found in the *total rape myth scale*. This regression suggests that those students who were female, non-athletes, lower-level students (freshmen and sophomores) held higher levels of total rape myth scores and these identity markers create that score through correlation and connection.

TABLE 4.3 Regression Analysis of Identity Variables in Study 3

Variable	B	SE B	B
Class Standing	5.319	1.582	0.186**
Gender Binary	−8.213	1.738	−0.272**
Athlete	−4.388	1.876	−0.132*
Greek life	1.112	3.242	0.019

$F = 11.529**$, $r^2 = 0.137$.
*$p \leq 0.05$, **$p \leq 0.001$.

TABLE 4.4 Regression Analysis of Identity Variables in Study 6

Variable	B	SE B	B
Class Standing	0.477	2.013	0.017
Gender Binary	−8.587	2.167	−0.285**
Athlete	−4.899	2.277	−0.158*
Greek life	0.287	3.647	0.006

$F = 5.632**$, $r^2 = 0.115$.
*$p \leq 0.05$, **$p \leq 0.001$.

Study 6 provides a check to study 3 for reliability and validity of the measures and findings. Independent t-tests and OLS regressions were completed with the identity variables in the study. Binary gender was a significant determinate of the mean differences for total rape myth scale, $t(177) = 4.137$, $p < 0.001$, providing that females have a higher scale score and thus disagreeing more with the rape myth. Class standing was not significant in mean differences of the total rape myth scale, $t(177) = -2.622$, $p < 0.535$. Being in sports created a difference in mean scores, $t(177) = 2.500$, $p < 0.013$, so that those not in sports held higher mean scores in the total rape myth scale. Being involved in Greek life on campus was not a predictor of mean difference in the total rape myth scale, $t(177) = -0.244$, $p < 0.807$.

The OLS regression analysis is viewable in Table 4.4. The model itself is significant with the identity variables that explained 11.5% of the variance in total rape myth scores. Both gender and athletic status are significant and negative predictors of rape myth. Both of these suggest that if you are a female and not an athlete on campus, you disagree more with the total rape myth. Class standing and Greek life, again, are not significant correlates of rape myth for this sample.

The qualitative perspective of identity starts with rape myths and rape culture. The focus groups were the clearest in explaining how identities develop our perceptions about rape myths, our safety, and the fear of sexual assaults. In these, faculty and staff hinged many beliefs on the university being safer than others because it was a small, midwestern, private campus with a religious affiliation.

Students would be kinder to each other and the campus would be safer with the lack of alcohol-fueled parties provided by fraternities and athletic teams. If students drink less and have less choices to party, they must be assaulted less. There might be some weight to this as about 9% of students from this university were assaulted, whereas the national sample of schools had close to 28% of students sexual assaulted. But it still happened here and perhaps due to the smallness, the social consequences were worse as they noted once they viewed the video depicting the aftereffects of assault.

Students of the first interviews, study 8, gave way to similar ideas when asked about the safety of the campus. The lack of parties and strong athletic teams or high affiliations to fraternity life kept students safer. Sexual assaults still existed but the ability to be on this type of campus provided them with a sense of safety and a lack of fear, which is also showcased in all surveys. Most of these females did not directly know a victim of assault from the campus and were not victims themselves. The two who did know others who were raped suggested that it was the friends' fault because of the alcohol they consumed, and she was asking for it in how she led the men around at a party; however, it was not on this campus. Both happened at parties at a larger, more urban, but still private and religiously affiliated campus; the city was blamed not the college.

The second set of interviews, study 14, with victims and survivors gave more direct information about identities as it was a focus of the questions and the conversations. The set of interviews told their stories of sexual assaults, including rape that might have happened while they were college students, but other times happened when they were in elementary school, high school, or the summer before college started. With their stories were their personal assumptions about why they did not report the assaults to law enforcement; none of the assaults were reported except for the rape of a child due to a social worker learning of the acts years afterward – crimes that have been investigated but unpunished due to lack of evidence. Most of the women have told family or friends or current partners, but for two of them, I was the first person they ever told. The power in me learning their stories was clear as victims are not to speak out due to the shame and stigma burned into them from the rape culture.

Four of the women interviewed identified with victim and the other three with survivor. This identity becomes part of who they are but hopefully less than other statuses held by the women such as daughter, mother, student, nurse, teacher, and so on. Women believed that by telling their stories, nothing would come from it and sometimes as in the case of the child sexual assault, they learned early that nothing would happen aside from their own pain, hurt, fear, and extra trauma. One woman explained,

> what you would have to deal with exactly [when you report it] ... I think it's very common for assaults to go unreported. I think a lot of people are pretty uneducated on the situation of like what is considered sexual assault and it's because the idea of reporting and also like the process of reporting

is almost impossible really, unless like you are already in the hospital or like got pregnant from it or like severely injured. Like would it do any good? ... The process looks difficult and I foresee the process as a lot of paperwork. A lot of people who are more busy with more important things like the police department is extremely overworked and they probably have a lot more important things than this assault or my crappy three hours of my life.

This one account is loaded with many of the other sentiments from the women student interviewees. Sexual assault goes unreported because that is the social norm; the perception is that the crime is not worth reporting. Police officers have more serious crimes and investigations to undergo suggesting that sexual assault is not important or the personal victimization the woman underwent is not a serious offense, especially when it does not fit the real rape script of stranger rape. They see reporting as a last resort and deemed possible when other factors from the assault occur such as physical injury or a pregnancy, both of which are less common in sexual assaults and rapes that are party rapes, date rapes, or acquaintance rapes. In the end, life experiences and the rape culture have told women that there is nothing to gain to go through the pain of telling their assault story. Many of the women commented that they completed this interview because they hoped that their voice would be heard, stories shared, and changes made.

Some of the women shared stories of friends making fun of others who report assault or not being believed because of her reputation. This is a difficult place knowing the truth about what happened but not trusting those close to you with the information. The interviewee thinks that this predicament is garbage – people do not lie about assault because

> why do you want to put yourself through that yeah so why is there this like community backlash almost just because nobody wants to deal with it because I know that I didn't want to do with me so I said why would that person who actually didn't want to admit it.

People would not choose to be victims and treated as outcastes for something someone did to them.

Another reason to not open up about victimization is because it changes the way people perceive you as a person. The shame and stigma are carried personally and socially. The rape culture assures that people who speak up are met with accusations of blame through the rape myths and often disbelief. From telling your story, you earn disrespect and a new identity many do not want to hold. One woman explains why her parents, especially her father, do not know of either rape she has experienced in life.

> My dad is the type of person who is not gonna like this situation. He will put it in your head, like that it's your fault just like it always is. He would say things like that, and he's really showed [in the past] how he doesn't

> care. He doesn't seem to like this, and I feel like I might not only disrespect myself to him but also to everyone else in my family. [He would let me know] I should've known what would happen when I went to the boy's house.

She was afraid to let her family know of this experience as a freshman in high school because how she would be viewed as a non-virgin, as someone who let this happen, as someone who was a slut or a whore. She feared what the boy's family would say as they were close friends of her own family. She was nervous about the ruined relationships. However, her largest fear was being seen as someone perhaps something she did not want to be perceived as a victim blamed for the action of another.

This was common among the survivors and victims. Many talked about their assault and rape as their fault, especially if drugs like alcohol were part of the experience. As a woman, you should have known better because you were raised better. You were raised to not be stupid and the importance to engage in protective patterns. As one woman describes it:

> I think that's almost like a global reaction to assaults. For some reason initial reactions are never blame the guy, which sounds as backward as hell, but I felt like I walked right into it. So instead of being like this piece of shit hurt me, it was I did this kind of thing, so I think I blamed myself and not him. I think that's for me where a lot of shame will come from as if I think I played a big role in not preventing it because then you get mad at yourself for in so much. And you like to see how clear as day the scenario is as a Monday morning quarterback. I think it was anger more at me than at him. I was mad at myself. I think I might've spoke up to him but speaking up felt just as wrong as the assault. I would've said 'you did this to me. This is what the fuck you made happen kind of thing'.

When she was asked why was she more angry with herself than her assaulter, she replied,

> I was warned you don't just take drugs from people so that I think was a big part of it [she was high at the time of the rape]. That led to me feeling I dug my own grave. You don't think you're gonna end up in that situations, but you do. You let him do it because I've been kind of warned him when you're younger, you don't act reckless, you don't takeoff clothes with older boys in their 20s. You be a nice girl. So, I was warned and now I have an attitude like dude you [I] should've known better.

This is the rape culture teaching young girls to be nice and to behave. To not act on sexual needs or desires or to not do drugs, especially when you are with an almost stranger. Protect yourself at all costs. She did not do this and so she feels to blame for the rape and physical assault; this is the strength of victim blame and the shame and torment it brings.

A few years later in college, a year before the interview, the woman, afraid of her dad's reaction, was raped by a boyfriend who often sexually coerced her into sexual intercourse and other sexual behaviors. I was the first person she told of this rape because who would believe her and trust her story when he was "*such a nice guy.*" It is amazing that so many of the women in my interviews, those who knew their assaulters well, were nice men or boys. Others viewed the assaulters as kind, strong, and nice, which made it harder for the women to open up about their assaults to those who knew them both – why would they believe them. In a rape culture, no one would.

Instead, what happens is victims stay quiet, fallen under their perceived shame and stigma of their assault. To use the words of an interviewee about the rape culture and why sexual assault continues to happen without reprimand:

> It's almost like the boys will be boys scenario that we just kind of shrugged and I think that a lot of people just like don't talk about it. I don't know why but I think that this probably adds to the freedom of doing [sexual assaults] and probably also the shame that people feel. In our culture you don't really talk about drama or stuff like that. You're supposed to just deal with it on your own. That's the rape culture.

As a female, you are not supposed to discuss aspects of life, including sexual desire, sexual behavior, or sexual assault. This is kept secret that vilifies women's bodies and identities. The rape culture ensures men have the right to speak and do while women remain hushed.

> I should say we were raised with the idea that our bodies are personal. We have private areas and anything that happens in those areas we don't feel like we can actively talk about with anybody especially with women … It's like the female body is a dirty thing and you can't talk about anything that happens to you. We were raised with it so much that you can't talk about the things that happened to your body and if you do you're bad if you want to walk.

If you cannot talk about the normal things that happen to your body as a woman, how do you talk about the trauma.

This becomes part of the female identity as a woman and especially as a victim in the rape culture. Women do not want to talk because she sees it as creating more trauma as a woman and not solving anything the assault created.

> I could but what's that going to do that she's going to prolong this tragedy that's gonna pull on my issue my trauma and have to keep talking about it keep thinking about it I want to get over it myself and then I feel doing this

and the things and not over it but I'm more comfortable With this I can't do anything because everything is gone.

She felt that many things before the rape no longer existed, as if her identity altered and fractured. She was the person she used to be but now on a different course marked with pain. She did not want to open that pain to others, so she, and most others, opted to remain silent.

Rape culture is boys will be boys and that includes taking advantage of women. There is not a strong traditional sense of femininity on the campus, but masculinity is shown through sports attire and general perceptions of uncaringness. Femininity is shown more during parties or when people go out or when dressed up for class. Otherwise, it is often hidden. Men are the dominant creatures who seek out women and try to hook up no matter what. *"Rape is about the power grab and victim blaming."* Men want the power and will blame the woman regardless of her actions. His aggression is expected and warranted but the female should remain docile and calm even if raped; it is her role and duty as a female. As such,

we live in kind of an overly aggressive patriarchal society so man dominated aggression. Men is good at dominating people with the rape culture. It argues that men are clearly here to dominate the world. If women cannot stop those behaviors, it easily leads to rape and it becomes acceptable.

The vision from this woman is that men hold the power in all relationships and rape can be inevitable. It is the woman who needs to find ways to control the man, so rape does not happen. She did not think that this is the way relationships should be but that the rape culture cultivates this working connection of sexual power and dominance through coercion.

Summary

There is something inside of us that wants to connect to the world around us through interactions and communication. This desire makes us compassionate toward our groups and finds ways for the members of these groups to like us. Expectation states and situated identity theories help demonstrate how identities connect and move through the social world together. The way we construct our reality is partially through the identities we create and the roles we embody. Our individual selves can only exist as part of the society; we are created because of the connections fostered.

The surveys provided support that rape myths are not agreeable in these samples. Yet, there were items in IRMA with the *he didn't mean to* and *she lied* scales that held higher levels of agreement. Those who held masculine identities as measured through a lack of empathy and social aggression were more likely to agree, or at least not highly disagree, with rape myths. Males were consistently on the lower end of the rape myth scales. Athletes, even female athletes, were less likely to highly disagree and their means moved closer to agreement and neutral categories. Not enough fraternity members were in the surveys, but sorority sisters were more likely to disagree with the rape myths.

Even though women were higher in the disagreement, all those interviewed fell into the socialized stereotypes of blaming victims and even themselves for the sexual assaults of others. Drinking, kissing, clothing, and dancing were seen as reasons the assaults happened. The lack of strength, both emotional and physical, was posited as why the victims and survivors were assaulted. Even though the women knew it was the man's fault, they still held the shame and stigma of being a reason and feared being blamed by others they loved and trusted.

Why can women rationalize the cause of assaults but still fall into the trap of victim blame? The study about perceived victim blameworthiness provides some light as identities of the victim, perpetrator, and survey participant mattered. There were connections of gender, sex roles, stereotypes, and situations that brought about blame. According to expectation states theory, we use social hierarchies to attribute decision making; the decision of assigned victim blame would not be different. If you look like a slut and act like a whore and move out of traditional sex roles such as a man being a rape victim, you deserved it – it was your fault. This is the argument of the rape culture.

Part of the reason women still victim blame might be because of feminism and the women's movement. It was the female athletes who quantitatively connected to the rape myths and all of the interviewees who spoke of the myths. As the quote by Steinman states, we are trying to make girls more manly but forgot to change the paths of boys and men. Athletes are in a world controlled by aggression and power, masculine traits. Other elements of masculinity are transferred into this culture perhaps including beliefs of locker room talk and boys will be boys. Personally, most of my coaches growing up were men and we were taught sports no differently than boys. Yet, it is not about making boys into girls or girls into boys as some people infer (Casey, 2020; Kipnis, 2017; Pagila, 2017). This is about equity of being your true self in a society stuck in traditional sex roles of masculinity and femininity. The misconception of making a man into a girl as a reason to not believe in toxic masculinity misses the point.

Alpha Girls (Kindlon, 2006) discussed the need for girls to become stronger and aggressive to change the path of women. Females needed to learn the ways of males to become successful in education and careers. The passive learner or quiet mouse would not be able to thrive in the workplace and make changes needed for equity of placements in powerful positions. The argument being that women are better at being men and are having an easier time making transition for their well-being.

In the book *Drinking* (Johnston, 2013), the author notes that females are surpassing men in drinking growth and trying to stay at par in the amount of alcohol consumed. This leads to more binge drinking by females as well as more blackouts, hospital visits, vomiting, and passing out. Biologically, women cannot drink as much as men, on average. What this leads to then are more females being raped either because they are unconscious or imbibed to a degree where it is hard to say not and fight people off from sexual advances. In a culture of consent where yes means yes and no means no but nothing means yes, more sexual assaults occur (Jozkowski, 2015; Keyser, 2019; LaFrance, Loe, & Brown, 2012; Little, 2005). *Unwanted Advances* (Kipnis, 2017) discussed the connection of drinking to rape. The more alcohol a female drink to keep up with men to prove herself, the more likely she is putting herself in danger. Finding yourself without friends or friends who also binge drink, passed out on a couch, puts women in precarious situations. This is not victim blaming but situational awareness. It creates a situation where a man who wants to rape can do so easily without little repercussion because she will not remember it happening or per the rape myths of victim blaming who would believe her (see Kantor & Twohey, 2019).

Women work hard at controlling and protecting their bodies according to their gender script. *Free Women Free Men* (Pagila, 2017) declared that the desire to be one of the boys harms women and men. In sexual assault, the harm is quite clear. For binge drinking, the harm is also clear. The issues are that we are stuck in social gender bounds until society and culture can catch up. Women are limited in the way we can act out in equal manners. For women, it is being more aggressive and trying to meet the status quo of strong, powerful men because they still are competing in a patriarchal world where crying and softness are not tolerated. People are still judged by the culture we are in (Mansfield, 2006).

Situated identity theory and expectation states theory provide a guide for why females still produce rape myth alibis for assaults. Women make decisions and show attitudes by the behaviors engaged in. If you want to be a strong feminist woman who is able to conquer all things, you need to demonstrate that powerful advantage. The image for power in culture and society still is manliness; females branding themselves in a patriarchal misogynistic culture as equal need to grab power through the rules developed by men.

You cannot be viewed as weak. You cannot be viewed as less than. Your need to demonstrate your strength by showing your attitudes of rape culture, in this instance. You need to be part of the group. Thus, you have some implicit bias that women who are raped are weaker. You are inclined to victim blame. You are part of the rape culture that believes in rape myths while not accepting of rape itself. For instance, she got so drunk and passed out on that dude's couch; she was stupid and deserved what she got. Or they both were so drunk and had sex. She just regrets her actions. He didn't really rape her. Females who see the rape myths as possible explanations are following her culture and society – she does not know how to speak out against it because she was not told to.

This is a tricky path for feminism. It is a route that our constructed identities and women marches left untouched. Women wanted equality without engaging in long-term efforts to cultural gender and corresponding sex roles. This was supported in the interviews; all the females said that they wanted equality in their relationships personal and professional. They discussed the need for homelife equality if they ever decided to have children. But they also discussed the sexual behaviors in their lives where their partner, often men, dominated and controlled their sexual experiences. Some consented after feeling coerced because they have to have sex in relationships and keep him happy. They opened up about not knowing what consent is supposed to look like if a woman initiated sexual behaviors because what man would say no. They talked about hookups and the extra pressure needed to give out sex whether in a relationship or not. This is against what is described as alpha girls. The women know how to show their force in classrooms but in the bedroom was a different story. They were lost and felt inadequate to navigate the sexual world. In short, these women all claimed to be feminists and wanted equality, but no one taught them the path.

This is the rape culture. It is a subtle nuance of knowing that rape is wrong morally and criminally but falling into created chasms of rape myth culture. Women are taught to be strong and move forward. Women are not taught how to fight their beliefs that boys will be boys and girls get raped when they do not protect themselves.

This type of toxic or aggressive or unforgiving masculinity destroys our culture and gendered perceptions. Pagila (2017) provided a solution to this; turn the discussion away from females and their strife to the needs of boys and men. We cannot focus solely on women and fix rape myths by telling women that it is not their fault. We need to create a true society where women can speak up loudly and proudly without men denying them a voice. (And yes, this is true for gender construction and the continuum we all fall onto to build our gender outside of the male/female dichotomy. Until we really see gender as cyclical, we will have a hard time building attitudes outside of rape myths.) We need to develop men who can be caring and soft while women accept this change. Men know not to rape, but they do it. Women know not to put themselves in danger, but they do it. The blame in on the rapists and sexual assaults, so we need a society that builds safe places for vulnerability (Brown, 2010; 2017). Vulnerability needs to be our new collective identity to help shatter the shame and stigma felt in our culture not just due to rape myths but because of the type of socialization that leaves us feeling untrue to ourselves.

References

Aronowitz, T., Lambert, C. A., & Davidoff, S. (2012). The role of rape myth acceptance in the social norms regarding sexual behavior among college students. *Journal of Community Health Nursing, 29*, 173–182. doi: 10.1080/07370016.2012.697852

Berg, N. (2005). *Non-response bias* (No. 26373). University Library of Munich, Germany.

Benedict, J. (2004). *Out of bounds: Inside the NBAs culture of rape, violence, and crime*. Harper.

Brown, B. (2017). *Rising strong: How the ability to reset transforms the way we live, love, parent, and lead*. Random House.

Brown, B. (2010). *The gifts of imperfection: Let go of who you think you're supposed to be and embrace how you are*. Random House.

Carmody, D. C., & Washington, L. M. (2001). Rape myth acceptance among college women: The impact of race and prior victimization. *Journal of Interpersonal Violence, 16*, 424–436.
Casey, G. (2020). *After #metoo: Feminism, patriarchy, toxic masculinity and sundry delights.* Ingram Book Company.
Chu, J. Y., & Gilligan, C. (2014). *When boys become boys: Development, relationships, and masculinity.* NYU Press.
Clay-Warner, J., & McMahon-Howard, J. (2009). Rape reporting: "Classic rape" and the behavior of law. *Violence and Victims, 24*(6), 723–743.
Crome, S. A., & McCabe, M. P. (2001). Adult rape scripting within a victimological perspective. *Aggression and Violent Behavior, 6*, 395–413. doi:10.1016/S1359-1789(00)0001
Dillman, D. A., Smyth, J. D., & Christian, L. M. (2014). *Internet, phone, mail, and mixed-mode surveys: the tailored design method.* John Wiley & Sons.
Ford, C. (2018). *Boys will be boys: Power, patriarchy and toxic masculinity.* Oneworld.
Ford, C. (2016). *Fight like a girl.* Oneworld.
Hechinger, J. (2017). *True gentlemen.* Public Affairs.
Hendra, R., & Hill, A. (2019). Rethinking response rates: New evidence of little relationship between survey response rates and nonresponse bias. *Evaluation Review, 43*, 307–330.
Johnson, K. C., & Taylor Jr., S. (2017). *The campus rape frenzy: The attack on due process at America's universities.* Encounter Books.
Johnston, A. D. (2013). *Drink.* Harper Wave.
Jozkowski, K. N. (2015). "Yes means yes"? Sexual consent policy and college students. *Change: The Magazine of Higher Learning, 47*(2), 16–23.
Kahn, A. S., Mathie, V. A., & Torgler, C. (1994). Rape scripts and rape acknowledgment. *Psychology of Women Quarterly, 18*, 53–66.
Kantor, J., & Twohey, M. (2019). *She said: Breaking the sexual harassment story that helped ignite a movement.* Penguin Publishing.
Keyser, A. J. (2019). *No more excuses.* Twenty-First Century Books.
Kindlon, D. (2006). *Alpha girls: Understanding the new American girl and how she is changing the world.* Rodale.
Kipnis, L. (2017). *Unwanted Advances.* Harper Collins.
Lafrance, D. E., Loe, M., & Brown, S. C. (2012). "Yes means yes:" A new approach to sexual assault prevention and positive sexuality promotion. *American Journal of Sexuality Education, 7*, 445–460.
Lanier, C. A. (2001). Rape-accepting attitudes: Precursors to or consequences of forced sex. *Violence against Women, 7*, 876–885.
Little, N. J. (2005). From no means no to only yes means yes: The rational results of an affirmative consent standard in rape law. *Vanderbilt Law Review, 58*, 1321.
Mac Donald, H. (2018). *The diversity delusion: How race and gender pandering corrupt the university and undermine our culture.* St. Martin's Griffin.
Mansfield, H. C. (2006). *Manliness.* Yale University Press.
McCaul, K. D., Veltum, L. G., Boyechko, V., & Crawford, J. J. (1990). Understanding attributions of victim blame for rape: Sex, violence, and foreseeability. *Journal of Applied Social Psychology, 20*, 1–26.
McMahon, S. (2007). Understanding community-specific rape myths: Exploring student athlete culture. *Journal of Women and Social Work, 22*, 357–370. doi:10.1177/0886109907306331
Murnen, S. K., & Kohlman, M. H. (2007). Athletic participation, fraternity membership, and sexual aggression among college men: A meta-analytic review. *Sex Roles, 57*, 145–157. doi: 10.1007/s11199-077-9225-1

Murphy, P. F. (Ed.). (2004). *Feminism & masculinities*. Oxford University Press.
Pagila, C. (2017). *Free women free men*. Pantheon Books.
Rossi, P. H. & Nock, S. L. (1982). *Measuring social judgments: The factorial survey approach*. Books on Demand.
Sexton, J. Y. (2019). *The man they wanted me to be: Toxic masculinity and a crisis of our own making*. Counterpoint.
Sperber, M. (2000). *Beer and circus*. Henry Holt and Company.
Stein, J. (2012). *Man made: A stupid quest for masculinity*. Grand Central Publishing.
Szymanski, L. A., Sloan Devlin, A., Chrisler, J. C., & Vyse, S. A. (1993). Gender role and attitudes toward rape in male and female college students. *Sex Roles, 29*, 37–57.
Weiss, K. (2009). "Boys will be boys," and other gendered accounts. *Violence against Women, 15*, 810–834. doi: 10.1177/1077801209333611
Workman, J. E., & Orr, R. L. (1996). Clothing, sex of subject, and rape myth acceptance as factors affecting attributions about an incident of acquaintance rape. *Clothing and Textiles Research Journal, 14*, 276–284. doi:10.1177/0887302X9601400407

5
OPENING THE UNIVERSITY CULTURE

This chapter explores a national sample of university students against data from the main university to determine if the presumptions presented are connected across universities in supporting a widespread rape culture and rape myths. It includes an additional survey from social media to try to bridge another gap of sampling outside of the university. What is found is that university life and beliefs are similar; the university presented so far is not unique in its attributes of student beliefs. Rape myths and rape culture surround us and infiltrate our social identities.

Study 10 – This study completed in Fall 2019 used social media such as Facebook to gain a broader audience that was not reliant on the university sample. The survey had a low response rate of 38% as 271 people started the survey and only 103 finished it. The response rate is concerning because of the nature of the study; it is assumed that those who completed the survey are different than those who did not complete it (Berg, 2005; Dillman, Smyth, & Christian, 2014). Perhaps those who completed the survey or even started the survey were interested in the topic of assault or rape myths or rape culture and thus are different than those who did not click and did not complete.

The sample was aged 18–66 with an average age of 28. The sample was mainly female at 77.7%. The sample held highest educational levels at 7.8% high school diploma, 5.8% had an associate degree, 28.2% taking some college credits (includes those currently in school), 38.8% having a bachelor's degree, 12.6% had a master's degree, and 3.9% with a doctorate. About 45% of the sample were current college students. These descriptive statistics of the sample are appropriate for this study as it is comparing university cultures, but it does not represent general society.

This sample viewed themselves as agreeing with feminist and socially liberal ideals; this connects to their educational attainment and proportion of females. Remember this is not a political party connection but how the participants perceive their beliefs about social concerns. A high percentage of the sample (43.7%) were victims of sexual assault and 41.7% were victims of other types of violent crimes. About 3% were convicted of sexual assaults and 11% were convicted of other types of violent offenses. Only 5% viewed themselves as criminals. Even with these numbers, most did not fear their current living situation. The average amount of fear was low at a mean of 26.78 out of 100. The range of fear in the sample was 1–97 with 76.7% under the value 50 and only 5% at 70 or higher. One-quarter of the sample valued their fear at or below 8/100, which is extremely low fear.

In respect to the IRMA, most people did not agree with the statements or the scales shown in Tables 5.1 and 5.2. All means were between disagree and strongly disagree. Most items had less than 10% agreement. A few items had percentages of 15 or higher in the agreement columns: items 4 (if a woman acts like a slut, eventually she is going to get into trouble), 6 (if a woman initiates kissing or hooking up, she should not be surprised if a guy assumes she wants to have sex), 7 (when guys rape, it is usually because of their strong desire for sex), 8 (guys don't usually intend to force sex on a woman, but sometimes they get too sexually carried away), 10 (if a guy is drunk, he might rape someone unintentionally), and 22 (women who are caught cheating on their boyfriends sometimes claim it was rape). These items are mostly in the *he didn't mean to* and *she asked for it* scales. This is slightly different than the other studies; it is unique to have two items in the *she asked for it* scale.

Examining the scales for study 10 does not seem to exhibit much difference than the other studies. All the means are above the midpoint levels suggesting disagreement with the scales. The ranges are typical for the studies and the alphas demonstrate strong reliability among the scale items. This illustrates that the main study university is not all that different from other types of samples and populations. It appears that our culture cultivates similar responses to rape myths as individual ideas and scales.

Study 10 included other scales that helped process some additional ideas which might be connected to rape myth beliefs. Table 5.3 displays the findings of these scales, including social desirability bias, consent, sex role traditions, empathy, sexual conservatism in behavior, and social (not physical) aggression. These variables provide a context to compare to studies 9 and 13 as well as further determine connections of rape culture through identities.

Social desirability bias is the likelihood a person is responding to survey items in a manner they think the researcher or society wants them to. It appears that this scale in the social media sample had a poor reliability score. The mean is in mid-range signifying no real presence of social desirability bias or the lack of it; it's on a neutral playing field. When examining the correlation between total rape myth scale and social desirability bias, there was small connection,

TABLE 5.1 Study 10 Fall 2019 IRMA Individual Items Percentages and Means

Scale		Items – Rape Myth Statements	SA 1	A 2	D 3	SD 4	Mean
She asked for it	1	If a woman is raped while drunk, she is at least somewhat responsible for letting things get out of hand.	1.0	2.9	20.4	75.7	3.71
	2	When women go to parties wearing slutty clothes, they are asking for trouble.	1.0	5.9	13.7	79.4	3.72
	3	If a woman goes to a room alone with a guy at a party, it is her own fault if she is raped.	1.0	0.0	13.6	85.4	3.83
	4	If a woman acts like a slut, eventually she is going to get into trouble.	1.9	13.5	20.4	64.1	3.47
	5	When women get raped, it's often because the way they said "no" was unclear.	2.9	3.9	20.4	72.8	3.63
	6	If a woman initiates kissing or hooking up, she should not be surprised if a guy assumes she wants to have sex.	1.9	20.4	30.1	47.6	3.23
He didn't mean to	7	When guys rape, it is usually because of their strong desire for sex.	4.9	15.5	32.0	47.5	3.22
	8	Guys don't usually intend to force sex on a woman, but sometimes they get too sexually carried away.	2.9	12.6	31.1	53.4	3.35
	9	Rape happens when a guy's sex drive goes out of control.	1.9	4.9	27.2	66.0	3.57
	10	If a guy is drunk, he might rape someone unintentionally.	1.9	21.4	22.3	54.4	3.29
	11	It shouldn't be considered rape if a guy is drunk and didn't realize what he was doing.	1.0	2.9	17.5	78.6	3.74
	12	If both people are drunk, it can't be rape.	2.9	2.9	19.4	74.9	3.66
It wasn't really rape	13	If a woman doesn't physically resist sex – even if protesting verbally – it can't be considered rape.	1.0	1.9	15.5	81.6	3.78
	14	If a woman doesn't physically fight back, you can't really say it was rape.	1.0	1.0	13.6	84.5	3.82
	15	A rape probably doesn't happen if a woman doesn't have any bruises or marks.	1.0	0.0	12.7	86.3	3.84
	16	If the accused "rapist" doesn't have a weapon, you really can't call it rape.	1.0	0.0	10.8	88.2	3.86
	17	If a woman doesn't say "no" she can't claim rape.	4.0	5.9	18.8	71.3	3.57
She lied	18	A lot of times, women who say they were raped agreed to have sex and then regret it.	2.9	9.7	35.0	52.4	3.37
	19	Rape accusations are often used as a way of getting back at guys.	1.9	5.8	36.9	55.3	3.46
	20	A lot of times, women who say they were raped often led the guy on and then had regrets.	1.0	6.8	28.2	64.1	3.55
	21	A lot of times, women who claim they were raped have emotional problems.	1.0	8.7	28.2	62.1	3.51
	22	Women who are caught cheating on their boyfriends sometimes claim it was rape.	2.9	22.3	23.3	51.5	3.23

TABLE 5.2 Study 10 Fall 2019 IRMA Scales

Scale	Alpha	Possible Range	Midpoint	Actual Range	Mean (Std. Dev.)
Total rape myth scale Items 1–22	0.953	22–88	55	22–88	78.73 (10.70)
She asked for it Items 1–6	0.863	6–24	15	8–24	21.57 (3.14)
He didn't mean to Items 7–12	0.819	6–24	15	6–24	20.84 (3.29)
It wasn't rape Items 13–17	0.917	5–20	12.5	5–20	18.89 (2.36)
She lied Items 18–22	0.916	5–20	12.5	5–20	17.13 (3.26)

TABLE 5.3 Study 10 Spring 2020 Survey Scales

Scale	Alpha	Possible Range	Midpoint	Actual Range	Mean (Std. Dev.)
Social Desirability Bias	0.035	10–20	15	12–18	14.49 (1.34)
Consent	0.890	18–72	45	23–72	38.09 (9.09)
Sex Role Traditions	0.546	9–36	22.5	12–30	17.78 (3.11)
Empathy	0.459	15–60	37.5	27–48	38.00 (3.64)
Sexual Conservatism	0.545	10–40	25	14–27	19.92 (3.16)
Aggression	0.867	9–36	22.5	9–36	11.52 (3.57)

$r(99) = 0.110$, $p = 0.282$. Thus, there might be some people whose rape myth responses are connected to the perceived correct answers and not their truths. However, with the lack of reliability in the social desirability bias, this can be questioned.

The consent variable measures the likelihood of a person using positive consent mechanisms in all of the sexual connections, including actions of kissing as well as intercourse. The higher the value of the scale, the more likely the person does not engage in positive consent practices such as asking if a kiss is alright or if clothes can be taken off. The mean is below the scale's midpoint illustrating poor use of consent practices in this sample. In fact, 87% of the sample has a consent scale measure of 45 or less; most of the social media sample engages in positive consent practices. For examples, item 5 states, "I believe that sexual intercourse is the only sexual activities that requires explicit verbal consent" of which 91.2%

disagreed; most were in strong disagreement (65.0%). Item 8 held almost 84% disagreement to the statement "I would have difficulty asking for consent because it would spoil the mood." Ninety percent of the sample agreed with item 18 of the consent scale which states, "I feel confident that I could ask for consent from my current partner." This sample was knowledgeable about the current platforms of how sexual consent should occur.

The variable of sex role traditions marks the way participants perceive traditional sex roles based on gender – what are men and women supposed to do in their daily lives. This sample was below the midpoint suggesting a lowered connection to traditional beliefs. Of the sample, 94% were at the midpoint scale measure or lower. For instance, item 3 held 91.3% disagreement to the statement "A woman should be a virgin when she marries" and item 7 had an 83.5% disagreement to "it is acceptable for a woman to have a career. But marriage and family come first." The social media sample was supportive of feminism and this scale supports that belief.

Empathy and aggression are used as measures of traditional femininity and masculinity; females are supposed to be empathetic and males are to be aggressive. Both of these scales have moderate support as the sample is neutrally empathic and barely socially aggressive. The measures for aggression are about verbal arguing and retaliation as this relates more to sexual coercion than traditional measures of physical aggression. For example, item 4 in the aggression scale (I have intentionally ignored a person until they gave me my way about something) held a 95.1% of sample disagreement. Empathy is in the mid-range demonstrating a presence of empathetic responses. For example, empathy item 2 (I am good at sensing how people feel) had an 80.6% level of agreement. The reason the scale is so close to the mid-range is because it acts as a level of agreement, implicit levels of empathy.

The last scale of the sexual behavior scale marks perceptions of conservatism in one's comfort level in particular sexual behaviors. The mean is below the midpoint with 95.1% of the sample being at or below the midpoint. This translates into a sample that does not align with conservative sexual behaviors and beliefs.

Study 10 was similar to the studies completed in the university even though its sample originated in social media and not university specific. Granted, almost 1/2 of the sample were college students, as they were friends of the student researchers helping distribute this study; this still demonstrates that the main university of the study is not different from other samples.

Study 13 –This study was a national sample of students from five different universities. It was hoped to have more universities represented but gaining approval from various schools and IRBs proved difficult due to diverse opinions about human welfare in the project. The survey and informed consent were altered per a few university requests but only when it did not change the meaning of the survey. Some universities wanted too much to change and disagreed with whole sections of the survey. These universities are not in the final sample because of the difficulty to work within their administrative and IRB guidelines.

132 University culture

This process was maddening as it limited the numbers in the sample and school participation for a study that already gained approval from one IRB.

The survey for study 13 was completed in 2019 and 2020, resulting in 398 completed surveys. The average age was 26 years with a median of 21 and mode of 19. The majority of the sample was female (71.8%) who believed in feminism (84.7%). It was split between liberal (50.5%) and conservative (46.2%) social identities. In this sample, 28.8% or 113 students have been victims or survivors of sexual assault and rape, and 34.2% or 136 students have been victims of other types of violence. Nearly all students stated that they were never convicted of a criminal offense (97.5%), including sexual and violent crimes but 11.4% (45 students) of the sample stated that they were engaged in a violent crime, whereas only 2 people or 0.5% admitted to sexually assaulting or raping a person. Most people do not fear their lives on campus. A scale of 0–100 held a mean of 33.58 with 1/4 of the sample having values of 11 or less and 1/4 having values of 55 or above; 90% of the sample held fear levels less than 70/100.

This student sample, like the other surveys, does not agree with rape myths. This is displayed in Table 5.4. The sample overall disagrees with each of the statements and the scales. Items 6, 7, and 22 have the lowest means which happen to be below 3. The IRMA items were measured as strongly agree (1), agree (2), disagree (3), and strongly disagree (4); thus, any means below 3 represents a level of agreement. However, all three are above 2.8 and thus are closer to disagree than agree on average. Nine of the 22 means are at or above 3.5, suggesting high levels of disagreement. The last ten items are between 3.03 and 3.42, illustrating that students disagree with those rape myth statements.

There are, however, numerous items that have agreement levels above 15%. These are 9 (rape happens when a guy's sex drive goes out of control), 10 (if a guy is drunk, he might rape someone unintentionally), 17 (if a woman doesn't say "no," she can't claim rape), 18 (a lot of times, women who say they were raped agreed to have sex and then regret it), 20 (a lot of times, women who say they were raped often led the guy on and then had regrets), and 21 (a lot of times, women who claim they were raped have emotional problems). Many also have agreement levels above 25%. These items were 4 (if a woman acts like a slut, eventually she is going to get into trouble), 6 (if a woman initiates kissing or hooking up, she should not be surprised if a guy assumes she wants to have sex), 7 (when guys rape, it is usually because of their strong desire for sex), 8 (guys don't usually intend to force sex on a woman, but sometimes they get too sexually carried away), 19 (rape accusations are often used as a way of getting back at guys), and 22 (women who are caught cheating on their boyfriends sometimes claim it was rape).

Nine of the items have strong disagreement levels above 65% of the national student sample. These are items 1 (if a woman is raped while drunk, she is at least somewhat responsible for letting things get out of hand), 2 (when women go to parties wearing slutty clothes, they are asking for trouble), 3 (if a woman goes to a room alone with a guy at a party, it is her own fault if she is raped), 5 (if a woman

TABLE 5.4 Study 13 Spring 2020 Survey items responses, percentages and means

Scale	Items – Rape Myth Statements	SA	A	D	SD	Mean
She asked for it	1 If a woman is raped while drunk, she is at least somewhat responsible for letting things get out of hand.	1.3	7.0	23.9	67.8	3.58
	2 When women go to parties wearing slutty clothes, they are asking for trouble.	1.3	9.3	20.9	68.6	3.57
	3 If a woman goes to a room alone with a guy at a party, it is her own fault if she is raped.	1.0	3.8	22.4	72.8	3.67
	4 If a woman acts like a slut, eventually she is going to get into trouble.	3.8	25.9	27.6	42.7	3.09
	5 If a woman goes to a room alone with a guy at a party, it is her own fault if she is raped.	1.0	5.5	25.4	68.0	3.60
	6 If a woman initiates kissing or hooking up, she should not be surprised if a guy assumes she wants to have sex.	5.0	28.6	29.4	36.9	2.98
He didn't mean to	7 When guys rape, it is usually because of their strong desire for sex.	9.6	28.2	27.7	34.5	2.87
	8 Guys don't usually intend to force sex on a woman, but sometimes they get too sexually carried away.	4.8	23.6	32.7	38.9	3.06
	9 Rape happens when a guy's sex drive goes out of control.	5.5	17.1	31.2	46.1	3.18
	10 If a guy is drunk, he might rape someone unintentionally.	2.3	18.6	32.7	46.3	3.23
	11 It shouldn't be considered rape if a guy is drunk and didn't realize what he was doing.	2.0	5.5	24.4	68.1	3.59
	12 If both people are drunk, it can't be rape.	3.8	9.6	27.8	58.8	3.42
It wasn't really rape	13 If a woman doesn't physically resist sex – even if protesting verbally – it can't be considered rape.	1.8	3.8	18.9	75.5	3.68
	14 If a woman doesn't physically fight back, you can't really say it was rape.	0.5	2.5	14.3	82.7	3.79
	15 A rape probably doesn't happen if a woman doesn't have any bruises or marks.	1.0	1.0	10.3	87.7	3.85
	16 If the accused "rapist" doesn't have a weapon, you really can't call it rape.	1.0	1.3	10.6	87.2	3.84
	17 If a woman doesn't say "no" she can't claim rape.	3.0	12.1	28.0	56.9	3.39
She lied	18 A lot of times, women who say they were raped agreed to have sex and then regret it.	2.5	20.4	40.1	37.0	3.12
	19 Rape accusations are often used as a way of getting back at guys.	5.0	23.4	35.3	36.3	3.03
	20 A lot of times, women who say they were raped often led the guy on and then had regrets.	1.5	16.3	38.2	44.0	3.25
	21 A lot of times, women who claim they were raped have emotional problems.	5.8	17.4	34.8	42.1	3.13
	22 Women who are caught cheating on their boyfriends sometimes claim it was rape.	5.0	32.2	31.4	31.4	2.89

goes to a room alone with a guy at a party, it is her own fault if she is raped), 11 (it shouldn't be considered rape if a guy is drunk and didn't realize what he was doing), 13 (if a woman doesn't physically resist sex – even if protesting verbally – it can't be considered rape), 14 (if a woman doesn't physically fight back, you can't really say it was rape), 15 (a rape probably doesn't happen if a woman doesn't have any bruises or marks), and 16 (if the accused "rapist" doesn't have a weapon, you really can't call it rape).

Survey items 14 (82.7%), 15 (87.7%), and 16 (87.2%) have the highest levels of strong disagreement among the students in this sample. These three items are part of the *it wasn't really rape* scale. Additionally, item 13 held a strong disagreement level of 75.5%, whereas item 17 held 56.9% of strong disagreement and 15.1% of agreement. This is comparable to study 9 completed at my university in Spring 2019. Students do not accept the blitz rape scenario or the script that the presence of physical harm and violence equates rape but some hold onto the concept that a woman must verbally state no for it to be rape. This connects to the visions of consent presented in Chapter 4.

This study shows higher levels of agreement in single survey items from the *he didn't mean to* and *she lied* scales. Looking at Table 5.5 shows the levels of scale connect with the findings as well. The means are similar to the means from previous studies and illustrate disagreement with rape myths. Students do not generally perceive the rape myths to be true. Obviously, this is not a statement for all. The individual items show that some students do agree with rape myth statements, which leads to lower mean values of the scales. All means for the scales are above the midpoint, but *he didn't mean to* and *she lied* scales are about one standard deviation away from the midpoint. Being below the midpoint suggests that the sample on average agrees with the scales, which is not the case here.

As addressed in prior chapters, it is not an all or nothing approach we are taking. It is expected that most people do not agree with rape myths; the concern

TABLE 5.5 Study 13 Spring 2020 Survey IRMA Scale

Scale	Alpha	Possible Range	Midpoint	Actual Range	Mean (Std. Dev.)
Total rape myth scale Items 1–22	0.917	22–88	55	25–88	73.73 (10.36)
She asked for it Items 1–6	0.832	6–24	15	6–24	20.48 (3.34)
He didn't mean to Items 7–12	0.749	6–24	15	7–24	19.34 (3.45)
It wasn't rape Items 13–17	0.815	5–20	12.5	5–20	18.53 (2.24)
She lied Items 18–22	0.874	5–20	12.5	5–20	15.41 (3.52)

*Any score below midpoint marks agreement with scale.

is with those who do and the implicit biases that result in this belief. Also remember that some who state disagreement might only be doing so because they know that it is the correct answer. In our society, even though the rape culture thrives, we also hold values of rape and sexual assault being horrible actions we are not to see as good. This might be why consistently the scale of *it wasn't really rape* has some of the highest levels of disagreement on average. This generation has accepted that physical harm and use of weapons are not always part of a rape; other forms of sexual assault such as date rape or acquaintance rape occur most often. Students are informed enough about what is and is not rape but not the foundational implicit biases held in this society.

Study 13 held six scales aside from IRMA as shown in Table 5.6. The consent scale represents the comfortability a person has with verbalizing consent during all sexual behaviors, from kissing to sex. The mean is 35.45, which is 10 points below the midpoint suggesting that the students in this sample are comfortable with asking for consent or at least perceiving themselves as being strong consent seekers. Only 5.2% of students or 22 students expressed themselves as having a hard time with consent practices with means at or above 54 (this number represents agreement with the positively coded items). For the midpoint, 87% of the sample sit at or below it. This scale was correlated positively with the social desirability bias scale stating that some people were likely providing answers they thought society would be proud about. They answered in ways they thought they should versus what they really believe about consent.

Sex role measures the connection to traditional beliefs about the binary sex roles of women and men. A number higher than the midpoint demonstrates commitment to traditional sex roles such as *a woman should be a virgin when she marries,* and *a wife should never contradict her husband in public.* A lower number shows agreement with items such as *there is nothing wrong with a woman going to a*

TABLE 5.6 Study 13 Spring 2020 Survey Scales

Scale	Alpha	Possible Range	Midpoint	Actual Range	Mean (Std. Dev.)
Social Desirability Bias	0.284	10–20	15	10–20	14.43 (1.64)
Consent	0.916	18–72	45	18–72	35.45 (10.31)
Sex Role Traditions	0.739	9–36	22.5	9–30	16.67 (4.33)
Empathy	0.755	15–60	37.5	28–58	42.78 (4.94)
Sexual Conservatism	0.804	10–40	25	10–34	18.90 (4.99)
Aggression	0.893	9–36	22.5	9–36	12.01 (4.29)

bar alone. The mean of 16.67 is below the midpoints, and in fact, 90.5% of the sample disagrees with traditional sex roles as measured in this study.

Empathy scale represents whether a person is empathic with higher values in the scale suggesting higher empathy. The mean is higher than the midpoint signifying that the students in this sample have empathy. Of the students in this sample, 12.8% are below the midpoint representing them holding little empathy. About 25% of the sample hold scale values at 45 or above, which means that students have higher levels of empathy.

The sexual behavior conservatism scale measures if you believe in behaviors that are more conservative. The statements include *men have a stronger sex drive than women* and *people should not have oral sex*. A higher scale value represents beliefs of sexual conservative behaviors. The mean of 18.90 is lower than the midpoint of 25 signifying low levels of conservative beliefs about sexual behaviors. About 63% of the sample had values of 20 or less so that 2/3 of students hold sexual values that are not conservative. Only 10% of the students have beliefs above 25 illustrating a conservative attitude about sexual behaviors.

The last scale is aggression. This scale measures social aggression not physical aggression. The higher scale value represents the more social aggression the student expresses in their life. The mean is 12 which is below the midpoint of 22.5. This student sample, thus, is not very socially aggressive. Only 3.6% or 19 students held levels at 22 or above suggesting that these students have higher levels of social aggression.

This sample can be described as one that does not agree with rape myths. The students have midlevel empathy and low levels of social aggression. The students demonstrated their engagement with positive consent practices. They disavow traditional binary sex roles and sexual behavior rules. These students match figures and presumptions for this generation (Ford, 2016; 2018; Freitas, 2018; Kindlon, 2006; Phillips, 2017). This sample is building norms outside of traditional sex roles and gender constraints. This provides hope that movement can continue out of the rape culture.

Comparison of studies: A quick way to note the similarities and differences is looking at the item means across and between the studies. Studies 9, 10, and 13 used the most similar measures of IRMA and other scales and thus will be compared. Table 5.7 showcases the means of the different studies for the individual items, so you do not have to page back and view them separately. You can view the scale means in Table 5.8 that displays the independent t-tests results.

In the individual items as well as the scale, some differences exist between the studies. For individual items, study 10 holds higher means in the items than both studies 9 and 10. To concentrate on the IRMA scales, small differences are apparent in every scale, some as miniscule as 0.10 for the she asked for it scale between studies 9 and 13 or as high as 3.29 in the total rape myth scale means of studies 9 and 10. This type of visual comparison is not enough statistically as comparison is needed to determine if the differences actually matter.

TABLE 5.7 IRMA Individual Items Means for Comparison

Scale	Rape Myth Statements	Study 9 Main University Mean	Study 10 Social Media Mean	Study 13 National Universities Mean
She asked for it	1	3.53	3.71	3.58
	2	3.58	3.72	3.57
	3	3.69	3.83	3.67
	4	3.18	3.47	3.09
	5	3.56	3.63	3.60
	6	3.03	3.23	2.98
He didn't	7	2.74	3.22	2.87
mean to	8	2.94	3.35	3.06
	9	3.13	3.57	3.18
	10	3.07	3.29	3.23
	11	3.61	3.74	3.59
	12	3.45	3.66	3.42
It wasn't really	13	3.68	3.78	3.68
rape	14	3.78	3.82	3.79
	15	3.82	3.84	3.85
	16	3.85	3.86	3.84
	17	3.28	3.57	3.39
She lied	18	3.05	3.37	3.12
	19	3.04	3.46	3.03
	20	3.18	3.55	3.25
	21	3.16	3.51	3.13
	22	2.86	3.23	2.89

Independent t-tests paired were completed between each of the study combinations of the scales. National universities means versus main university means produced no significant differences between the means. Social media sample versus main university sample held a significant mean difference in all scales. Finally, social media versus national universities sample had a significant difference in all means except the scale *it wasn't rape*.

The lack of significance in the means between the main university and the national university is supportive of the hypothesis covered for this chapter and brings to light some ideas from the rest of the book. This means that the main university studied is presumably no different than the sample of universities in this book and due to rules of inference and generalizability no different than universities in general. Although the main university is small and private, the national universities are public and private, small and large, and religiously affiliated and secular. The data demonstrates that the findings could be population-based in how rape myths and thus rape culture are viewed among young adults in college.

138 University culture

TABLE 5.8 Study Comparisons through Independent T-tests of Scale Mean Differences

	Study 9 Main University		Study 13 National Universities		Independent t-test	
	M	SD	M	SD	t	df
Total rape myth	73.44	9.03	73.73	10.36	0.453	933
She asked for it	20.58	2.93	20.48	3.34	−0.487	977
He didn't mean to	18.95	2.92	19.34	3.45	1.834	960
It wasn't really rape	18.42	1.91	18.53	2.24	0.888	983
She lied	15.32	2.99	15.41	3.52	0.454	973
	Study 9 Main University		Study 10 Social Media		Independent t-test	
	M	SD	M	SD	t	df
Total rape myth	73.44	9.03	78.73	10.70	−5.197★★	647
She asked for it	20.58	2.93	21.57	3.14	−3.102★★	683
He didn't mean to	18.95	2.92	20.84	3.29	−5.872★★	670
It wasn't really rape	18.42	1.91	18.89	2.36	−2.178★	688
She lied	15.32	2.99	17.13	3.26	−5.570★★	681
	Study 10 Social Media		Study 13 National Universities		Independent t-test	
	M	SD	M	SD	t	df
Total rape myth	78.73	10.70	73.73	10.36	−4.241★★	480
She asked for it	21.57	3.14	20.48	3.34	−2.956★	496
He didn't mean to	20.84	3.29	19.34	3.45	−3.956★★	494
It wasn't really rape	18.89	2.36	18.53	2.24	−1.376	491
She lied	17.13	3.26	15.41	3.52	−4.467★★	496

★$p \leq 0.05$; ★★$p \leq 0.001$.

The social media study held different means in most of the scales when compared with the other two studies. This denotes that something about the social media sample created higher means in the scales. Looking for variances in the social media sample with the total rape scale, statuses of age and being a college student, $t(95) = -0.637$, $p < 0.526$, did not produce significant mean differences through independent t-tests. Those who were less than 25 or greater than and equal to 25 years did not hold significant differences in the total rape myth scale means, $t(96) = 1.323$, $p < 0.189$. Gender/binary did showcase that females were more likely to agree or have higher scores in the total rape myth scale, $t(93) = -2.916$, $p < 0.004$, but this is typical of the other studies. Those who held a bachelor's degree or higher in education were more likely to hold higher scores demonstrating higher agreement with the scales, $t(95) = 3.046$, $p < 0.003$. Confusingly, my other studies suggest that upperclassman have lower numbers on the scales – this is a bit puzzling. The other supposition of difference or response error is that the sample being taken from social media impacted the results because of who decided to take the survey and who did not.

Subsequently, one reason might be because only 38% of the interested sample completed the full survey. Those who completed the survey might be those who disagree more with rape myths and have stronger anti-rape opinions and identities. Also, those who completed the social media survey might be more interested in the topic and be baited to click more than samples that took it by paper (university sample) or online university connections (national sample) (Sue & Ritter, 2012). Are you willing to take a survey and waste 20 minutes of your life about sexual assault and rape myths if you do not care about the topic or do not want to be tested and have your perceptions known? If you love rape myths, are you going to let me know – probably not as a consideration of socialization, social identity, and rape culture. Regardless, larger studies using social media and other national samples must be engaged in to see these findings endure.

Other bits of university life

There is more than the rape myths and culture to see in examining a culture of campus. Most of my studies questioned students about their perceptions of safety and fear. Some studies gather information about victimization and perpetrator rates for sexual assaults and other violent crimes. Some studies asked about drinking and other drug use. Some of these tidbits might help untangle that what can we do to move forward.

Study 13 also provides a reliability check on the markers of identity in connection to the total rape myth scale as discussed originally in Chapter 4. Binary gender identity was significant in mean differences for the *total rape myth* scale, $t(372) = 4.698$, $p < 0.000$, with males scoring lower in the scale means so that females disagree more with the scale. Holding a more liberal social view was connected significantly to higher means in the *total rape myth* scale, $t(499) = -6.373$, $p < 0.000$. Agreeing with the ideals of feminism created a higher mean score in *the total rape myths*, $t(380) = -4.867$, $p < 0.000$. Being a victim of sexual assault also impacted the means of the scale, $t(377) = -3.969$, $p < 0.000$, those who were a victim held a higher mean tending to disagree with the scale more so than those who were not victims of sexual assault. Thus, the higher means and those who disagreed the most with rape myths were females who were sexual assault victims that believed in feminism and liberal ideologies.

Table 5.9 displays the results from the identity variables OLS regression analysis with the dependent variable of *total rape myth* scale. All variables were significant in the model, the model itself was significant, and the variables explain about 14.3% of the variance in the *total rape myth scale* measures. Thus, all identity variables in this study correlate with the scores found in the total myth scale, adding reliability to what was found in Chapter 4 with the main university findings and demonstrating that the main university in this study is not unique despite

140 University culture

TABLE 5.9 Regression Analysis of Identity Variables in Study 13

Variable	B	SE B	B
Gender	2.255	0.901	0.125★
Feminism Belief	4.260	1.454	0.147★
Social Liberal	−4.759	1.029	−0.231★★
Sexual Assault Victim	2.819	1.140	0.124★

$F = 15.043$★★, $r^2 = 0.143$.
★$p \leq 0.05$, ★★$p \leq 0.001$.

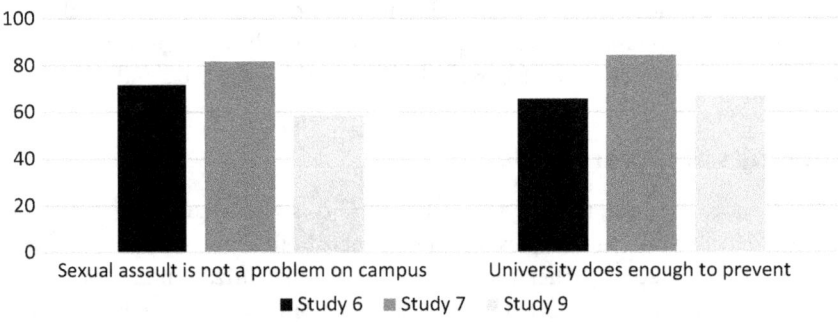

FIGURE 5.1 Perceptions of sexual assault and programming.

its standing as small, private, religious institution. Different in this study, which might be due to the larger sample size and a higher percentage of sexual assault victims, the variable of sexual assault victim remained statistically significant in the regression model and not just the independent t-tests giving this variable more weight in this sample. To reiterate, those students who identify as females that hold liberal and feminism ideals and who happen to be victims of sexual assaults disagree with the rape myths the most.

The university holds other types of information that aids in creating the culture and social group environment for the students; see Figures 5.1 and 5.2. Students on the main university surveys declared loudly that sexual assault was not a problem on the campus and that the university does enough to prevent sexual assault on campus. The majority of students, around 3/4, could not remember ever attending a program dedicated to sexual assault awareness, prevention, and education but believes the campus enough. One reason might be that students do engage in work in their dormitory halls that perhaps they did not count as programs; only a few wrote this as a program attended when asked in the surveys. It might be connected to the belief that their own campus is safe from these horrible activities and thus the university does not have to engage in too much student protective factors. During interviews, those who were victims or knew

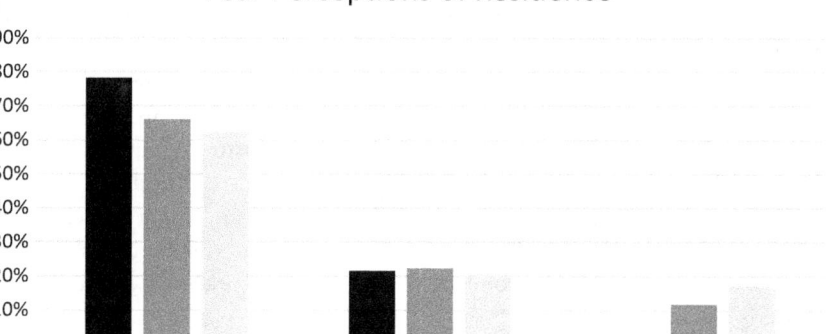

FIGURE 5.2 Perceptions of fear in participants' residences.

of student victims were more negative in view of what the campus does and can do for them. Those who know the predicament are more aware of shortcomings and needs.

As a whole, people surveyed were not fearful of their residence whether on a college campus or off, as a student or not; see Figure 5.2. There is a subtle ability of humanity to feign ignorance and not want to see the ugliness of society. Remember, only 8.3% experienced sexual assault victimhood in study 9, the social media sample in study 10 was nearly 45%, and the national university sample in study 13 experienced it at a higher rate of 28.8%. These rates suggest why the prevalence and incidences are unknown about sexual assault; survey results are often difficult to note trends of reporting. Lower numbers in study 9 could be that the sample was in a classroom setting sitting next to students with the researcher in the room. Higher numbers in sample 13 could be the autonomy of online surveys. The highest numbers in study 10 could be due to social media sample and who was interested; the topic draws more victims. Also, the majority of our population are not criminals nor victims of other types of crimes. Hence, not everyone shares victimization as part of their identity.

It is assumed that students know there is a department for victims and violence on campus as the office presents to classes and places posters around campus, including in all bathrooms. Perhaps, this and a counseling center is enough for students who do not think that sexual assault is a problem. However, there is discontent under the service, as exists in other universities detailed in other books about Stanford, Baylor, Missoula, Harvard, Duke, and countless others. The data in this chapter highlights that universities have similar backdrops, rape cultures, perceptions of rape myths, and beliefs about consent, sex, gender/sex roles, empathy, and aggression.

Earlier studies (studies, 1, 2, 3) gathered information from universities about their sexual assault and rape program initiatives. Study 1 demonstrated that universities are not collecting appropriate data about the effectiveness and outcomes of their sexual assault programs. Studies 2 and 3 suggested that students do not note the programs attended beyond leaving the program; students might like the programs, but this is not the true measure of success. Crossing of a to-do list for Title IX does not evoke change in a cultural thread. When the students who were interviewed knew something about the university programming and handling of assault cases, they presented statements that their university was not different from the others; lots of work must be done if rape culture is to change.

Knowledgeable women in the interviews spoke with me about how their university does not do enough for them as victims and survivors. Partially their beliefs stemmed from rumors and assumptions that the university does not want to do anything more than what is done or cannot do anything more than what they do or mishandles the situations of their friends and peers who do report their sexual assaults. For instance,

> I guess to put it on a scale of 1–10 10 being a huge problem, I'd probably put it at a 5, so it's a big problem. With a campus like this it should, I think, really be at 0 shouldn't have to worry about that whatsoever. Again, with the whole confidential thing that makes it a huge problem, just escalates it 1,000 times especially when you have predators on the campus. I guess it's also you can't drill it in enough, I know at the beginning of freshman year they did the whole speech on "Oh here's the [counseling center]" I think no one takes it seriously until [a sexual assault] actually happens. So I guess if they would kind of give a voice to what happens and telling people like "This is not ok" like "If you're in this situation you can get out of it" just emphasize you can get help and totally prevent the situation from happening. So, I guess making it more well known that is a problem because I know as a freshman I thought "Oh I'll never need to go and see a psychologist or the [counseling center]". So, it's like you don't think that it's possible until it actually happens.

Further, another student interviewee rightly does not believe in the statistics presented by the Clery Act and university:

> And so I mean each year there are like, maybe 3 reported? Like between sexual assault, attempted sexual assault like total under any of the categories covered in this. Three to five tops. But I do think that it is vastly under reported, I think a lot of people don't talk about it enough in part because of all the uncertainty in what the process looks like and there's a lot of distrust that anything will be done and then a lot of times it's only going to make things worse.

She is talking about the belief that reporting a rape or assault does not help anyone as there is nothing to be done; the distrust created by the assault is fed into the system of resolving it. This part of rape culture does not help the perception of the university; you are wrong no matter what you do.

Students thus felt a sense of discontentment if they are in the unfortunate group of holding knowledge of sexual assault on campus. As one student declared,

> just actually doing something about it when it happens instead of just letting it go, like there's been so much stuff in the news and like about the perpetrators just getting off because the judge didn't want to ruin their college career or they were an athlete and all this other stuff I feel kind of makes it seem like it's okay, as long as you're like a white male that's in college and an athlete, you're gonna get away with it and that's kind of [this university's] thing, it's white males that are athletes so um I feel like that definitely doesn't help here at [this university] with stuff like that.

The stereotype of white male athletes being assaulters was a large idea in the interviews as well as anecdotical stories around campus. This is a concern for so many universities and they must find ways to reckon with it. If students think only certain groups are protected on the campus, that perception hurts the university. This perception runs through this campus, even though it is not perceived as a large party school with athletes and fraternities running the show; these groups have a large enough base connected with socialized stereotypes to blame them for assaults – regardless of the size, these groups still run a lot of the parties.

For instance,

> I mean I've seen a couple posts on social media and stuff like that like from guys in like fraternities or things like that have been pretty like disgusting about like how they like talk about women on social media and like they'll have like a caption and I'll be like 'wow that's disgusting'. in terms of like campus wide like I don't I can't think of any like examples that would encourage rape culture or that like we don't do so I'm not sure like how to answer that question. do you think like could you give me like an example or like lead me to something that maybe could be applicable to another situation or campus or something like that?

When asked about programming for prevention, she responded:

> I think that the office of victim services which is new I think that's going to help a lot especially like with their healthy masculinity programs that they're implementing. I know I was talking to {a staff member] the other day and they're implementing it in like the football team and stuff like that because I think probably if anything it's probably sports and like Greek

life that may be encouraging it but again like I don't I'm not in Greek life and I'm not in sports and I don't like attend like sporting events like male sporting events so I'm not really sure what that culture is and I don't think I have a place to like say like 'oh the football team is like really bad because x y and z' so I don't really want to like draw any conclusions if I don't have evidence.

When asked about toxic masculinity, she added:

> I definitely think that like we did that documentary where we like displayed that documentary last year for wee about healthy masculinity and versus toxic masculinity and I 100% believe that masculinity can be toxic and like the way we raise men in this country is disgusting, quite frankly, and you know there's all of these, we actually have like pretty high expectations of men and like of boys as they're growing up and those expectations like stick with them for a very long time and we don't realize the implications of what we're doing psychologically to boys and to like our young men and I definitely think that like if we focused a little bit more on like teaching men and boys like emotional intelligence and empathy and things like that that would be implemented through the toxic masculinity program or the healthy masculinity program rather, I think that that would help a lot and just like educating them on like consent and like all those other things as well, I think that would help a lot.

All of this perceived power and prestige, as connected to ideas from expectation states and situated identity theories, has a silencing effect on students and disallows for reality to be seen. The rape culture wins because shame and stigma again override the truth to be told. One student discussed the need to bring a voice to sexual assault and truth to the numbers because otherwise it will never be seen as a real issue on this campus.

> But yeah and just giving a voice to the people who it has affected, I'm sure there's plenty of people who don't know and I don't know of other people who it's happened to because it's such an awful topic that nobody ever really wants to talk about it so kind of making it more conversational be like 'Yes this did happen' and kind of realize like 'Oh my gosh this has happened to so many people' and kind of relating to it and like hearing their stories. Then if you were to ever find yourself in a similar situation be like 'Oh this happened to my friend' and like people out here. Just kind of more education and more… What's it called. Cracking down on people who do.

Another student discussed the role the campus has in perpetuating the rape culture because of those who are afraid to speak up about their assaults. The campus environment itself – being small, private, upper middle class, religious – inhibits victims from speaking against their fellow students.

> we don't have a lot of diversity here, obviously. we're a very upper middle class white school and if you're not upper class you're here basically on scholarship and so I feel like here we don't' really talk about a lot of stuff like that because we don't want to believe that here in our perfect university like 'look at us with our high stats and our programs' that stuff like this actually happens to our students, so I guess that's kind of what I meant by close minded is that we just don't want to believe that bad things can happen on campus.

When asked about this mentality, she followed with,

> I think it like with us being so close minded it does help rape culture around here just because we don't talk about it so how are we supposed to know if it's happening, I feel like victims are probably too afraid to come forward and say anything and then the people that are doing it are just getting away with it and then they might do it again because they got away with it the first time and the second time, and it's just kind of a big cycle and um same with like sexual assault like you know there's definitely things that happen on this campus but nobody like reports it because they don't always know that it is considered sexual assault or sexual harassment, they just kinda figure people are joking around um and you know like I said we don't really talk about it here and so like not knowing what is considered sexual harassment or considered sexual assault I feel like is a big influence in people getting away with it.

It is hard for universities as institutions to admit that they are not protecting students to the best of their ability or engaging in difficult learning lessons surrounding cultural change. Roadblocks existed though with the perceptions of students, as not all students think that rape myths or rape culture need to be addressed (see Kipnis, 2017; Mac Donald, 2018; Paludi, 2016). Many families and students hold beliefs that universities should attend to traditional education for their career paths not for personal and societal well-being. Liberal arts is choosing a path that is filled with red tape and business needs. Universities need to attract students; if you admit you are fixing the rape culture, you have to admit you are part of it. Which university has the strength to do this first?

This type of conversation led to student interviewees discussing possible events or programming the campus can do to encourage truth around sexual assault and real prevention, which is what is needed on university campuses. One student discussed the need for consent programming but also the unwillingness of students to attend programming of this nature.

> That's a tough one, man... I don't think there is an easy answer to that. I think a lot of it has to do with educating people, but also it's very hard to reach a lot of people because short of orientation week when all of the freshmen are like required to go to like the school shooting like how to throw chairs at people video and like short of like presenting things during that there's not time where you can be like "Hey everybody let's gather to talk about consent" I mean I'm an RA (Resident Assistant) and trying to get people to come to a program on consent, and guess how well that worked out, you know? ... It's not something that people want to talk about and a lot of it I think I mean again people do it intentionally, it's not like you accidently assault somebody so even if you educate them to the moon and back, it's not saying that they are still going to want to have that power over somebody else.

This includes the discontent with programs and the disbelief that the programs will change people's actions; if people want to rape another person, they will. To a degree, this is correct; college programming is not necessarily meant to stop sexual assault, but it can limit rape myths and the impact of rape culture on perceptions of assaults and victims (Anderson & Whiston, 2005; Breitenbecher, 2000; Exner & Cummings, 2011; Foubert, Langhinrichsen-Rohling, Brasfield, & Hill, 2010; Gidycz, Orchowski, & Berkowitz, 2011; Lonsway, 1996; O'Donohue, Yeater, & Fanetti, 2003; Paludi, 2016).

It is not just programming that will aid students; it is how the campus is perceived in their responses to sexual assaults on campus. For behavior to change, students need to be within an environment of change, not just thrown information and education (Allport, Clark, & Pettigrew, 1954; Pettigrew & Tropp, 2006). A woman interviewee suggested accountability in the actions of assaulters because she did not see that happening in the assault stories they knew about.

> Definitely kicking off any predators, first of all, so yeah if anything would happen you expel them you don't allow them to come back to school and continue their education. I think and all that information should go on their public record. Right now, if you do something on campus all that it shows is that you missed a whole semester of classes, like why is that? You can come up with any story you want as to why you were kicked off. They should definitely be like "Yes, this student is a sexual assault person, he's assaulted women before" so that should on their public record. Yeah making it more well-known and just emphasizing on how to avoid and get out of that situation regardless of what the other person is saying, like you should always have some sort of escape if you ever find yourself in that situation, because I know they can be like "Oh there's no way out of this" but there's plenty of ways out of it, just kind of isolating yourself from that person.

Many universities are not viewed as being accountable; it is why books exist whistleblowing the concerns of campus and sports and fraternities. People want to see the truth to experiencing it.

Yet, students remained skeptical of anything working in this population.

> I feel like you could do some sort of program, but I don't know how effective those always are. Especially I think we talked about sexual assault in freshman orientation or something, but you don't have to go to anything after that and in reality maybe it's a bigger deal for people that are juniors and seniors because you have that habitual thing – oh I had sex with him sophomore year, but now he's still thinking I'll still have sex with him his senior year. That's a long stretch of time without people being reminded that it's both parties' type of thing. So maybe targeting something more towards old people might be effective more so. Yeah. That's my idea for you.

While another had a difficult time reckoning that sexual assault was a problem and that victim blaming should not happen. This is common and expected in a rape culture.

> I think that it's not again I don't think it's a campus problem, I have heard of these types of situations though on campus and I know that from what I've heard action has been taken which I think is good obviously for like a campus to do in something like this. I don't think really it's a problem on the campus because at the same time if an individual is accused of it… it's you… kind of while giving the victim the benefit of the doubt, they are innocent until proven guilty so it's a tricky situation. Yeah that's all I have to say I think about that.

This also is so true, people deserve due process, people deserve to be believed, and it is not the place of a university to figure this all out when they have their own interests at hand. An independent panel or investigative team that rests outside of the university, like law enforcement, might just be a better organization to figure this all out (Mac Donald, 2018; Paludi, 2016).

This is part of the reason this book exists; angered students wanted answers and were tired of turning to Title IX red tape that did not help their wounds or academic progress (Fisher, Daigle, & Cullen, 2010; Paludi 2016). Anecdotally, students in my classes seem to be in two camps – (1) unknowledgeable about sexual assaults on campus and what the campus does in connection to them or (2) knowledgeable about sexual assaults on campus and unsatisfied with what the campus does in response. Many students, outside of research, have expressed concerns over their knowledge of sexual assault processes on campus and the number of victims who have been hurt when they come forward, express their story numerous times to strangers, and then be told that there is not enough evidence for the university to do anything. The only case I know of where a person was expelled from the university was a case that had a video of the incident and he was later found guilty in criminal court. I am not stating that the university is wrong in their actions; if evidence does not exist, it does not exist. Many sexual assault cases are "he said, she said" and a university cannot investigate similarly as law enforcement and courts. Title IX might demand that the university does so, but it did not equip administrators, scholars, and staff to figure out the means to do so; this was the partial impetus for the 2020 changes to Title IX.

The first study completed called a sample of universities to determine what programming they offered students and how they complied with Title IX; it was not different from the main university. Universities understood the basic requirements of Title IX and the Clery Act; protect your students through education and report sexual misconduct in all forms (Fisher, Daigle, & Cullen, 2010; Paludi, 2016). The education was directed at freshman, athletes, and those in Greek life, mostly fraternities. It held many stereotypes about drinking, partying, walking in pairs, get home before dark, make safe friends, and do not ever be by yourself. Lots of fear in the warnings. Universities also taught about the concerns of sexual misconduct, what to do if it happens to you or a friend, and a bit about bystander intervention.

What was neglected was the assessment of effective programming. No universities measured long-term outcomes of their programs offered to freshmen, athletes, or Greek life participants. Most did not even examine the short-term impacts. This is not saying that research does not happen, but the 50 national schools we spoke with via the phone did not engage in any systematic review of their programming. Some had questionnaires students could fill out after the program to rate their perception and likability of the program, my university included. This was part of the impetus of my research and why this book exists – how can universities which house academic researchers not engage in research about these programs and their outcomes. Literature reviews showed similar trends – it is hard to find good research about the outcome and effectiveness of sexual assault and prevention programming. Sexual assault programming should be uncomfortable; students should not like it or enjoy it.

Campus Action (Paludi, 2016) declared that programming at the university level needs to include education about the individual campus and the larger university picture. It needs action plans and goal setting. It needs rigorous research initiatives set against appropriate goals. The goals should be more than lower sexual assault, as that might not happen. Outcomes include lowering rape myths, being able to openly discuss sexual assault, being able to describe rape culture and rape myths, and appreciating our own implicit biases that impact sexual assault and rape myth values and beliefs. When speaking with faculty, staff, and students, this is what was wanted. Programs of worth and substance. People need to know what they do not know and their personal ideologies before restructuring cultures. This society needs better-focused programs, not less.

Campuses also need to step outside of their implicit biases held from socialization of the rape culture and rape myths. We need to move beyond sexualization of women and victim blaming for the way they look and act. For instance, a few women in the interviews discussed new initiatives on campus that were aimed at women and the clothing they wear to student work placements. In response to whether campuses are doing anything to limit the impact of rape culture and sexualization, a woman stated,

> I don't think that it happens here, I do feel like with a lot of places besides this campus there is more of like trying to, I'll describe after, the kind of like sexualizing women because for example I heard the front desks no longer allow women to wear the tight fitting leggings.

Part of this is the regulation of women's clothing and what is professional wear. Can women wear pants? Leggings? What do their shirts have to look like? Can we see their shoulders or cleavage? What about male counterparts in clothing – can men where joggers? Tanks? Short sleeves? Tight shirts? This is the rape culture and rape myths scrounging around victim blaming; people should be professional in their work but blaming specific clothing choices might be more gendered than realized.

The other part of this comment is the idea that our university is not creating appropriate policies to help men and women transition into more positive connections to sex, relationships, and assaults. Their polices are misguided and not benefiting the general student body. What are the goals and outcomes of the policies? Why are the policies occurring? Why is women clothing being examined as too tight for sitting at a front desk, but male clothing is not being viewed as too messy? Part gendered norms and part rape culture impact the decisions – women are in charge of limiting their sexualization, while men are not charged with limiting their brains from viewing women that way. Socialization does not provide males with many choices but to view females through sexual lenses. Part of victim blaming is looking for clues in woman's wardrobes that would have turned a man sexually frustrated. This is the rape culture, limit the options of females while letting men prowl.

At the university, and presumably others similar to it – small, midwestern, private, religiously connected, students have a tough time dealing with the dichotomy knowing that sexual assaults occur on university campuses versus the safeness of their own campus. There was a difference in perceptions of fear of other places and the role of safe places you are part of and live within. Students, as well as the faculty and staff, spoke about their known safety on the campus because crime, including sexual assaults, was simply not a problem. Other schools that were bigger, where students could be more anonymous, and held larger, crazier parties connected to athletics and fraternities were less safe and students should be more fearful. It was a story of the unknown as well as not in my backyard. The interviewed women felt safe in the care taken in constructing the data collection method. The surveyed students felt safe. They did not perceive a reason to fear.

This is in direct opposition to the arguments presented in books such as *The Diversity Delusion* (Mac Donald, 2018), *Sex Matters* (Charen, 2018), *The Campus*

Rape Frenzy (Johnson & Taylor; 2017), and *Unwanted Advances* (Kipnis, 2017). These authors claimed that college students live in fear of sexual assault and that campuses have become agents of fear where women need to protect themselves against the scary strong men. These authors alleged that too much emphasis upon sexual assault brings students into a culture of fear. This does not match the studies presented herein. None of the studies suggest strong fear of their campus or residence. None of the studies show understanding and utter savvy of rape culture and rape myths. It displays concerns of not being knowledgeable enough about the world that surrounds them and the risk of sexual assault. The definitions are unclear, and sex is murky. They are young adults finding their paths and sometimes it includes pain. The campuses are not riddled with fear nor causing it to happen. Their arguments suggested that universities have little time educating students in the traditional aspects such as Shakespeare because they are too busy fighting against structural isms that simply do not exist. These fights against sexism, homophobia, racism, classism, and ableism are ill fought and poorly conceived. The data disagrees that students do not live in fear and want more education about life, culture, and society.

The female survivors discussed the safety of the campus in convoluted terms (Fisher, Daigle, & Cullen, 2010). Yes, they felt safe. Most of their assaults did not happen on campus. Yes, they knew their attacker. No, it was not necessary, while they or the attacker were students on campus. No, they did not think that the university could protect them if they spoke out about their story. No, the cops would not care or believe them. No, family would not be inclined to help them but instead ridicule them and call them a slut for letting it happen. Yes, most were in current relationships they viewed as positive. Yes, they did not view themselves as needing to take extra precautions, but many showed me pepper spray and how they held their keys when walking. Yes, they felt scared and scarred but hopeful that it would not happen again because they learned how to speak their voice.

Many students, faculty, and staff thought that the university did not do enough to prevent sexual assault (Fisher, Daigle, & Cullen, 2010; Paludi, 2016). In both sets of interviews, women wanted more education about what really happened on this campus; they wanted to hear the stories of victims and aggressors. They wanted real numbers but realized that would not happen because if they do not speak up, why would others. For instance,

> I feel like because it is kind of more of a close minded school that you know we don't really hear about it much, we don't talk about it much so people feel like they can get away with it, because it's not a topic often talked about.

Another woman acknowledged,

> Yeah. Like 'It's a problem everywhere else, but not here' and so, I mean you can't say it's like that one things fault they did like specifically mention that when people pump that out and say it's not happening on my campus,

sexual assault not at my campus, I mean it can very easily be misread as like it doesn't happen here.

Students also recognized that sexual assaults do happen but limited their scope to being within the presence of parties, alcohols, and drugs (Johnston, 2013; Keyser, 2019).

> Just that like I think a lot of the time if say just because it typically happens at parties, because that's when people are most vulnerable. You're at a party, you wake up in the morning and like "Shit happened" and if you don't have that much to go off of three's just a feeling of like "Well if I have to go talk to (head of student conduct) and spill my guts out about everything that happened but I don't know anything of what actually happened how are they going to be able to do anything, how are they going to be able to help anything, how are they able to fix anything?"

Within this statement, there is also the disbelief that anyone, especially, the university, could help with the painful aftermath. If students were drunk, and potentially underage, it provides more reason to not report what happened. If it happened in the dormitories and alcohol was consumed, which is against rules, reports will be less likely (Kaysen, Neighbors, Martell, Fossos, & Larimer, 2006; Wolitzky-Taylor et al., 2011). Women do not want to get in trouble for their choices before the assault occurred. The increase in feminine freedom has connected with more alcohol consumption but this does not excuse being assaulted (Grigoriadia, 2017; Johnston, 2013; Pagila, 2017). The pain of the rape might be less than the pain of coming forward and explaining what happened to administrators, conduct boards, police officers, friends, strangers, parents, and medical health professionals. It is hard to breach the belief that no one can help, which is part of the values and beliefs learned through the rape culture.

The rape culture not only allows people to feel safe as they blame the victim for various actions that led to a rape or sexual assault; it also connects to a culture where people do not have to believe accusers on campus. Even though these are fellow students and peers on a small campus, the inherent disbelief was present in the interviews,

> in general I also think that it's being less than normalized like people are coming out more, you know like on the news and stuff. People are describing their experiences, again it's only fair to give them the benefit of the doubt but I don't… yeah I don't think that there's like a perpetual rape culture on this campus.

This statement renounces the rape culture while supporting the rape culture. The problem is that people link rape culture to the prevalence and incidences of rape and not the values and beliefs that predispose us to misunderstanding sexual assaults. It is true that more people are coming out about their attacks; it is in the media more often than in the past; it is something our society is paying more attention to. Attention does not mean fixing or caring. Movements that do not bring action are not enough (Fileborn & Loney-Howes, 2019); it is time to carry on the power of #metoo and similar movements to create lasting change.

Another example of what occurs on this campus and in case you still are in disbelief of the existence of rape culture,

> I've seen a couple posts on social media and stuff like that like from guys in like fraternities or things like that have been pretty like disgusting about like how they like talk about women on social media and like they'll have like a caption and I'll be like 'wow that's disgusting'. In terms of like campus wide like I don't, I can't think of any examples that would encourage rape culture.

This woman again was supporting the existence of the rape culture and then dismissing it. Rape culture develops in the forms of locker room talk, boys will be boys, they are just talking, or other idealized statements that connect to the "disgusting things" the guys in the fraternities were stating on social media. They were describing women they had sexual encounters with and the things they would do to them next time. Some of this is banter and the creation of a presence and identity on social media, typical in this age group (cite). The stating of volatile ideas against women is the privilege of men in a rape culture.

This banter is supported in *Beer Campus* (Sperber, 2000), *True Gentlemen* (Hechinger, 2017), and *Blurred Lines Rethinking Sex* (Grigoriadis, 2017). This campus is nothing out of the ordinary for young adults in this age group, but typical and normed can still be wrong and unhealthy. In Vanasco's (2019) experiences with sexual assault, the men in the stories were likable to various degrees. We have to stop looking for the scary stranger with a deformed face lurking behind bushes with ropes and teethers; this is not all rapes. Date or acquaintance or party rapes happen in trusted environments with recognizable people. Remember all the women raped and assaulted by people they knew either in a relationship, friendship, or through a dating app. These were not prowling strangers. Assaulters use their familiarity and trust to hurt others (Adams-Curtis & Forbes, 2004; Armstrong, Hamilton, & Sweeney, 2006; Brownmiller, 1975; Gay, 2018; Vanasco, 2019); this might be one of the hardest things to wrap heads around in the rape culture.

Part of these truths are learned through college experiences. In surveys, upper-level students were more likely to agree with rape myths and have higher numbers in the scales. It was collaborated with interviewees who stated as freshman that they felt safer and secure on campus. Through personal and vicarious experiences during college, students saw the way college life is harmful and painful. Women who were assaulted or had friends who were assaulted learned the unforgiving nature of the rape culture. Women in the focus group video shared the shame and stigma provided by their peers when they dared to come forward and tell their assault stories. Ignorance is easier to live with and part of the reason the rape culture is so hard to accept.

Summary

This chapter highlights the rationale that the university of study is not alone in its tendencies to disagree with rape myths and feel safe on campuses. The sample aligned with the presumed populations. These findings develop the reliability of the IRMA scales and potentially the validity especially through of construct and criterion validities. The scale measures react in a predictable manner for different samples. Essentially, this means that we can trust the results of the studies as ranked against themselves.

Although there is disagreement among theorists and authors about the role rape culture and rape myths have in social life and the university, this study reaffirms our social need to limit their impact. I ponder if those who are against the worth and reality of the existence rape culture because of the existence and subtly of rape myths. If the rape culture tells us to not care about sexual assault especially if it is not "real" rape. If the rape culture encourages victims to remain silent even in the presence of "real" rape. If the rape culture tells us that the rape culture is not real. If the rape culture tells women to be quiet, be nice, do not cause a stir, and let men rule – how is this managed? If those women who do speak out are faced with ridicule and shame, do you want to follow suit. Thus, why would we want to believe it exists.

As constructed and measured by IRMA, rape myths exist. As developed over decades of research, rape myths exist. The ideas connected to women lying about sexual assaults, that men did not mean to assault a woman, that the rape or assault did not even happen, and that the woman asked for the assault to happen because she is a slut all are alive. The majority might disagree with the statements but not everyone. Students, faculty, and staff still are able to select neural, agree, or strongly agree in response to the IRMA scale items. Social desirability scales suggest that the numbers of agreement might even be higher that was found in these surveys. People are willing to agree especially with the beliefs that women lie about assaults and that he did not mean to assault her. What does this state about the rape culture – that it exists.

Remember the rape culture is not saying that society and culture is an industrious factory pumping out rapists on an assembly line. Rape culture states that we are unaware of the reality of sexual assault, we trivialize sexual assault, we pretend that rape myths do not exist while believing them, and we do not acknowledge what this all means for society. Rape culture at its most basic form is the values and beliefs that allow for rape myths to survive alongside patriarchy, sexism, and misogyny. Is it shocking that those who disavow rape culture also do not perceive systemic sexism being a problem any longer; it was a thing of the past; we are beyond that now. But we are not.

Universities should be aware of the resources and time spent on the messaging and programming of sexual assault and rape culture. By making programming through typical freshman orientation-type PowerPoint presentations limits the effectiveness. It demonstrates the bureaucratic nature of necessity in the programming. Students must attend this rote lecture that checks off an item on a to-do list not made by the students in attendance. The university is checking off boxes of requirements created for them by the government that allows federal funding to be obtained. It is on a topic that people are trained to not discuss or talk openly about, and this is further illustrated by the routine boring lectures over PowerPoint given in person or through an online program. What is missing from all of this is heart.

For programming to work, it has to be connected to ideas that are practical, necessary, and novel. We need programming that people want to attend because they want to make a change. For this to happen, people first must be woken to the concerns and their involvement in them. This is not going to be everybody; there is a place for mandated programming but there is also a need to programming that is effective in altering beliefs and make people want to change our society. Universities have power and structure; it is their role to teach the classics while educating for the future. This is not a political cry but one for equity and compassion toward others and us. By limiting the role of rape culture, we can improve lives of not just women, but the men held back by gender-normal and traditional social identity constructions.

References

Adams-Curtis, L. E., & Forbes, G. B. (2004). College women's experiences of sexual coercion: A review of cultural, perpetrator, victim, and situational variables. *Trauma, Violence, & Abuse, 5*, 91–122.

Allport, G. W., Clark, K., & Pettigrew, T. (1954). *The nature of prejudice.* Perseus Books Publishers.

Anderson, L. A., & Whiston, S. C. (2005). Sexual assault education programs: A meta-analytic examination of their effectiveness. *Psychology of Women Quarterly, 29*(4), 374–388.

Armstrong, E. A., Hamilton, L., & Sweeney, B. (2006). Sexual assault on campus: A multilevel, integrative approach to party rape. *Social Problems, 53*, 483–499.

Berg, N. (2005). *Non-response bias* (No. 26373). University Library of Munich, Germany.

Breitenbecher, K. H. (2000). Sexual assault on college campuses: Is an ounce of prevention enough?. *Applied and Preventive Psychology, 9*(1), 23–52.

Brownmiller, S. (1975). *Against our will.* Fawcett.

Charen, M. (2018). *Sex matters.* Crown Forum.

Dillman, D. A., Smyth, J. D., & Christian, L. M. (2014). *Internet, phone, mail, and mixed-mode surveys: The tailored design method.* John Wiley & Sons.

Exner, D., & Cummings, N. (2011). Implications for sexual assault prevention: College students as prosocial bystanders. *Journal of American College Health, 59*(7), 655–657.

Fileborn, B., & Loney-Howes, R. (Eds.). (2019). *#MeToo and the politics of social change.* Springer Nature.

Fisher, B. S., Daigle, L. E., & Cullen, F. T. (2010). *Unsafe in the Ivory Tower*. Sage Publications.
Ford, C. (2018). *Boys will be boys: Power, patriarchy, and toxic masculinity*. Oneworld.
Ford, C. (2016). *Fight like a girl*. Oneworld.
Foubert, J. D., Langhinrichsen-Rohling, J., Brasfield, H., & Hill, B. (2010). Effects of a rape awareness program on college women: Increasing bystander efficacy and willingness to intervene. *Journal of Community Psychology, 38*(7), 813–827.
Freitas, D. (2018). *Consent on campus: A manifesto*. Oxford.
Gay, R. (Ed.). (2018). *Not that bad: Dispatches from rape culture*. Harper Perennial.
Gidycz, C. A., Orchowski, L. M., & Berkowitz, A. D. (2011). Preventing sexual aggression among college men: An evaluation of a social norms and bystander intervention program. *Violence against Women, 17*(6), 720–742.
Grigoriadis, V. (2017). *Blurred lines: Rethinking sex, power, and consent on campus*. Houghton Mifflin Harcourt.
Hechinger, J. (2017). *True gentlemen*. Public Affairs.
Johnson, K. C., & Taylor Jr., S. (2017). *The campus rape frenzy: The attack on due process at America's universities*. Encounter Books.
Johnston, A. D. (2013). *Drink*. Harper Wave.
Kaysen, D., Neighbors, C., Martell, J., Fossos, N., & Larimer, M. E. (2006). Incapacitated rape and alcohol use: A prospective analysis. *Addictive Behaviors, 31*, 1820–1832.
Keyser, A. J. (2019). *No more excuses*. Twenty-First Century Books.
Kindlon, D. (2006). *Alpha girls: Understanding the new American girl and how she is changing the world*. Rodale.
Kipnis, L. (2017). *Unwanted advances*. Harper Collins.
Lonsway, K. A. (1996). Preventing acquaintance rape through education what do we know. *Psychology of Women Quarterly, 20*(2), 229–265.
Mac Donald, H. (2018). *The diversity delusion: How race and gender pandering corrupt the university and undermine our culture*. St. Martin's Griffin.
O'Donohue, W., Yeater, E. A., & Fanetti, M. (2003). Rape prevention with college males: The roles of rape myth acceptance, victim empathy, and outcome expectancies. *Journal of Interpersonal Violence, 18*(5), 513–531.
Paludi, M. A. (Ed.). (2016). *Campus action against sexual assault: Needs, policies, procedures, and training programs*. Abc-clio.
Pettigrew, T. F., & Tropp, L. R. (2006). A meta-analytic test of intergroup contact theory. *Journal of Personality and Social Psychology, 90*(5), 751–783. https://doi.org/10.1037/0022-3514.90.5.751
Phillips, N. D. (2017). *Beyond blurred lines*. Rowman & Littlefield.
Sperber, M. (2000). *Beer and circus*. Henry Holt and Company.
Sue, V. M., & Ritter, L. A. (2012). *Conducting online surveys*. Sage.
Vanasco, J. (2019). *Things we didn't talk about when I was a girl: A memoir*. Tin House Books.
Wolitzky-Taylor, K. B., Resnick, H. S., Amstadter, A. B., McCauley, J. L., Ruggiero, K. J., & Kilpatrick, D. G. (2011). Reporting rape in a national sample of college women. *Journal of American College Health, 59*, 582–587.

CONCLUSION

To gain anything from this book, I hope it is this – rape culture is alive and thriving in our communities. It provides the impetus to presuming that women are weaker than men and women can be controlled. This control might come from sexual assault and rape, but it exists in many other forms such as domestic violence both physical and verbal, gaslighting, workplace challenges such as glass ceilings and sexual harassment, and the simple child playground of not letting girls play with the boys. Many of these elements are part of the rape culture as it allows patriarchal rhetoric to thrive in misogynistic manners. These actions might seem benign and far from rape, but the behaviors come from similarly placed values, beliefs, and attitudes about the women's role and place in society and culture.

A larger goal of this book is that once rape culture is accepted as still thriving, we must get to a point at appreciating the end game. Reducing paradigm of rape culture in itself is enough. Think about this for a spell; most research and many books discuss that the end effort is reduction of sexual assaults and rape. This is a superb goal, but it discredits the outstretched arms of rape culture and the force it has on so many other elements of life. It makes rape culture appear not as important because the goal is to stop rape. Many who discredit the rape culture do so because most people are not rapists and some (very, very few) women do lie about rapes. Those who do come forward to report their rapes and assaults are too few. These declarations become enough justification to think that rape culture is a farce. Those arguments are weak.

For instance, *Diversity Delusion* (Mac Donald, 2018) presumed that rape culture is a misnomer that does not exist. The vast amounts of research about sexual assault and rape myths that coincide with theories of rape culture are wrong, ignorant, and discount realities of human existence. She claimed the dark figure of rape that exits due to a lack of reporting is because women know that their stories are not rape. The lack of evidence in sexual assault cases is simply because the women were not raped and not because physical evidence often does not exist. Mac Donald believed that women who do not come forward to report their assaults are not by-products of rape culture but rather liars who do not appreciate the true definition of rape. The author speaks much to the blitz rape scenario and blames women for falling victim to feministic goals of equity in the games of drinking, parties, and hookups. She uses incorrect wording about rates of sexual assault by claiming it is rates of rape and fails to clarify the distinction between the two terms. In short, the rape culture does not exist, and the gravity expressed about sexual assault is ill worn and unnecessary; universities have more vital educational goals to attain.

Similarly, *The Campus Rape Frenzy* (Johnson & Taylor, 2017) proclaimed that universities are too preoccupied with rape and sexual assault that other aspects of its duties become ignored. Universities are unable to provide students appropriate programming that impacts rape myths, rape culture, and sexual assault. Programs out of Title IX and the Clery Act receive much focus from administration but then fail to meet goals. However, the book states that these should not be goals of a university as the sexual assault statistics are a farce, many women lie about victimhood, many men lives become ruined out of false claims, and due process cannot be secured by university processes. Administrators and students have been spellbound by the current climate of rape culture, which is inherently false and does not exist.

Others (Bevacqua, 2000; Charen, 2018; Grigoriadis, 2017) dismantled the university infrastructure about Title IX, Clery Act, and the need for victim programming on campuses. The author proposed that too much effort is placed on the scariness of campus by focusing on sexual assaults, rapes, #metoo, rape myths, and rape culture. Feminism is ruined through bureaucracy found at the university. Universities were ill-equipped at aiding students with the emotional, social, and educational impacts of sexual assault; the university should spend its time meeting its true goal of education in the classics and science. Administrators need to focus away from the fear mongering of rape as the rape culture only creates concerns and makes false claims of rape increase due to female sexual desires while partying and hooking up.

Another line of books argue that the rape culture itself is killing true feminism (Murphy, 2004; Pagila, 2017). These argued that too much research, time, money, and concern are brought to the topic of sexual assault and not sexual freedom. That by teaching to fear rape and sexual assault, females are unable to recognize their sexual power and use desire positively. This fear turns sex scary when feminism is supposed to allow women to harness their sexual freedoms. The authors presumed that feminism is moved backward when women are made aware of their social placement in social hierarchies of roles and status. That by focusing on the power taken historically, women cannot move forward and beyond. In essence, it is time to stop discussing rape culture as it is ruining the positive vibe of womanhood.

Another argument runs against the #metoo movement by claiming that it is founded on lies and convenient half-truths (Casey, 2020). Men are fine and toxic masculinity is a farce. Women want to be controlled in households and earn freedoms elsewhere. Men and women have different abilities, and this is why equity cannot be found. Power cannot be equal; men have the skills and knowledge to be leaders and women lack the ability. That is, women could be powerful; they would not be assaulted because they would have the fight to leave. Also, that #metoo was a bunch of whiny women who need to deal with the complexities of the business world if equity it desired. Women cannot expect rules to change just because they are part of the environment.

Those who fight against the rape culture seem to carry a similar thread – there are not enough rapists for us to be concerned and not enough real victims for us to worry with. Think about this for a moment – close the book – hold the page – and really think. What is a real victim? What is real sexual assault? What is real rape? Is it the legal definition? A personal perception of an event? Does it matter if someone is convicted? Does it destroy the victim's life any less? (Read *Know my Name*, Miller, 2019 for a personal account to find your own compelling answers.)

Rape myths invade our mental processes. Sexual assaults and rape are negative life-changing moments. Rape is rape regardless of how physically painful it was. Sexual assault is negative even if it is viewed not as serious as rape. Sexual coercion, sexual harassment, domestic violence, patriarchy, and misogyny are all factors of lifelong socialization which impact the core foundational ideas of ourselves, our identities, our personalities, and our systems or institutions.

Those who advocate for the rape culture's existence are not proclaiming that the rape culture turns all into rapists. It instead does something more nuanced and subtle to the whole of a society and culture. It allows individuals and groups to accept one of the highest disregards of human sanctity, the act of taking sex, as not important. Rape and sexual assault do not matter. It does not matter because she asked for it. It does not matter because it was not really rape. It does not matter because she lied about it. It does not matter because he did not mean to do it. It does not matter because it simply does not matter.

The rape culture suppositions need to go as rape and assault do matter. It is time to stop the victim blaming. If someone has the strength and fortitude to tell their story of abuse or assault, how do we react? We as a society are aghast when someone yells rape, when and if it fits into the script of forcible, harmful rape by a stranger, we believe. With any other account, we become angered with the victim that she dare tell her story. With each additional compelling story, we must find a way to reexamine our conceptualization of sexual assault. It is on us to lift this veil of thinking that the rape culture only leads to rape. The rape culture leads to so much more pain than rape itself can unfold; the naysayers of rape culture's existence must become woke.

Consequently, fighting against and limiting the power of rape culture is the end goal. Limiting the train of thought that dismantles people into things and turns sex into power is enough. The current paradigm of rape culture shouts that women are submissive in all aspects of life and need to be coerced into having sex. Women are conquests and not seen powerful autonomous beings outside of their connection to men. This paradigm must go.

As Kuhn (2012) elaborated in his book about paradigms, worlds change and new order is found, we cannot hold onto thought systems that no longer serve communities. For instance, the world is round and rotates around the sun. This was not always the normed belief. Our patterns and presumptions must change as life evolves and we gain scientific evidence that the current paradigm is wrong and hurtful. This book took care in delivering news about how rape culture is destroying us all and creating identities that are not mentally healthy.

Dismantling rape culture would allow the works of feminism and the women's right movement to come into full existence. Granted, this means different ideals for some than for others as it depends on what type of feminist you are. However, let us just sink into a moment of reflecting upon equity. Even this thought that women can be on a level field with all other women, men, and non-binary genders becomes scary. Fear often is the setback of paradigm shifts. It is not easy to look at a culture and the normed way of being and say it is time for alterations as we are doing something wrong. A huge something – we are placing blame on those who do not hold power simply to maintain the status quo of power.

Paradigm shifts transform societies and cultures into new creations where answers are unknown and full pictures of what it will be cannot be developed. Paradigm shifts allow people to socially construct our new reality. This unknown is difficult and takes time to achieve (there are still people who believe that the earth is flat). Theories have described this notion of not holding norms in social situations and the sense of anomie and doom that follows. Crime is often seen as a result of this loss of norms and social control, including rape in social learning theory (Akers, 1973; Akers & Jensen, 2011), social disorganization theory (Kubrin & Weitzer, 2003; Sampson & Groves, 1989; Shaw & McKay, 1942); general strain theory (Agnew, 2005; Agnew & White, 1992), and collective efficacy (Durkheim, 1973; Sampson, 2006). When we do not know what to expect or do not think people care, trouble flourishes. However, trouble can be good.

Paradigm shifts are active; we are a society and culture cannot sit idle and wait for it to happen. Women's right to vote was not easily won by suffragists, Blacks right to attend equal and not separate schools was a battleground, marriage equity laws were fought for, and today in our society, the Black Lives Matter movement is not smooth and easy going. Paradigms shake the foundational beliefs encoded in our socialization. The implicit biases that speak young is better than old, healthy is better than sick, men are better than women, white is better than Black, and rich is better than poor are not often seen, understood, and fought against. When people become woke, it is a deliberate process on the individual's educational path to see the turmoil of groups. Ending rape myths and rape culture will be no different especially since it is imbedded in so many of the -isms this culture holds dear.

The data in this book demonstrated that when people attend programs, students do not remember the educational value or even attending. Rape myths disagreed with less and as lower scores by senior and junior students. Interviewees continued to claim how the university cannot meet the needs of victims on a campus; there are too many rules to support all students in the fact-finding process. Thus, some presumptions about the worth of university programming to move students' perceptions of rape culture are appropriate. The university is still learning how to use programming and help develop more positive ideologies of equity and fairness.

For instance, rape myths might be altered by specific types of programs such as bystander intervention but when people are in college, this creates short-term changes in attitudes that rarely last beyond the start of the next semester (Burn, 2008; Coker et al., 2011; Exner & Cummings, 2011; Foubert, Langhinrichsen-Rohling, Brasfield, & Hill, 2010). Even when athletes and those in Greek life engage in more programming as forced by Title IX, the messages eventually become background noise against foundational socialization of youth that creates the original support for rape myths and rape culture (Anderson & Whiston, 2005; Breitenbecher, 2000; Lonsway, 1996; Lonsway & Kothari, 2000). Colleges appear not to be the best place to make the longstanding changes, but it can plant seeds to alter ideals of patriarchy, feminism, and power.

Many so-called troublemakers, those women and men who spend their lives trying to make our world better and stronger, have said similar things to the quotation below, but I turn to Ruth Bader Ginsberg who observed, "real change, enduring change, happens one step at a time." Paradigms cannot be crushed in a day, a week, or even a year. Seeds must take root to build the beautiful trees of enlightenment. Enough people must think that the change is valid and truthful to turn it into their reality. Reality is shaped by values, norms, and beliefs of culture. Longstanding views are not conquered easily; disagreements must occur. People must be willing to fight for and engage in the new paradigm. These same people must be ready for the backlash that comes with fighting against norms. Change can occur only at the pace enough people are willing to accept it. People need to be willing to chip away at rape culture's hold, so we can have enduring change; we all deserve it. Trouble must be created.

Women have been trying to claw their way to equity and to be noticed for their strengths and abilities. Traditional sex roles place people into typologies hurting the potential of all. Another tidbit by RBG provides advice on why changes are important: "a gender line… helps to keep women not on a pedestal, but in a cage." Rape culture is a vestige of the lines drawn in the sand between the duties of a woman and the privileged life of a man. It is not about chivalry and protecting the delicate nature of women. Rape culture continues to perpetuate the dominance of sex roles based in binary views of gender. This is a cultural ramification of patriarchy and misogyny; women are not equal, and men hold privilege. These are social truths. Women are not to speak about the negative actions of men such as rape or else they deserve the outcome of telling, shame, and stigma. Women still are in a cage.

Social identities still hold on to the fabric of decision making and viewing people in the social world and groups around us. Chivalry and the placing of women was a result of women being less than men; the weaker, more emotional, less intelligent sex. Rape culture thrives on this foundation of culture and society. Women would be raped less in a world where men thought their actions were truly wrong and where rape was not trivialized. If something is not that big of a deal – if sexual conquests are a way to obtain power and prestige – if women are not supposed to let their sexual beings thrive – what is the result? Pain. Suffering. Callousness. It is the time to break out of the cage.

Similar to arguments in *The Campus Rape Frenzy* (Johnson & Taylor, 2017), Title IX and the bureaucratic decisions made by universities are not helpful. They waste resources and build resentment against students and administrators. Both sides perceive the other as not being responsible and caring for each social group. Students have a negative view of administrators and the university in being able to take care of sexual assaults responsibly and firmly. The programs, that were not even remembered by students, are useless in combating rape myths, rape culture, and educating students about the processes of how to report rape and who is a mandatory reporter.

Faculty, staff, and students want a means of education to gain knowledge and skills in understanding the rates of sexual assault and rapes on the campus. These invested partners want appropriate programs to know what to do on their campus and how to solve the problem. The issue is that the programming available to students, Greeks, and athletes is inadequate to create longstanding changes (Johnson & Taylor, 2017; Mac Donald, 2018; Paludi, 2016). A program that lasts an hour or given through a mandatory PowerPoint or signs displayed on campus is not enough to combat lifelong socialization of the rape culture. The focus is not to end rape and sexual assault but to limit the authority of rape myths and bring to surface implicit biases. You cannot do that in short-term programs.

Programs must be created thoughtfully and given over time (Paludi, 2016). It must be an environment fostered by the university, its actors, and students. People must buy into the necessary change and the tasks needed for change. Similar to the ideas of affirmative action and diversity, if people do not want to admit to their own biases and need for change, the university as a system cannot do much.

One effective strategy would be a freshman seminar and other programming throughout their university careers. An even better strategy would be to start this in high school or middle school or elementary school. However, to change the tide of beliefs, we need to start with those who will raise the next generation. We need to use programming that does not solely focus on rape myth busting but the creation of attitudes that support diversity, inclusion, and equity.

Men hold privilege to not worry about sexual assault in the same manner women do. Do you lock doors in neighborhoods that look downtrodden? Do you attend late night gatherings in sketchy areas? Do you drive in neighborhoods where residents do not look like you in fear of being pulled over? Do you hold your keys between fingers when walking to your car or apartment? We learn protective factors based on our social identities of sex, gender, wealth, race, ethnicity, sexual orientation, age, and ability.

Programs to reverse rape myths must adhere to these cultural and social group norms, values, beliefs, and paradigms (Paludi, 2016). There is a reason bystander intervention groups such as Green Dot work better than others; its taught by peers with a mindset for what works for college students (Black, Weisz, Coats, & Patterson, 2000; Burn, 2008; Coker et al., 2011). To limit the power of rape myths and rape culture, we need to view it through the eyes of those in the group; think social identity and expectation states theories. We also need to be cognizant of who is teaching the material. A room full of women students taught by a man will not be as well received; what does he have to share about being a woman taught to fear him and rape?

This is why we lump together athletes in learning experiences about sexual assault with their coaches. The players need to see the investment made by coaches to believe that this is something to be mindful about and to learn (Berkowitz, 1994; Burnett, 2009; Cantor, et al. 2015; Choate, 2003; Jaime et al., 2015). A professor or administrator will not be received the same way; social identities do not allow it. There is a subconscious gruffness to outsiders or those in different hierarchies. A coach is different than a professor and different from an administrator; our socialization ensures that we act differently according to the social identities and expectations of the group. Locker room talk belongs in the locker room (if even there) not in a classroom or the president's office. If you want to get to the nitty gritty of these topics for learning and exploration, you need to pay attention to whom you are speaking to and who you are conversing with.

For instance, my first interviews were conducted by students of students. I believed students would be more willing to discuss the campus and their fears or safety to other students who shared the same rank in hierarchies. I thought the students would be calmer and able to tell their truths. Even though I was in the room, the students seemed to often forget I was there, and the interviews provided valuable data about perceptions. Yet, students in the second interview shared their sexual assault stories with me, a female professor, researcher, and academic, in confidence without much hesitation. To me, the difference is in the stories being shared; the more personal story would not be so easily told to students as there is less ability to ensure confidence and trust necessary in interviews. The same holds true for programming; the director speaks to the level of education, knowledge, respect, and other attributes. The goals and format need to be considered.

We cannot change the course of culture in a day as we could not simply land on the moon because of a desire. Skills and knowledge need to be built. Ideas need to crash and burn. Mistakes need to be made and learned from and made again. This is the process. Society needs to hold onto the ride as well as be active and able participants in forming the ride. Shifts of culture take risk and hardships.

It takes thick skin and work. People will not want to be on the ride and perhaps try to dismantle it from its very core. This is why #metoo was met with mockery and anger – it is the fear of change. It has been time for women to move forward out of the cage, but it is time for men to move with them. It is time to broaden gender lines and move into identities of love, empathy, and compassion. We need to trust one another, so we can become ourselves as an individual and as a society. It is time to disavow the rape myths and crush the rape culture. Freedom is there, lurking in the shadows; we have to be brave enough to fight through the dark.

References

Agnew, R. (2005). *Pressured into crime: An overview of general strain theory*. Oxford.
Agnew, R., & White, H. R. (1992). An empirical test of general strain theory. *Criminology, 30*, 475–500.
Akers, R. L. (1973). *Deviant behaviors: A social learning approach*. Wadsworth.
Akers, R. L., & Jensen, G. F. (Eds.). (2011). *Social learning theory and the explanation of crime* (Vol. 1). Transaction Publishers.
Anderson, L. A., & Whiston, S. C. (2005). Sexual assault education programs: A meta-analytic examination of their effectiveness. *Psychology of Women Quarterly, 29*, 374–388. doi:10.1111/j.1471-6402.2005.00237.x
Berkowitz, A. D. (1994). The role of coaches in rape prevention programs for athletes. *Rape, 101*, 61–65.
Bevacqua, M. (2000). *Rape on the public agenda*. Northeastern University Press.
Black, B., Weisz, A., Coats, S., & Patterson, D. (2000). Evaluating a psychoeducational sexual assault prevention program incorporating theatrical presentation, peer education, and social work. *Research on Social Work Practice, 10*, 589–606.
Breitenbecher, K. H. (2000). Sexual assault on college campuses: Is an ounce of prevention enough? *Applied and Preventive Psychology, 9*, 23–52. doi:10.1016/s0962-1849(05)80036-8
Burn, S. M. (2008). A situational model of sexual assault prevention through bystander intervention. *Sex Roles, 60*, 779–792. doi:10.1007/s11199-008-9581-5
Burnett, A. (2009). Communicating/muting date rape: A co-cultural theoretical analysis of communication factors related to rape culture on a college campus. *Journal of Applied Communication Research, 37*, 465–485.
Cantor, D., Fisher, B., Chibnall, S. H., Townsend, R., Lee, H., Thomas, G., et al. (2015). *Report on the AAU campus climate survey on sexual assault and sexual misconduct*. The Association of American Universities, Westat.
Casey, G. (2020). *After# MeToo: Feminism, Patriarchy, Toxic Masculinity and Sundry Cultural Delights*. Societas.
Charen, M. (2018). *Sex matters*. Crown Forum.
Choate, L. H. (2003). Sexual assault prevention programs for college men: An exploratory evaluation of the men against violence model. *Journal of College Counseling, 6*, 166–176. doi:10.1002/j.2161-1882.2003.tb00237.x
Coker, A. L., Fisher, B. S., Swan, S. S., Williams, C. M., Clear, E. R., & Bush, H. M. (2011). Multi-year evaluation of "green dot" bystander intervention on college campuses. *American Journal of Preventive Medicine, 50*, 295–302. doi: 10.1037/e529382014-080
Durkheim, E. (1973). *Morality and society*. University of Chicago Press.

Exner, D., & Cummings, N. (2011). Implications for sexual assault prevention: College students as prosocial bystanders. *Journal of American College Health, 59*, 655–657. doi: 10.1080/07448481.2010.515633

Foubert, J. D., Langhinrichsen-Rohling, J., Brasfield, H., & Hill, B. (2010). Effects of a rape awareness program on college women: Increasing bystander efficacy and willingness to intervene. *Journal of Community Psychology, 38*, 813–827. doi:10.1002/jcop.20397

Grigoriadis, V. (2017). *Blurred lines: Rethinking sex, power, & consent on campus*. Houghton Mifflin Harcourt Publishing.

Jaime, M. C. D., McCauley, H. L., Tancredi, D. J., Nettiksimmons, J., Decker, M. R., Silverman, J. G., ... & Miller, E. (2015). Athletic coaches as violence prevention advocates. *Journal of Interpersonal Violence, 30*(7), 1090–1111.

Johnson, K. C., & Taylor Jr., S. (2017). *The campus rape frenzy: The attack on due process at America's universities*. Encounter Books.

Kubrin, C. E., & Weitzer, R. (2003). New directions in social disorganization theory. *Journal of Research in Crime and Delinquency, 40*, 374–402.

Kuhn, T. S. (2012). *The structure of scientific revolutions*. University of Chicago press.

Lonsway, K. A. (1996). Preventing acquaintance rape through education: What do we know. *Psychology of Women Quarterly, 20*, 229–265. doi:10.1111/j.1471-6402.1996.tb00469.x

Lonsway, K. A., & Kothari, C. (2000). First year campus acquaintance rape education: Evaluating the impact of a mandatory intervention. *Psychology of Women Quarterly, 24*, 220–232. doi:10.1111/j.1471-6402.2000.tb00203.x

Mac Donald, H. (2018). *The diversity delusion: How race and gender pandering corrupt the university and undermine our culture*. St. Martin's Griffin.

Miller, C. (2019). *Know my name*. Viking Press.

Murphy, P. F. (Ed.). (2004). *Feminism & masculinities*. Oxford University Press.

Pagila, C. (2017). *Free women free men*. Pantheon Books.

Paludi, M. P. (2016). *Campus action against sexual assault: Needs, policies, procedures, and training programs*. Praeger.

Sampson, R. J. (2006). Collective efficacy theory: Lessons learned and directions for future inquiry. *Taking Stock: The Status of Criminological Theory, 15*, 149–167.

Sampson, R. J., & Groves, W. B. (1989). Community structure and crime: Testing social-disorganization theory. *American Journal of Sociology, 94*(4), 774–802.

Shaw, C. R., & McKay, H. D. (1942). *Juvenile delinquency and urban areas*. University of Chicago Press.

RESEARCH NOTES

The data and ideas from this book originated in 14 studies which collected data from one main institution, including its students, faculty, and staff, two national studies of universities, and a social media sample study. The main university is a midwestern, small, private, religiously connected institution. Its students are mostly female, white, and middle to upper class. Many students play sports either collegiately or intermural. Greek life consists of approximately 10% of the student body. The studies are explained below to gain insight about their methodologies. All studies gained IRB approval.

For all quantitative studies, the Illinois Rape Myth Acceptance (IRMA) Scale was utilized as developed by McMahon and Farmer (2011). This is a 22-item scale traditionally measured through (1) strongly agree, (2) agree, (3) neutral, (4) disagree, and (5) strongly disagree. In the later surveys from data analysis and comparison, the neutral category was removed as it was hiding data. Studies 9 and after measured IRMA with (1) strongly agree, (2) agree, (3) disagree, and (4) strongly disagree. It holds five scales: total rape myth, she asked for it, he didn't mean to, it wasn't rape, and she lied. In study 6 and beyond, two items were added to IRMA measures but not included in the total rape myth scale. These items measured the perceptions of male rape and consent. The finalized form of IRMA is in Appendix C in the survey used for study 9 and beyond.

1 Spring 2015 Quantitative study about programming on campuses and rape myth perceptions. Preliminary study completed as a pre-test for Spring 2016 study. This study was developed mostly by the student Bri Hotchkiss. The paper survey was a convenient sample of students known to the student researcher. Data was entered into SPSS to look at descriptive statistics of the rape myth using IRMA and opinions about programming on campus.

Study supported that students did not accept rape myths and did not attend, or remember attending, rape programming on campus.
2 Summer 2015 ($n = 30$) Qualitative interviews with national sample of universities to learn about rape prevention programming on campuses. This study was developed mostly by the student Bri Hotchkiss. This study connected with 50 universities via phone calls and emails to gather information about their sexual assault programs, how the programs were evaluated, and plans for new programs. Thirty universities chose to participate. The conclusion was that universities engage in required activities of Title IX and little research is complete about their projects and programs aside from student satisfaction surveys.
3 Spring 2016 ($n = 316$) Quantitative survey of students to collect foundation rape myth measures and see differences of perceptions in lower-level students and upper-level students and to measure university program connection. Surveys were distributed across campus during class time when professors allowed researchers in. Surveys were entered into SPSS for data analysis. There were three research questions: (1) What is the level of rape myth acceptance on campus; (2) does attending programs or remember attending programs impact rape myth agreement; and (3) do upper-level students (juniors and seniors) have different levels of acceptance of rape myths than lower-level (freshman and sophomores) students? Most students did not remember attending any programs sponsored by the university about rape or sexual assault. This is despite that all freshmen must attend a program and all those living in dormitories attend at least one program a semester. Most who did remember attending one program remember a human trafficking speaker brought to campus by the criminal justice and sociology programs that occurred about a month before the survey. This sample did not accept rape myths and mostly disagreed with the scales. Upper-level students did have lower means than lower-level students showing more acceptance or less disagreement with the rape myth scales.
4 Spring 2016 ($n = 75$) Quantitative survey of faculty and staff to collect foundation rape myth measures. Surveys were distributed at the end of faculty and staff meetings, which limited the amount of data collected. Faculty and staff leave at various points during the meetings. The completion rate of these surveys was 98%; however, these surveys included more missing data and neutral responses especially from the staff than what was in student surveys. When this survey was distributed, a piece of paper asking for name and email was included to volunteer for the focus groups of study 5. The survey showed that staff and faculty highly disagreed with rape myths, felt safe on the campus, and did not perceive sexual assault as a problem on campus.
5 Spring 2016 Four focus groups of faculty and staff to see their connections to rape culture and rape myths. Three focus groups were of faculty and one was of staff. The staff appeared more knowledgeable about sexual assault but many of them worked with student affairs. One faculty group were more

knowledgeable than the other two but those in the one group conversed about their personal connections to sexual assault as students. The focus groups supported the direct disagreement with rape myths but adherence to stereotypes of drinking, partying, and victim blaming in those situations. Focus groups did see the campus as safe and did not see sexual assault as a major concern on campus. A video was shown to the focus groups that shared two stories of campus rape victims; this changed the mood of the focus groups and demonstrated that sexual assaults did happen on campus and students were not kind to victims. This prompted a call for education and programming to become more knowledgeable about this campus.

6 Fall 2017 ($n = 187$) Quantitative survey of students to develop stronger measure of rape myths and continue to create a stronger survey. Of the students who completed the surveys, there was a 99% completion rate and there were 2% students who were not in classes. This survey removed the neutral category in IRMA. It included information about Greek life, athletics, student organizations, music, and theater. The surveys were distributed to freshman and senior seminars to gain students. Freshman in this fall semester survey remembered the programming stronger than in previous studies. The research questions were (1) what are the levels of rape myth acceptance; (2) does student groups impact the level of acceptance; (3) how does removing the neutral category impact acceptance? The study had typical disagreement with IRMA and the means were slightly higher when weighted. Social groups did not impact rape myth acceptance except for males and athletes.

7 Spring 2018 ($n = 147$) Quantitative survey of overlap students to develop stronger measure of rape myths. Neutral was returned to IRMA. Study included mostly freshman from the freshman English course. This connected to those in the freshman seminar courses from the prior fall survey. This was the same survey as study 6 except that students could respond to IRMA statements with neutral. About 8% less students remember attending a program. Students disagree with IRMA but like study 6 males and athletes had lower means suggesting increased acceptance or lowered disagreement.

The neutral categories across studies 6 and 7 (as well as 3 and 9) were examined using a POMPS syntax in SPSS. POMPS standardizes the scores of similar scales when different measurement is used such as a 4-item Likert or 5-item Likert as is the case when not using neutral or using neutral for IRMA. The syntax is found at https://osf.io/eaxgb/. The syntax is run in SPSS to create scores out of 100 so that comparison can be accomplished. This comparison demonstrated that means were different when using neutral response category. Neutral tended to lower the amount of disagreement in the samples. Hence, neutral was removed from scales starting in study 9.

8 Spring 2018 Qualitative interviews with seven female students to see their connections to rape culture, rape myths, sexual assault definitions, and consent. This was a study to explore how campus students define and explain sex, consent, sexual assault, rape myths, rape culture, and their ability to

connect all these terms. The study was open to every student on campus but only women showed up for the interviews. Three men signed up for interviews but did not attend. The study was conducted in my office with student researchers engaging with the interviewees. I was in the office as well taking notes and helping with follow-up questions if needed at the end of interviews. Interviews were audio recorded and transcribed. No names were kept or recorded. This study supported the need for education, but also personal experience is a true learning tool. The campus was viewed as safe and sexual assaults were not viewed as a problem on campus. The students explained the generalities of the terms, but nuances became confusing to them. They knew the right answers but often talked about consent and assault as being gray areas they did not understand.

9   Spring 2019 ($n = 597$) Quantitative survey of student body to measure rape myth and its connected characteristics (sex roles, sexual behaviors, consent, aggression, empathy, self-esteem) and social identities (masculinity, femininity, social liberal ideology, feminist). The research question was how do social identities impact rape myth acceptance? IRMA held disagreement in this sample again and neutral was not used as an option for responding to the statements of the scales. Surveys were distributed across campus during class time when professors allowed researchers in. Surveys were entered into SPSS for data analysis. Social group identity seemed to impact acceptance rates, including feminism, masculinity (mid-range social aggression and lower empathy), consent, and social liberalism. Students were not conservative nor traditional in sex roles and sexual behaviors but half considered themselves socially liberal. This study supported that more conservative students held lower means in the IRMA items and scales especially when male. That scales of she lied and he didn't mean to held the lowest disagreement or highest acceptance in mean scores.

10 Fall 2019 ($n = 103$) Quantitative survey of social media sample to measure rape myth and its connected characteristics (sex roles, sexual behaviors, consent, aggression, empathy, self-esteem) and identities (masculinity, femininity, political ideology, feminist). This was an electronic version of study 9 created in RedCap and distributed via Facebook from the researchers' profiles and others who might have shared the original post. All participants had informed voluntary consent and were adults (age 18 plus). Completion rate was 38%, which is high for electronic surveys of this sort. Response bias is assumed as the sample was educated higher than typical population and nearly 50% were victims of sexual assault. It cannot be generalized to the general public but provides data and collaboration of prior studies that suggest conservative people tend to agree with rape myths. This sample was highly educated and socially liberal; they held some of the highest means of all studies in disagreement to IRMA items and scales. The scale of debate in this study was he didn't mean to which connects to all other surveys.

11 Fall 2019 ($n = 200$) Quantitative vignette research about perceived victim blameworthiness dependent on gender of victim, aggressor, and participant. This study was developed mostly by the student Leah Witthuhn through an independent study. It used a factorial survey approach in three vignettes that provided a rape script. Each scenario included information about the victim and aggressor that altered perceived gender to see how the survey participant perceived victim blameworthiness. It used a scale created by yes/no questions to measure perceived blame. This study supported that the gender of the victim and aggressor altered perceived blame as well as the gender/sex of the participant. Male participants were more likely to blame the victim in all three scenarios with scenario 2 instigating the most perceived victim blame with a male victim and female aggressor. It supported the theories used in the book of expectation states and situated identity and the overall presumption that social identities matter in rape myths.

12 Spring 2020 ($n = 35$) Quantitative survey of faculty and staff to measure rape myth and its connected characteristics (sex roles, sexual behaviors, consent, aggression, empathy, self-esteem) and identities (masculinity, femininity, political ideology, feminist). This study was to check the reliability of study 4. It is not included in the book as the data collection proved difficult. It was to occur in Spring 2020 but then could not happen after the school shutdown in March 2020 due to Covid-19. The survey was transferred from a paper version into an electronic survey through RedCap to distribute in Fall 2020. The survey relied on forwarded emails from deans and chairs as well as a campus electronic bulletin board. When the link was opened, an error message shown that many were not willing to bypass. As a result, only 35 surveys were completed with an additional 12 not completed. Survey non-response bias and sample bias were assumed so the data was not placed in the book. Descriptive statistics suggest that faculty and staff were in high disagreement with IRMA scales similar to study 4.

13 Spring 2020 ($n = 398$) Quantitative survey of national university sample to measure rape myth and its connected characteristics (sex roles, sexual behaviors, consent, aggression, empathy, self-esteem) and identities (masculinity, femininity, political ideology, feminist). This was an electronic version of study 9 distributed through RedCap. Other university networks and colleagues were targeted to gain information from 25 universities with a potential sample of 1,500. However, working through the guidelines and rules of other universities proved insurmountable even though IRB approved the study. Five universities distributed the survey through the aid of faculty with a completion rate of around 65%. Faculty forwarded an email with the survey link. The study supported the findings of study 9. Students disagreed with the rape myths but those who held more masculine and conservative ideologies held lower means for IRMA items and scales. This study collaborated the presumption that social identities connect to and develop perceptions of IRMA.

14 Spring 2020 Qualitative interviews with seven victims/survivors to see how identities and ideologies connect to their experiences. Twenty interviews were hoped for in this study and 15 were scheduled. The advertisement for the study included any students of the university and requested victims, survivors, and bystanders of sexual assault. No bystanders were interviewed but some made appointments. The data collection was cut short due to Covid-19 and the university shut down face-to-face events. Thus, seven interviews were completed and eight were cancelled. The interview guide is shown in Appendix D. The interviews were audio recorded and transcribed automatically into word documents. Data pulled from the interviews included stories of the victims and survivors and how they related to concepts of rape myths, consent, feminism, masculinity, femininity, and rape culture. The data showed the stigma and shame felt by victims and survivors as a result of victim blame by self and their community and their own reliance on rape myths to share their experiences.

APPENDICES

Appendix A – Illinois rape myth acceptance scale

Statement	Strongly Agree	Agree	Disagree	Strongly Disagree
1 If a woman is raped while she is drunk, she is at least somewhat responsible for letting things get out of hand.				
2 When women go to parties wearing slutty clothes, they are asking for trouble.				
3 If a woman goes to a room alone with a guy at a party, it is her fault if she is raped.				
4 If a woman acts like a slut, eventually she is going to get into trouble.				
5 When women get raped, it's often because the way they said "no" was unclear.				
6 If a woman initiates kissing or hooking up, she should not be surprised if a guy assumes she wants to have sex.				

(Continued)

Statement	Strongly Agree	Agree	Disagree	Strongly Disagree
7 When guys rape, it is usually because of their strong desire for sex.				
8 Guys don't usually intend to force sex on a woman, but sometimes they get too sexually carried away.				
9 Rape happens when a guy's sex drive goes out of control.				
10 If a man is drunk, he might rape someone unintentionally.				
11 It shouldn't be considered rape if a guy is drunk and didn't realize what he was doing.				
12 If both people are drunk, it can't be rape.				
13 If a woman doesn't physically resist sex – even if protesting verbally – it can't be considered rape.				
14 If a woman doesn't physically fight back, you can't really say it was rape.				
15 A rape probably doesn't happen if a woman doesn't have any bruises or marks.				
16. If the accused "rapist" doesn't have a weapon, you really can't call it rape				
17 If a woman doesn't say "no" she can't claim rape.				
18 A lot of times, women who say they were raped agreed to have sex and then regret it.				
19 Rape accusations are often used as a way of getting back at guys.				
20 A lot of times, women who say they were raped often led the guy on and then had regrets.				

21 A lot of times, women who claim they were raped have emotional problems.
22 Women who are caught cheating on their boyfriends sometimes claim it was rape.
23 Only females can be victims of sexual assault and rape.
24 If consent is given once, consent for sex is always there.

Appendix B – Study 8 interview guide Spring 2018

1 What do you think you are here to speak about today? (use this to warm up the room and build rapport)
2 What is a sexual assault? Provide examples please
3 What is the difference between sexual harassment and assault? Provide examples please
4 What is the difference between sexual assault and rape? Provide examples please
5 What do you think causes sexual assaults and rapes? Why do you think this?
6 Why do you think sexual assaults and rapes occur on this campus? Anything else to add?
7 Do you think most of your friends believe sexual assault is not real if people are drunk? Explain
8 Do you think most of your friends believe rape is not real if there is no physical abuse? Explain
9 Do you think only females can be sexual assaulted? Explain this idea for us. Do you think your friends agree with you?
10 Do you think victims lie about being sexually abused? Explain this to us?
11 When men sexually abuse a female, do you think they mean to? Do you think they know it is sexual abuse or rape? Explain for us
12 If we ask about rape myths – do you know what that means?
13 Rape culture is the shared attitudes, behaviors, and beliefs that leads someone to believe that sexual assaults are normalized or not that big of a deal. Do you think this perception is shared on this campus? Why do you think this? Do you think most of your friends would agree with you?
14 Is there something this campus does or doesn't do to encourage rape culture?
15 What do you think about consent processes? What does that look like? Do the ideas surrounding consent lead to sexual assaults and blurred lines?
16 Does knowing the definition of sexual assault change your answers to any of the above questions or make you think differently?

17 How much of a problem are sexual assaults on Carroll's campus? Why do you think this? Please do not include any personal stories.
18 How much of a problem are rapes on Carroll's campus? Why do you think this? Please do not include any personal stories
19 How would you limit sexual assault and rape on campus?

Appendix C – Survey for study 9

Thank you for your participation in this study. Your time and honesty are appreciated.

Please mark your level of agreement or disagreement to the following statements.

Statement	Strongly Agree	Agree	Disagree	Strongly Disagree
1 If a woman is raped while she is drunk, she is at least somewhat responsible for letting things get out of hand.				
2 When women go to parties wearing slutty clothes, they are asking for trouble.				
3 If a woman goes to a room alone with a guy at a party, it is her fault if she is raped.				
4 If a woman acts like a slut, eventually she is going to get into trouble.				
5 When women get raped, it's often because the way they said "no" was unclear.				
6 If a woman initiates kissing or hooking up, she should not be surprised if a guy assumes she wants to have sex.				
7 When guys rape, it is usually because of their strong desire for sex.				
8 Guys don't usually intend to force sex on a woman, but sometimes they get too sexually carried away.				
9 Rape happens when a guy's sex drive goes out of control.				
10 If a man is drunk, he might rape someone unintentionally.				

11 It shouldn't be considered rape if a guy is drunk and didn't realize what he was doing.
12 If both people are drunk, it can't be rape.
13 If a woman doesn't physically resist sex – even if protesting verbally – it can't be considered rape.
14 If a woman doesn't physically fight back, you can't really say it was rape.
15 A rape probably doesn't happen if a woman doesn't have any bruises or marks.
16 If the accused "rapist" doesn't have a weapon, you really can't call it rape
17 If a woman doesn't say "no" she can't claim rape.
18 A lot of times, women who say they were raped agreed to have sex and then regret it.
19 Rape accusations are often used as a way of getting back at guys.
20 A lot of times, women who say they were raped often led the guy on and then had regrets.
21 A lot of times, women who claim they were raped have emotional problems.
22 Women who are caught cheating on their boyfriends sometimes claim it was rape.
23 Only females can be victims of sexual assault and rape.
24 If consent is given once, consent for sex is always there.

Please mark True or False to the following statements.

Statement	True	False
1 I'm always willing to admit it when I make a mistake.		
2 I always try to practice what I preach.		
3 I never resent being asked to return a favor.		
4 I have never been irked when people expressed ideas very different from my own.		
5 I have never deliberately said something that hurt someone's feelings.		

(Continued)

Statement	True	False
6 I like to gossip at times.		
7 There have been occasions when I took advantage of someone.		
8 I sometimes try to get even rather than forgive and forget.		
9 At times I have really insisted on having things my own way.		
10 There have been occasions when I felt like smashing things.		

Please mark your level of agreement or disagreement to the following statements.

Statement	Strongly Disagree	Disagree	Agree	Strongly Agree
1 I feel that I am a person of worth, at least on an equal plane with others.				
2 I feel that I have a number of good qualities.				
3 All in all, I am inclined to feel that I am a failure.				
4 I am able to do things as well as most other people.				
5 I feel I do not have much to be proud of.				
6 I take a positive attitude toward myself.				
7 On the whole, I am satisfied with myself.				
8 I wish I could have more respect for myself.				
9 I certainly feel useless at times.				
10 At times I think I am no good at all.				

Please mark your level of agreement or disagreement to the following statements.

Statement	Strongly Disagree	Disagree	Agree	Strongly Agree
1 I think that obtaining sexual consent is more necessary in a new relationship that in a committed relationship				
2 I think that obtaining sexual consent is more necessary in a casual sexual encounter than in a committed relationship				
3 I believe the need for asking for sexual consent decreases as the length of an intimate relationship increases				
4 I believe it is enough to ask for consent at the beginning of a sexual encounter				
5 I believe that sexual intercourse is the only sexual activity that requires explicit verbal consent				
6 I believe that partners are less likely to ask for sexual consent the longer they are in a relationship				
7 If consent for sexual intercourse is established, making out or fondling can be assume without new consent				
8 I would have difficulty asking for consent because it would spoil the mood				
9 I am worried that my partner might think I am weird or strange if I asked for sexual consent before starting an sexual activity				
10 I would have difficulty asking for consent because it doesn't really fit with how I like to engage in sexual activity				
11 I would worry that if people knew I asked for sexual consent before starting sexual activity, that they would think I was weird or strange				

(*Continued*)

Statement	Strongly Disagree	Disagree	Agree	Strongly Agree
12 I think that verbally asking for sexual consent is awkward				
13 I have not asked for sexual consent (or given my consent) at times because I felt that it might backfire and I wouldn't end up having sex				
14 I believe that verbally asking for sexual consent in a sexual encounter reduces the pleasures of the encounter				
15 I would have a hard time verbalizing my consent in a sexual encounter because I am too shy				
16 I feel confident that I could ask for consent from a new sexual partner				
17 I would not want to ask a partner for consent because it would remind me that I'm sexually active				
18 I feel confident that I could ask for consent from my current partner				

Please mark your level of agreement or disagreement to the following statements.

Statement	Strongly Disagree	Disagree	Agree	Strongly Agree
1 A man should fight when the woman he's with is insulted by another man				
2 It is acceptable for the woman to pay for a date				
3 A woman should be a virgin when she marries				
4 There is something wrong with a woman who doesn't want to marry and raise a family				
5 A wife should never contradict her husband in public				
6 It is better for a woman to use her feminine charm to get what she wants rather than ask for it outright				

7   It is acceptable for a woman to have a career, but marriage and family come first
8   It looks worse for a woman to be drunk than for a man to be drunk
9   There is nothing wrong with a woman going to a bar alone

Please mark your level of agreement or disagreement to the following statements.

Statement	Strongly Disagree	Disagree	Agree	Strongly Agree
1 I can tune into how someone else feels rapidly and intuitively				
2 I am good at predicting how someone will feel				
3 I can easily work out what another person might want to talk about				
4 I can sense if I am intruding even if the other person doesn't tell me				
5 I am quick to spot when someone in a group is feeling awkward or uncomfortable.				
6 Seeing people cry doesn't really upset me				
7 I tend to get emotionally involved with a friend's problem				
8 I really enjoy caring for other people				
9 I usually stay emotionally detached when watching a film				
10 If I say something that someone else is offended by, I think that that's their problem, not mine				
11 I do not tend to find social situations confusing				
12 I find it hard to know what to do in a social situation				
13 Friendships and relationships are just too difficult, so I tend not to bother with them				
14 I often find it difficult to judge if something is rude or polite				
15 I find it difficult to explain to others things that I understand easily, when they don't understand it first time				

180 Appendices

Please mark your level of agreement or disagreement to the following statements.

Statement	Strongly Disagree	Disagree	Agree	Strongly Agree
1 A woman who initiates a sexual encounter will probably have sex with anyone				
2 A woman shouldn't give in sexually to a man too easily or he'll think she is loose or slutty.				
3 Men have a stronger sex drive than women				
4 A mice woman will be offender or embarrassed by dirty jokes				
5 Masturbation is a normal sexual activity				
6 People should not have oral sex				
7 I would have no respect for a woman who engages in sexual relationships with no emotional attachment				
8 Having sex during menstrual periods is unpleasant				
9 The primary goal of sex is to have children				
10 Women have the same needs for a sexual outlet as men				

Please mark how often you participate in the following

How often have you …	Never	Rarely	Sometimes	Often
1 My friends know that I will think less of them if they do not do what I want them to do.				
2 When I want something from a friend of mine, I act "cold" or indifferent towards them until I get what I want.				
3 I have threatened to share private information about my friends with other people in order to get them to comply with my wishes.				
4 I have intentionally ignored a person until they gave me my way about something.				
5 When I am not invited to do something with a group of people, I will exclude those people from future activities.				

6 When I have been angry at, or jealous of someone, I have tried to damage that person's reputation by gossiping about him or her or by passing on negative information about him/her to other people.
7 When someone does something that makes me angry, I try to embarrass that person or make them look stupid in front of his/her friends
8 When I am mad at a person, I try to make sure she/he is excluded from group activities (going to the movies or to a bar).
9 I have spread rumors about a person just to be mean.

Please complete the following questions about yourself by circling your response

1. What is your class standing?
   Freshman   Sophomore   Junior   Senior
2. What is your gender?
   Male   Female   Transgender   Other   Prefer not to answer
3. Do you believe in feminism (meaning that women and men should be equal in all aspects of life)?   Yes/No
4. Do you drink alcohol?   Yes/No
5. Do you use any drugs illegally?   Yes/No
6. Do you live on campus?   Yes/No
7. Do you connect to a more liberal or conservative social identity? Liberal Conservative
8. Have you been a victim of sexual assault while a college student? Yes / No /Prefer not to answer
9. Have you committed an act of sexual assault while a college student? Yes / No /Prefer not to answer
10. How much of a problem is sexual assault on this campus?

0	1	2	3	4	5	6	7	8	9	10
No Problem										Large Problem

11. How much do you fear for your safety on this campus?

0	1	2	3	4	5	6	7	8	9	10
No Fear										Mega Fear

12 Do you think the university does enough to prevent sexual assaults and rapes on campus?   Yes/No
13 Do you think the university does enough to protect your safety on this campus?   Yes/No

Appendix D – Interview guide for study 14

(Read informed consent)
[Audio record approval process for interview and audio recording]
Thank you very much for agreeing to participate in this interview. During our time, we will be discussing several areas related to sexual assault, rape myth, and rape culture. Specifically, I will touch on questions about your experience as a survivor and/or bystander and how it impacted your personal, professional, and academic life. We will be taking written notes along with the audio recording. You have already voluntarily consented to this process. Remember, your participation is voluntary, and you can stop the interview or skip questions if you feel the need to do so. Again, thank you very much for coming here. Your knowledge is invaluable to us and others.

- Do you have any questions before we start?
- Are you comfortable?

(Start the formal interview)
Intersectionality Questions:

1 If you don't mind telling me, what year were you born?
2 Are you currently employed? What type of job?
3 Please describe the community that you currently live in. Is it on campus or off campus?
4 What gender do you identify with? (Male, female, transgender, other)
5 What race and ethnicity do you identify with?
6 How would you identify your sexual orientation? (Straight, gay, lesbian, bisexual, other)
7 What is your marital/partner status? Can you tell me about your relationship?

Now thinking about why we are here today.

8 Are you a victim or survivor of sexual assault?
9 Have you ever been a bystander or witness to a sexual assault situation?

Thank you. (if the person is a survivor or bystander tailor the following questions accordingly)

10 Did you know the offender/assailant? Was the person a stranger? How/explain?
    a   How did you know the survivor/victim?
11 Please explain the environment the experience occurred in.
12 Why do you think this happened?

I really appreciate that you agreed to participate in this project. Now I am going to ask you a few questions about the assault. Are you ready?

13 Would you mind telling me what happened to you? (Probe about assailant, how the victim responded, how it ended, what the victim did first.)
14 Were you on campus at the time of the attack/attacks? Were you enrolled in this school?
15 Did you ever tell anyone about it?

If yes:
- Please tell me about that who you told and why? How did you explain the situation?
- Why did you choose to confide in that person? (What did that person do/say?
- Who did you tell?
- How did this help/not help you?
- Please walk me through their responses.
- What did you think, say to them at the time?
- Did talking about the incident lead to any consequences for the offender?
- Did you tell anyone else? (repeat questioning)

If no:
- Why not?
- Looking back to the event, do you wish you would have told someone from your school?

16 Did anyone from within the criminal justice system become involved in your case?

If yes:
- Who? Why?
- Can you please walk me through their responses? What did they do to help?
- What could have been done differently, if anything?
- Did reporting the incident lead to any consequences for the offender?

If no: Why not?

17 Did you tell the university? Did the university investigate the assault?
   a Why or why not?
   b Who? Why?
   c Can you please walk me through their responses?
   d What, if anything, did they do to help?
   e What could have been done differently, if anything?
   f Did reporting the incident lead to any consequences for the offender?
18 Did anyone ever place blame on you for the sexual assault? Can you tell me about that experience?
19 Did you experience any after affects or trauma after the assault?
   - For example, how did you feel mentally?
   - How did you feel socially?
   - How did you feel physically?
   - Did these symptoms affect your schoolwork?
   - Did these symptoms affect employment?

20 Did your relationships with friends change after the sexual assault? How/explain
21 Did your relationship with your parents change after the sexual assault? How/explain
22 How did it impact your education or school life? How/explain
23 How did it impact your work life? How/explain
24 How, if at all, does the assault impact your life today?
25 Is there anything else you think we need to know about this sexual assault experience?

Thank you for telling us about those experiences. We appreciate the information and now want to move onto more general perceptions you might hold about rape and sexual assault.

26 What is your definition of sexual assault? What does it include? What does it not include?
27 Where did you learn these beliefs?
28 What causes sexual assaults? Explain
29 If anyone, who is to blame for sexual assaults? How/explain
30 Does our culture or society create opportunities for sexual assaults? How/explain
31 Do you know what rape myths are? Can you provide an example?
    a How does this relate to your situation explained above?
    b Why did the experience you address above happen?
32 How do you see masculinity in the United States culture?
    a What about at college?
    b Does this connect to rape? How/explain
33 How do you see femininity in the United States culture?
    a What about at college?
    b Does this connect to rape? How/explain
34 Can you define feminism?
    a Does this connect to rape? How/explain
35 How does your gender/sexuality/race/ethnicity – your social identity – impact how you see this incident?
36 What can this university do to help survivors?
37 What can this university do to help bystanders?
38 Do you think the university or education structure cares about sexual assault? Why/why not?
39 Do you think our culture cares about sexual assault? Why/Why not?
40 What needs to change in our society and culture to impact sexual aggression? Masculinity? Femininity? Feminism? Politically? Educationally? Other ideas?

Thank you so much for your time and energy. If you know of someone who also could do this interview, please ask them to contact us. I appreciate your time.

How are you feeling? Do you need any assistance or care? Please remember the information on the informed consent if you need help processing this experience or the interview.

INDEX

acquaintance rape 21, 98, 135
aggression 7–9, 20, 23, 60, 77, 105–108, 121, 122; *see also* social aggression
alcohol 31, 60, 62, 63, 72, 74, 78, 88, 94, 95, 112, 117, 122, 123, 151
athletes 2, 10, 27, 28, 29, 73, 80, 105–109, 112, 115, 122, 143, 148, 160, 161, 162
athletics 5–7, 27–28, 67, 95, 108, 112, 115, 149, 167; *see also* sports

Baylor University 2, 68, 107, 141
blameworthiness *see* perceived blameworthiness
Blassey Ford, Dr. 3, 81, 98
blitz rape 21, 32, 45, 48, 66, 78, 98, 111, 134, 157; *see also* real rape or classical rape
Boys will be Boys see Ford, C.
Brownmiller, S. 20, 25, 36, 37, 62, 91, 94, 95, 152
bystander intervention 8, 28, 75, 148, 160, 162

Campus Action see Paludi
campus programming *see* programming
class standing 45, 109, 112, 114–116
classic rape *see* real rape
Clery Act 27, 67, 107, 142, 148, 157

dark figure of crime 67, 156
date rape 21, 98, 135
definitions of constructs: aggression (social) 113, 114, 136; consent 114; empathy 114, 136; feminism 100; gender (binary) 115, 116, 138; self-esteem 113; sex role traditions 135; sexual assault 84; sexual behavior conservatism 136; rape 84; rape culture 84; rape myths 84
due process 3–4, 34, 81, 147, 157
Duke University 3, 107, 141
Durkheim, E. 12, 14, 81, 159

expectation states theory 13, 16–18, 36, 93, 104, 110, 112, 121–123, 144, 162, 169

fear *see* perceptions of fear
Fight like a Girl see Ford, C.
Ford, C. 23, 24, 38, 63, 89, 93, 95, 96, 106, 107, 112, 136
FRATERNITY 27–29, 71, 73, 95, 105–109, 112, 115, 117, 143, 147–149, 152; *see also* Greek life

gender (binary construction) 115, 116, 138
gender construction 7, 13, 124
Greek life 6–10, 42, 74, 108–110, 112, 115–116, 144, 148, 160, 165, 167

Harvard 68, 141
hookup culture 5–6, 9, 14, 28–30, 60, 71, 88, 89, 101, 108
Hunting Ground, The 67, 107

identity *see* social identity
ignorance 37, 46, 77–78, 82, 95, 99–100
implicit bias 3, 18–20, 55, 59, 60, 66, 123
IRB (institutional review board) 42, 131, 132, 165, 169

Kavanaugh, Brett 3, 19, 81, 98
Krakauer, J. 2, 28, 80
Know my name see Miller, C.

Lavigne & Shlabach 2, 28, 68, 80
locker room talk 20, 64, 105, 106, 122, 152, 162

master status 15–16
#metoo 99, 152, 157–158, 163
Missoula see Krakauer, J.
Missoula University 68, 141; *see also* Krakauer, J.
Miller, C. 2, 19, 68, 80, 83, 108, 158
Mills, C.W. 12, 14, 78
misogynistic 32, 35, 105, 106, 123, 156
misogyny 20, 37, 41, 49, 62, 153, 158, 160

Netflix and chill 30

Paludi, M. 8, 145, 146, 147, 148, 150, 161, 162
paradigms 13, 26, 100, 101, 156, 159
parties 5, 6, 14, 19, 29, 49, 62, 63, 71, 75, 83, 89, 95, 97, 105, 113, 117, 121, 132, 143–151, 157
party rape 21, 78, 118, 152
patriarchal 1, 4, 7, 8, 10, 13, 22, 32, 35, 62, 77, 95, 105, 106, 121, 123
patriarchy 20, 37–38, 49, 101, 158, 160; *see also* patriarchal
perceived blameworthiness 20, 111–112, 122, 169
perceptions of fear 70, 82, 84, 79, 117, 119, 128, 132, 141, 149–150
perpetrator 19, 86, 97, 98, 111, 122, 139
POMPS analysis 58, 167
prevention 141, 143–145, 148
program attendance 43, 45–46, 154
programming 1, 8, 10, 28, 42, 43, 66, 73–75, 109, 140–148, 154, 157, 160–162, 165–167
protection *see* self-defense

real rape 21, 25, 29, 30, 48, 78, 86, 97–100, 118, 153, 158; *see also* blitz rape
reliability 39, 40, 48, 49, 53, 54, 55, 59, 67, 109, 116, 128, 130, 139, 153, 169; *see also* reliable
response bias 111, 168, 169
Ruth Badger Ginsburg (RBG) 160

self-defense 8, 28, 63, 94, 96
self-esteem 9, 108, 113, 168, 169
sexism 20, 60, 62, 64, 150, 153
sexual assault programming *see* programming

sexual coercion 5, 6, 20–21, 25, 26, 30, 45, 61–62, 65–66, 87, 95, 101, 105, 131, 158
shame 3, 4, 8, 29, 32, 61, 62, 63, 65, 67, 74, 78–81, 86, 94–99, 101, 118–124, 144, 153, 161, 170
situated identity 15–17, 169
situated identity theory 13, 16–17, 36, 93, 104, 110, 112, 121, 123, 144
slut 30, 52, 60, 68, 119, 122, 128, 132, 150, 153
slut-shamed (and slut-shaming) 20, 37, 62–64, 74, 78
social aggression 109, 112–113, 121, 128, 131, 136, 141, 168, 169
social constructionism 7, 9, 12, 16, 23, 24, 97, 100
social desirability bias 58, 128, 130, 135, 153
social groups 13, 18, 31, 38, 105, 108, 167
sociological imagination 14, 78, 102
sorority 73, 105, 109, 122; *see also* Greek life
sports 9, 23, 28, 71, 105–106, 109, 116, 121–122, 143–144, 147, 165; *see also* athletics
stanford university 68, 108, 141
stereotypes 1, 3, 13, 17, 22, 61, 71, 74, 108, 109, 122, 143, 148, 167
stigma 4, 16, 18, 32, 61, 63, 65, 67, 71, 74, 78–81, 95, 101, 117, 118, 120–124, 144, 153, 161, 170
subconscious bias *see* implicit bias
symbolic interactionism 12–16, 23, 58, 104

Take Back the Night 73
Title IX 1, 8, 27–28, 67, 73, 107, 142, 147–148, 157, 160, 161, 166
toxic masculinity 13, 99, 105, 108, 113, 122, 144, 158
Turner, Brock 12, 19, 83, 108

unconscious bias *see* implicit bias
university programming *see* programming

validity 8, 39, 40, 54, 59, 109, 116, 153
Vanasco, J. 80, 89, 91, 93, 98, 152
victim blame 1, 2, 20, 21, 31, 36, 94, 97, 111–112, 119–123; *see also* perceived blameworthiness
victimization 1, 21, 67, 80, 97–100, 118, 139, 141
Violated see Lavigne & Shlabach
vulnerability 124

Wade, L. 29, 31, 88, 96
Weinstein, Harvey 3, 19

Yes means Yes movement 8, 19, 28, 123

For Product Safety Concerns and Information please contact our EU
representative GPSR@taylorandfrancis.com
Taylor & Francis Verlag GmbH, Kaufingerstraße 24, 80331 München, Germany

www.ingramcontent.com/pod-product-compliance
Lightning Source LLC
Chambersburg PA
CBHW070831300426
44111CB00014B/2518